Table of Contents

continued on next page

continued on next page

continued on next page

continued on next page

continued on next page

continued on next page

continued on next page

continued on next page

Glossary and Answer Key are located in the back of the book .

Reading   **English**   **Math**   **Spelling & Writing**   **Comprehension**   **Thinking Skills**   **Citizenship**   **Environmental Science**

These symbols are located at the top of every lesson page and represent the subject area for each lesson.

Color Code

Directions: Color the B words orange. Color the M words yellow. Color the L words blue. Color the S words black.

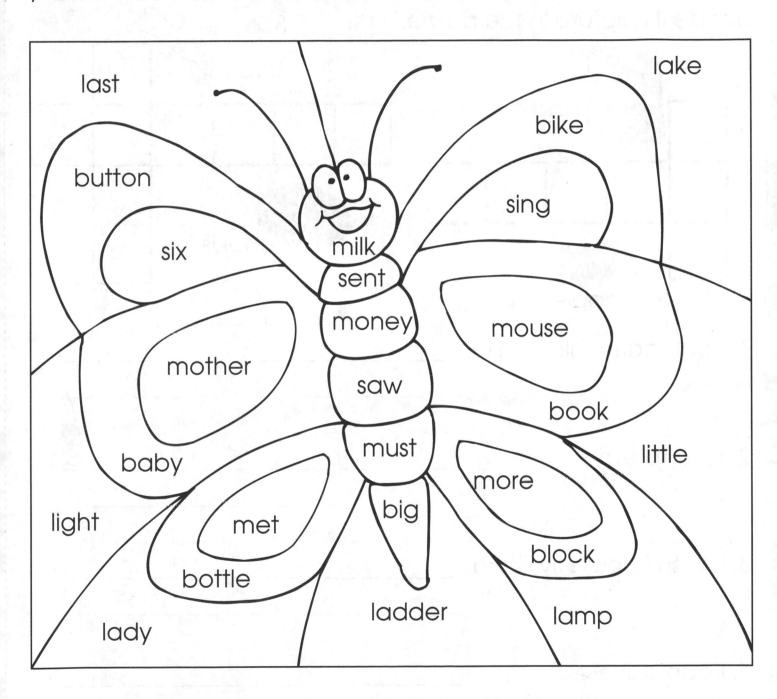

Name: _____

Things I Know About

Directions: 1. Say each of the 4 words aloud. 2. Write each word where it belongs in the blanks. 3. Now write each word beside its picture in the puzzle.

3.
bird

1.
bag

2.
apple

4. cookie

1. I can carry things in a _____ .

2. I like to eat an _____ .

3. I wish I could fly like a _____ .

4. I can bake a _____ .

Number Recognition

Directions: Write the numbers 1-10. Color the bear.

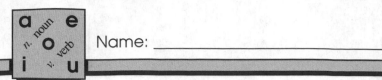

Name: _____

ABC Order

Directions: Draw a line to connect the dots. Follow the letters in **ABC** order.

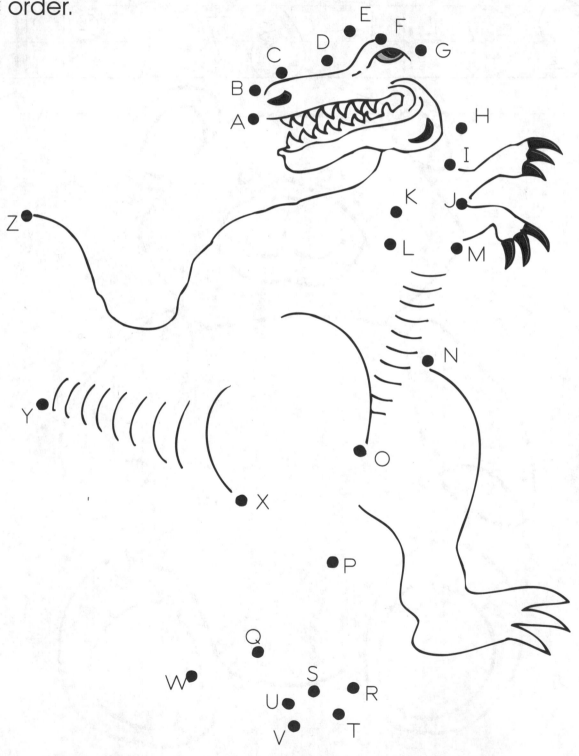

I Can Write The Names Of Pets!

Directions: 1. Follow the lines to write the name of each pet.
2. Write each name again by yourself. 3. Color the pictures.
4. Read the words to someone.

Like this:

frog   frog

dog

fish

cat

bird

Name: _____

Following Directions

Directions: Put a box around the circle ○.

   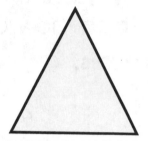

Put a box around the square □.

Put a box around the triangle △.

Put a box around the half-circle ◗.

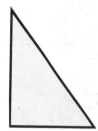  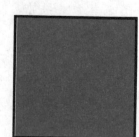 

Building A Snowman

Directions: Read the sentences. Do what they tell you to do.

Bob is making a snowman. He needs your help. Draw a black hat on the snowman. Draw red buttons. Now, draw a green scarf. Draw a happy face on the snowman.

Name: _____

Snow Is Cold!

Directions: Read about snow. Then answer the questions.

When you play in snow, dress warmly. Wear a coat. Wear a hat. Wear gloves. Do you wear these when you play in snow?

1. Snow is
    warm.
    cold.

2. When you play in snow, dress
    warmly.
    quickly.

3. List 3 things to wear when you play in snow.

_____

_____

_____

_____

Number Recognition 1, 2, 3, 4, 5

Directions: Use the color code to color the parrot.

Color:
1's red
2's blue
3's yellow
4's green
5's orange

abc Order

Directions: Draw a line to connect the dots. Follow the letters in **abc** order.

Name: _____

Citizens Now

Your country is called the United States of America. The United States of America is different from most other countries because it is made up of people from all over the world.

People who are members of our country are called citizens. Did you know that you don't have to wait until you are a grown-up to become an American citizen? You already are a citizen of the United States of America. You are a **citizen now**!

Do you think it is good that the United States has all kinds of citizens? Tell why you think as you do.

ACTIVITY 1

Citizens Now

Directions: Look at the citizen's face. Make the face look like yours. Next, cut it out and paste it on a large outline map of the United States with other citizens' faces to show that you are all **Citizens Now**!

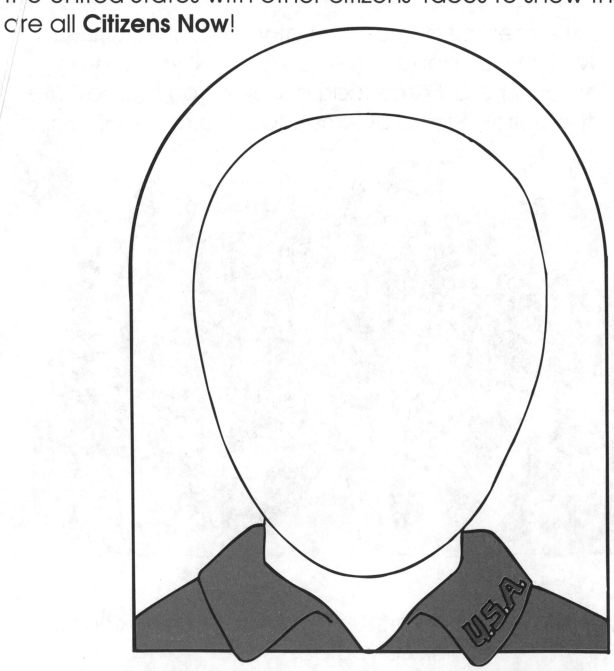

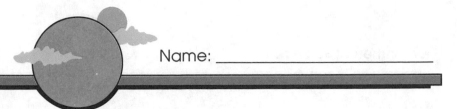

Name: _____

Lesson 1

Your Environment

The Earth is where we live. The Earth is made of many things. People made some of the things. Other things were made by nature. Some of these things are living. Others are not alive.

Your environment is everything around you. People, plants and animals are all parts of your environment. Air, water and soil are parts of your environment, too.

Name some things in your school environment.

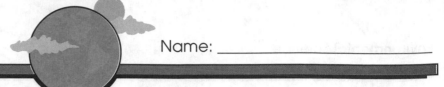

Name: _____

All Around Me

Directions: Mark an **X** next to the picture of each thing you see in your environment. Then draw two pictures of other things you see in the boxes at the bottom of the chart.

snake
☐

skyscraper
☐

bird
☐

mountains
☐

traffic light
☐

trees
☐

fireperson
☐

taxi
☐

mailbox
☐

snowman
☐

tractor
☐

ocean waves
☐

Color The Eggs

Directions: Read the words. Color the picture.

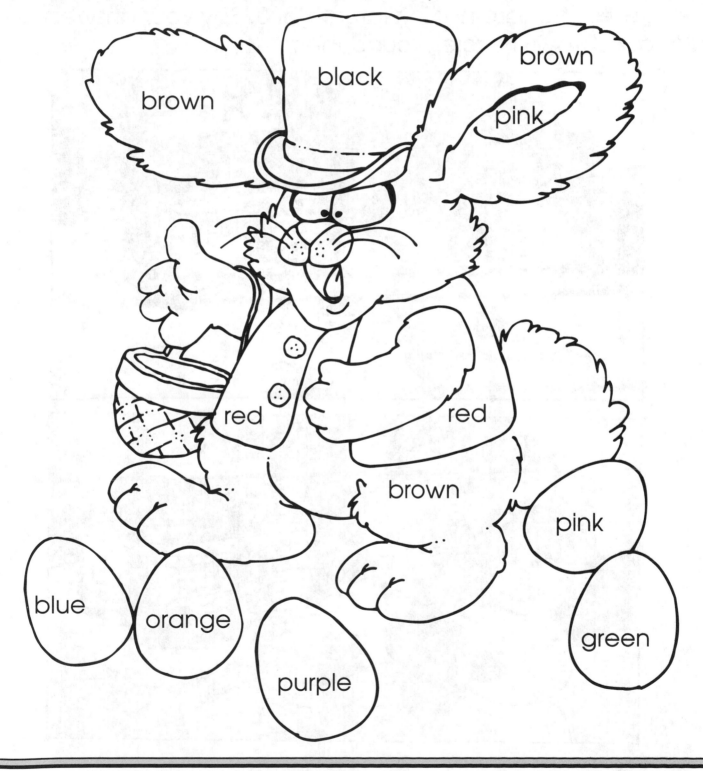

brown

black

brown

pink

brown

pink

red

red

brown

pink

blue

orange

green

purple

Name: _____

Look And See

Directions: 1. Look at both pictures. 2. Find five things in picture # 1 that are not in picture # 2. 3. Say your answers aloud. 4. Draw a circle around them.

1

2

Name: _____

Number Recognition 6, 7, 8, 9, 10

Directions: Use the code to color the carousel horse.

Color:
6's purple
7's yellow
8's black
9's pink
10's brown

Name: _____

Beginning Consonants Bb, Cc, Dd, Ff

Beginning consonants make the sounds that come at the beginning of words. Consonants are the letters b, c, d, f, g, h, j, k, l, m, n, p, q, r, s, t, v, w, x, y, z.

Directions: Say the name of each letter. Say the sound each letter makes. Draw a circle around the letters that make the beginning sound for each picture. Say the name of someone you know whose name begins with each letter.

Bb   Cc   Dd   Ff

Bb Dd   Ff Cc   Cc Dd   Ff Bb

Bb Dd   Ff Cc   Cc Dd   Ff Bb

Name: ____________________

Color The Pictures

Directions: Color each picture the correct colors. Draw and color another picture like the first one.

1
blue
2
yellow
3
green
4
orange
5
black
6
red

1
3
5
6
2
4

2
5
3
3

1
3
6
4
2

2
2
4
5
4
2
2

4
1
6
1
4

5
2
2
3
4

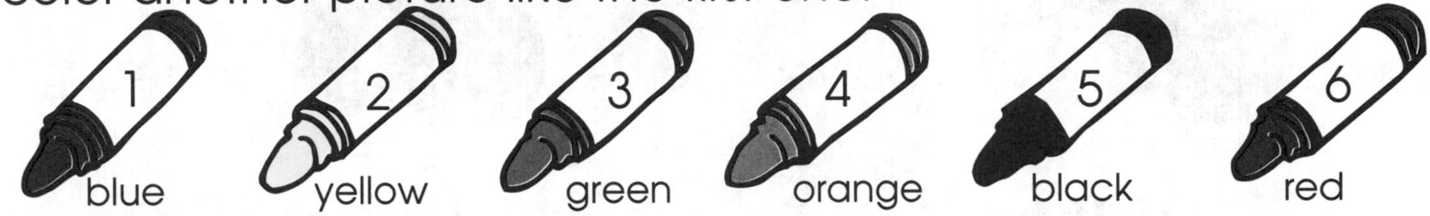

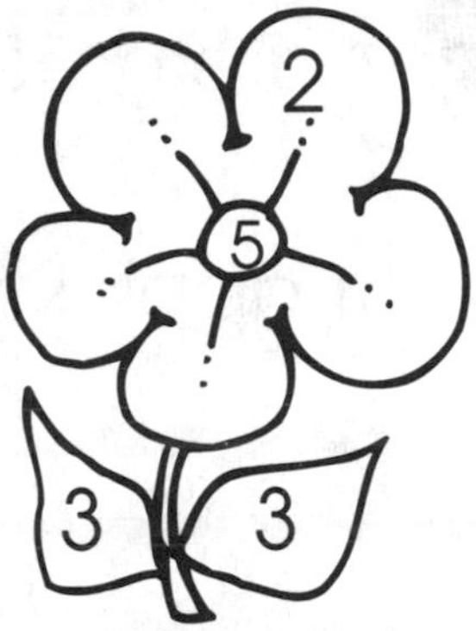

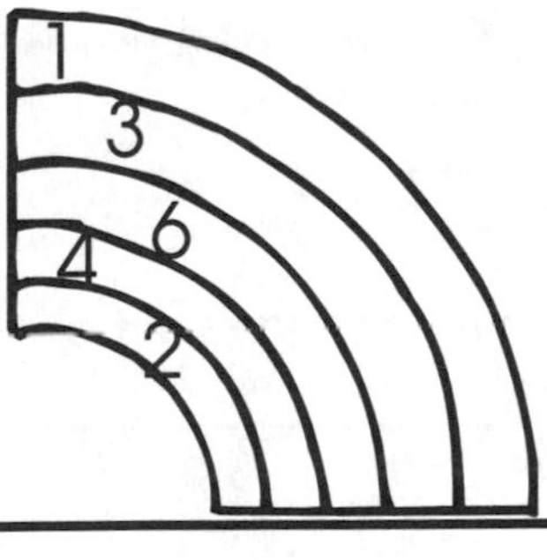

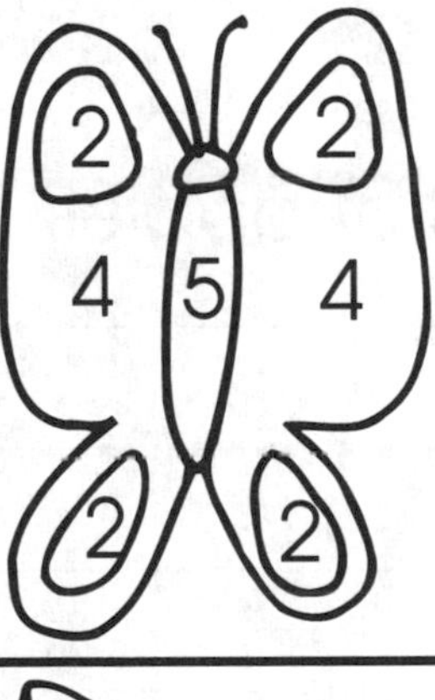

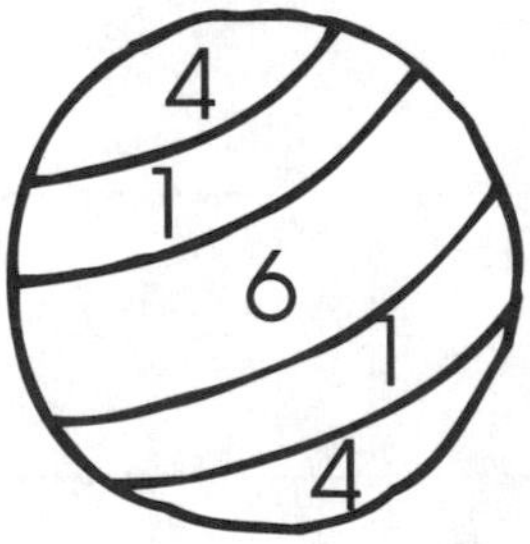

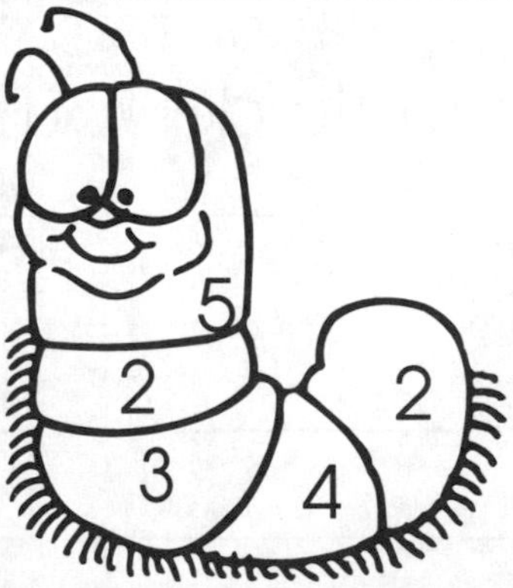

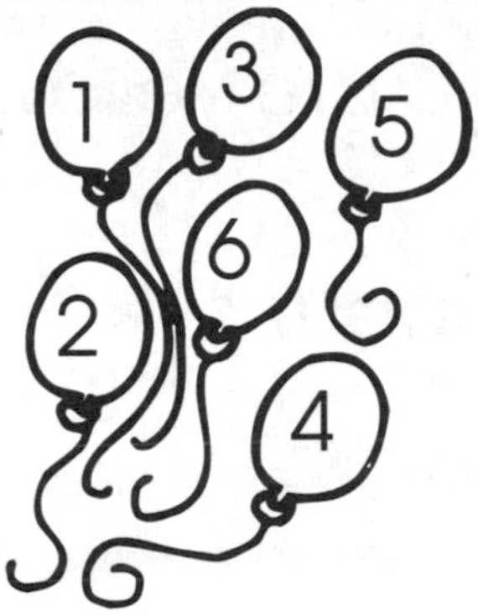

Name: _____

I Like Apples

Directions: Read about apples. Then answer the questions.

I like  . Do you? Some  are red.

Some  are green. Some  are yellow.

1. How many kinds of apples does the story tell about?

_____

_____

_____

2. Name the kinds of apples.

_____ _____ _____

_____ _____ _____

_____ _____ _____

3. What kind of apple do you like best?

_____

_____

_____

Name: _____

Number Recognition

Directions: Count the number of objects in each group. Draw a line to the correct number.

1

2

3

4

5

6

7

8

9

10

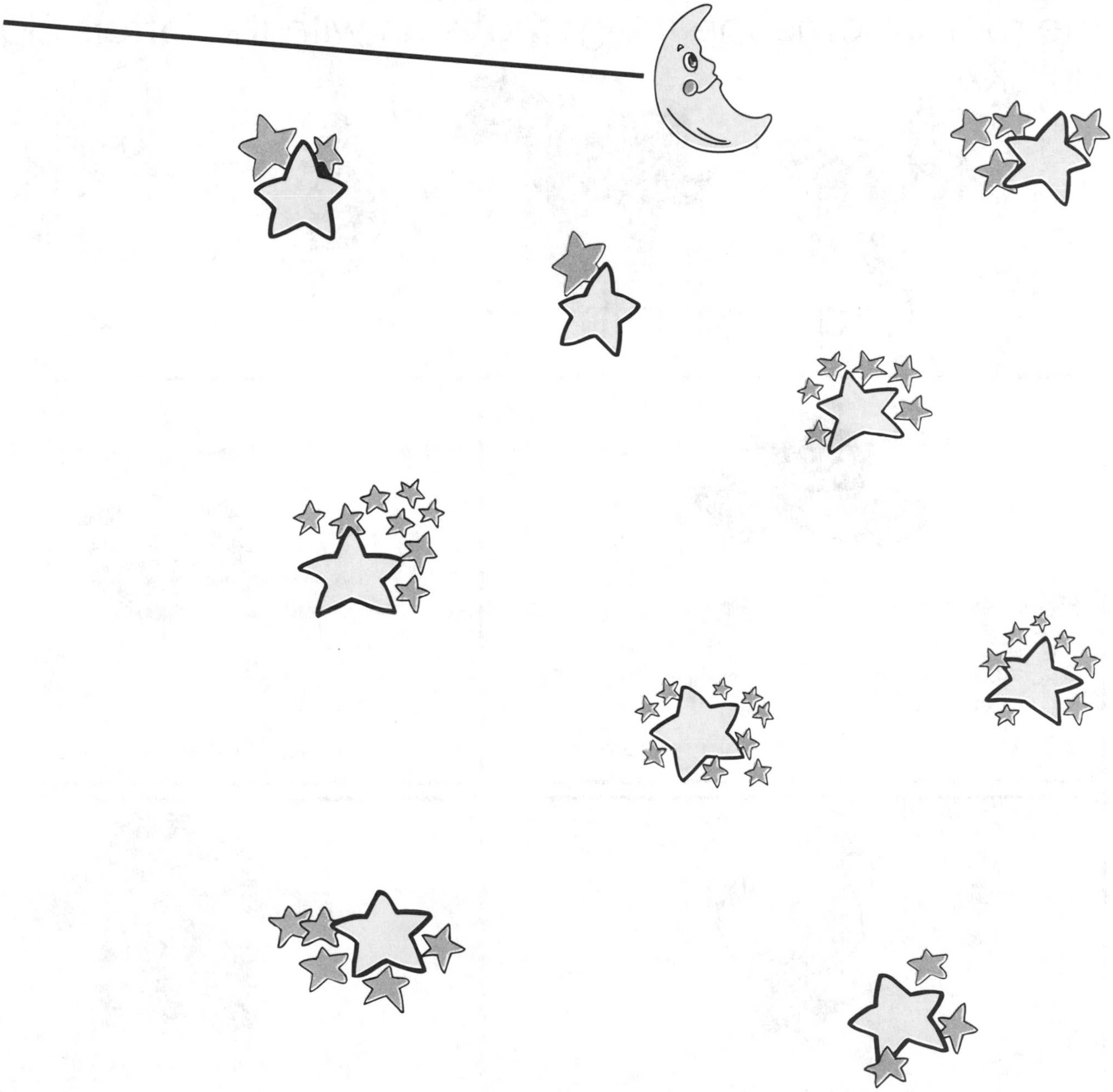

Name: _____

Beginning Consonants Gg, Hh, Jj, Kk

Directions: Say the name of each letter. Say the sound that each letter makes. Then, trace the letter that makes the beginning sound in the picture. After you finish, look around the room. Name the things that start with the letters Gg, Hh, Jj, and Kk.

Gg   Hh   Jj   Kk

Kk   Hh   Gg   Kk

Gg   Hh   Jj   Gg

I Know Which Letters Are Missing!

Directions: Fill in the missing letters for each word. Then write the word by yourself.

Like this:

frog frog frog

fi___   f___   ___h

___d   ___g   ___og

bi___ d___b d___

___at c___ ___t

Name: _____

Same/Different

Directions: Color the shape next to it that looks the same as the first shape in each row.

 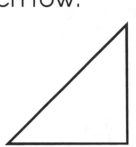  

 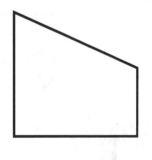  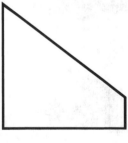

Name: _____

Counting

Directions: How many are there of each shape? Write the answers in the boxes. The first one is done for you.

Name: _____

Beginning Consonants Qq, Rr, Ss, Tt

Directions: Say the name of each letter. Say the sound that each letter makes. Then, trace each letter in the boxes. Color the picture which begins with the sound of the letter.

Name: _____

LESSON 2

AMERICA 2000

In 1989, George Bush became President of the United States. President Bush thought that education was important, so he helped make a plan for the future called AMERICA 2000.

Since people need to learn to read to be good citizens, part of the plan says that every grown-up will know how to read by the year 2000.

Look at the citizens waiting to vote. Name the different items in the picture that can be read.

Why do you think it is important for citizens to know how to read?

ACTIVITY 2

AMERICA 2000

Directions: Pretend it is the year 2000. You are much older now and want to share a book with someone you know who is in first grade. Draw a picture of the cover of the book you would read with the first grader.

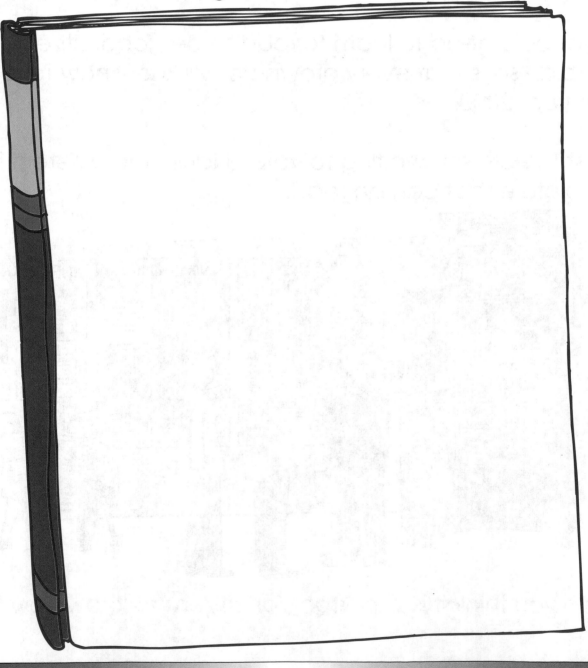

Lesson 2

Water

People need water to stay alive.
People use water for drinking, cooking and cleaning.
People use water for fun, too.

Animals need water to live.
Plants need water to grow.
Some animals and plants live in water.
All living things need clean water.

But not all water is clean.
Some water is very dirty, or polluted.
Polluted water makes people sick.
Animals and plants that live in polluted water can die.

How does water become polluted?

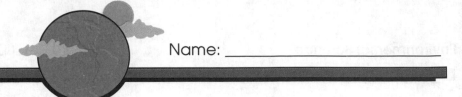

Name: _____

Activity 2

Living Things Need Clean Water

Directions: You will need cups, two bean seeds, water, soap suds, and oil. Follow each step in order.

1. Fill two cups with soil.

2. Mark the cups 1 and 2.

3. Plant a bean seed in each cup.

4. Water cup 1 with clean water.

5. Water cup 2 with water that has some soap suds and oil mixed in it.

6. Watch your seeds each day.

7. Always water cup 1 with clean water.

8. Always water cup 2 with polluted water.

Draw what you think will happen to the seeds in each cup?

Counting

Directions: How many are there of each shape? Write the answers in the boxes. The first one is done for you.

Name: _____

Beginning Consonants Vv, Ww, Xx, Yy, Zz

Directions: Say the name of each letter. Say the sound the letter makes. Then, trace the letters. Now, draw a line from the letters that match the beginning sound in each picture.

Vv Ww Xx Yy Zz

V v

W w

X x

Y Y

Z z

Name: _____

Skills Review: Following Directions, Color Word Vocabulary

Directions: Read the sentences. Follow the directions.

1. Color one house red.
2. Color two cars green.
3. Color two jets blue.
4. Color a big truck orange.
5. Color a bus yellow.

Name: _____

Review

Directions: Read the story. Then follow the instructions.

Some things used in baking are dry. Some things used in baking are wet. To bake a cake, first mix the salt, sugar and flour. Then add the egg. Now add the milk. Stir. Put the cake in the oven.

1. Circle the things that are wet.

2. Tell the order to mix things when you bake.

_____   _____   _____

1) ——————————   2) ——————————   3)——————————

_____   _____   _____

4) ——————————   5)——————————

3. The first things to mix are

       dry.   wet.

                              _____

4. Where are cakes baked?   _____

                                          _____

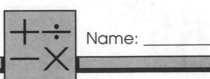

Name: _____

Review

Directions: Count the shapes and write the answers.

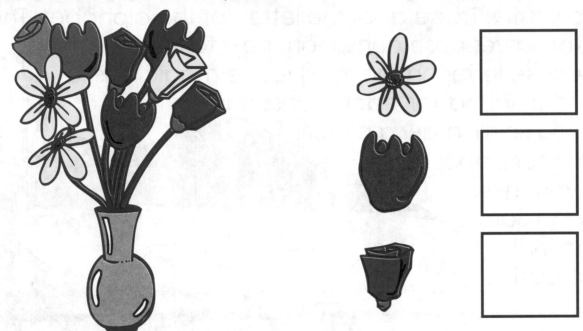

Directions: Fill in the missing numbers. Connect the dots to finish the picture.

Review

Directions: Help Meg and Kent and their dog, Sam, get to the magic castle. Trace all of the letters of the alphabet. Then, write the lower case consonant next to the matching upper case letter on the road to the magic castle. Make the sound for each consonant. After you finish, draw a picture on another paper of what you think Meg and Sam will find in the magic castle.

Name: _____

Review

Directions: Use the words in the pictures to write a sentence about each pet. Can you spell the name of the pet by yourself? Put a period at the end of each sentence.

Like this:

The 🐸 eats bugs   The frog eats bugs.

The 🐱 drinks milk

_____

_____

The 🐦 eats an apple

_____

_____

_____

The 🐭 jumps out

_____

_____

_____

The 🐟 sees a friend

_____

_____

_____

Name: _____

Review

Directions: Color the circles ○ red.

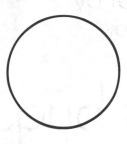 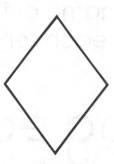 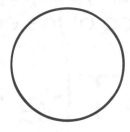 

Draw a triangle △. Color it. | Draw a square □. Color it.

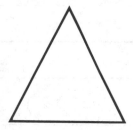 

Color the shapes that match.

 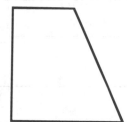 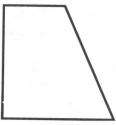 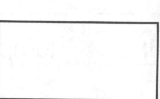

Put an **X** on the shape that is reversed.

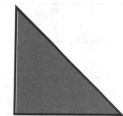  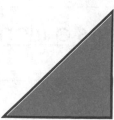 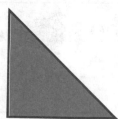

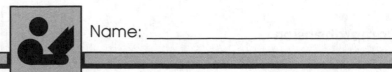

Which Are Opposites?

Directions: Draw a line between the opposites.

day

happy

big

open

front

little

closed

night

back

sad

Name: _____

I Like Cats

Directions: Read the story. Then answer the questions.

Do you like cats? I do. To pet a cat, move
slowly. Hold out your hand. The cat will
come to you. Then pet its head.
Do not grab a cat! It will run away.

1. To pet a cat, move   fast.

                              slow.

2. Give directions on how to pet a cat.

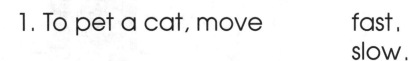

_____

1) Hold out your _____ .

_____

_____

2) The cat will _____ .

_____

_____

3) Pet the cat's _____ .

_____

_____

3. Do not do this _____
   to a cat!   _____

Name: _____

Game Of Opposites

Directions: Write each word from the word box under its opposite.

no	bad	hot	up	in	went	go	off

good

came

yes

stop

down

on

out

cold

Name: _____

Where Flowers Grow

Directions: Read about flowers. Then answer the questions.

Some flowers grow in pots. Many flowers grow in flower beds. Others grow beside the road. Some flowers begin from seeds. They grow into small buds. Then they open wide and bloom. Flowers are pretty!

1. Name 2 places flowers grow.

_____

_____

_____

2. Some flowers begin from _____ .

3. Then flowers grow into small _____ .

4. Flowers then open wide and _____ .

I Can Finish A Sentence!

Directions: Use the color words to finish these sentences. Then put a period at the end.

Like this: My new are _____ orange _____ .

 green tree    blue bike    yellow chick    red ball

1. The baby  is _____ □

2. This  is _____ □

3. My  is big and _____ □

4. My sister's  is _____ □

Name: _____

Classifying

Directions: Color the stars ☆.　　How many stars?_____

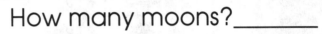

Color the moons ☾.　　　　　How many moons?_____

Color the half-circles ⊃.　　How many half-circles?_____

  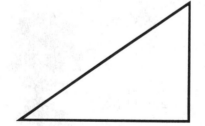 

Color the diamonds ◇.　　　How many diamonds?_____

 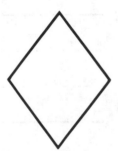 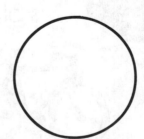 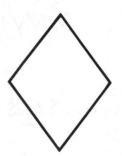

Name: _____

LESSON 3

The United States Flag

The United States flag stands for our country. It is a symbol of the United States and its people.

The flag can be seen in many places. Draw pictures of places where you have seen the American flag.

Why do you think Americans like to display the United States flag?

ACTIVITY 3

The United States Flag

Look at the astronaut on page 79. She is Sally Ride, the first American woman to orbit the earth. Sally Ride went to school for many years. She studied and worked hard to be an American astronaut and wear her country's flag during space travel.

Directions: Make a flag patch like the one on Sally Ride's suit. Wear your flag patch proudly!

Name: _____

Air

Living things need air to live.
People and animals need clean air to breathe.
Plants need clean air to grow.
Some air is not clean.
It is very dirty.

This air is polluted.
It may have dust, dirt and smoke in it.

Polluted air can be harmful to living things. It can make people sick.
Polluted air can harm plants and animals, too.

How can people help to keep our air clean?

Name: _____

Activity 3

Stop Air Pollution

Directions: Read the words in the bus. Read the sentences. Use the words in the bus to complete the sentences.

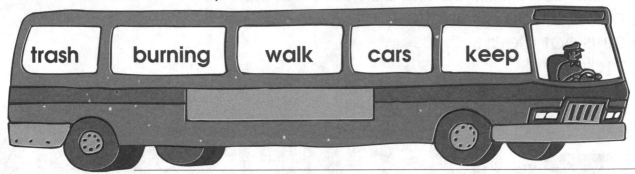

People can use _____ less.

They can _____ more.

Factories can _____ dirt out of smoke.

People can stop burning _____

People can stop_____ leaves.

Name: _____

Classifying

Directions: Draw a circle around the correct pictures.

What Can Swim?

What Can Fly?

Flower Puzzle

Directions: Re-read the story about flowers on page 74, Then fill in the puzzle with the right answers about flowers.

Across
1. Flowers do this when they open wide.
2. Some flowers grow from these.

Down
1. Before they bloom, flowers grow ___.
3. A flower can grow in a flower bed or a __.

Name: _____

I Know Which Words Sound The Same!

Directions: Circle the words that start with the same sound.

Like this:

red   blue   green   brown   black   yellow

Directions: Circle each word that has two letters the same in it. Write the two letters under the word.

Like this: (happy)   man   (feet)   boat

pp   ___   **ee**   ___

red   blue   green   brown   black   yellow

___   ___   ___

Directions: This time, circle the words that end with the same sound.

Like this:

red   blue   green   brown   black   yellow

Name: _____

Classifying

Directions: Mary and Bob are taking a trip into space. Help them find the stars ☆, moons ☾, circles ○, and diamonds ◇.

Color them: Use yellow for ☆.   Use blue for ☾.
Use red for ○.   Use purple for ◇.

How many stars ☆? _____   How many moons ☾? _____

How many circles ○? _____   How many diamonds ◇? _____

Name: _____

I Know Which Ones Are Sentences!

Directions: Some of these sentences tell the whole idea. Others have something missing. If you think something is missing, draw a line to a word that would finish that sentence. Remember to put a period after the last word in the sentence.

1. He is holding up his

2. Ken has a new puppy.

3. I can read a

4. We like to play games.

5. Pat wants to eat some

6. I will color the

7. This is my birthday.

book

hand.

tree

cake

Name: _____

Classifying

Directions: Help Mary and Bob sort their shapes. Draw a line from each shape to the basket it should go in.

Alphabetical Order

Directions: Look at the words in each box. Circle the word that comes first in a-b-c order.

A-B-C Order

duck	chair	peach
four	apple	this
rock	yellow	walk

game	light	mouse
boy	come	ten
pink	one	orange

angel	zebra	foot
table	watch	boat
hair	five	mine

look	who	book
blue	dog	tan
rope	black	six

Name: _____

Clowning Around

Directions: Look at the pictures of the clowns. Find 4 things that are different in picture 2. Color the things that are different.

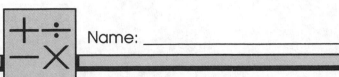

Shapes: Triangle

A triangle is a figure with three corners and three sides. This is a triangle △.

Directions: Find the triangles and put a circle around them.

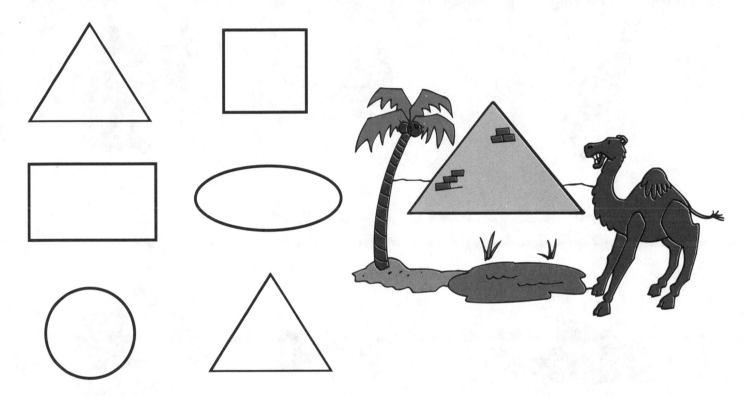

Directions: Trace the word.   Write the word.

triangle

Beginning and Ending Sounds Discrimination

Directions: Say the name of the picture. Draw a blue circle around the picture if it begins with the sound of the letter. Draw a green triangle around the picture if it ends with the sound of the letter.

w

l

m

k

n

u

t

s

z

Name: _____

I Know Which Words Begin The Same!

Directions: Say the name of the color and the picture beside it. If they begin with the same sound, write an **X** in the box.

Like this:

red   **X**   ☐   **blue**

yellow   ☐   ☐   **black**

green   ☐   ☐   **brown**

Name: _____

Classifying

Directions: Look at the shapes. Answer the questions.

How many white shapes? _____
How many blue shapes? _____
How many half-white shapes? _____
How many blue stars? _____
How many white circles? _____
How many half-blue shapes? _____

Name: _____

I Know How To Start A Sentence!

A sentence starts with a capital letter.

Directions: 1. Read the words by each picture. 2. Write them to make a sentence that tells about the picture. 3. Start each sentence with a capital letter—and end with a period.

Like this:  the girl coat a red has

The girl has a red coat.

1. box sees he a blue

2. picks the flower yellow she

3. green house colors he the

105

 Name: _____

Classifying

Directions: Look around your home or school. Find some pencils, pens, straws, toothpicks, paintbrushes, and crayons. Count them.

How many:

pencils ![pencil] ?_____   straws ![straw] ?_____

paintbrushes ![paintbrush] ?_____   pens ![pen] ?_____

toothpicks ![toothpick] ?_____   crayons ![crayon] ?_____

Draw a picture of each thing you found.

LESSON 4

The Declaration of Independence

In 1776, American leaders asked Thomas Jefferson to write the Declaration of Independence. The Declaration of Independence was an important paper. It said a new country called the United States of America had been formed. In the Declaration, Thomas Jefferson wrote that people have the right to be free. American citizens will always remember Jefferson's famous words.

Why do you think American leaders chose Thomas Jefferson to write the Declaration of Independence?

ACTIVITY 4

The Declaration of Independence

Directions: The Declaration of Independence reminds us that we are free. Write a "Declaration" that tells what ***being free*** means to you.

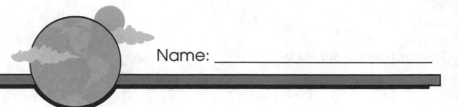

Name: _____

Lesson 4

Keep Our Land Clean

Things people throw away can cause pollution.
Pollution makes the environment unclean.
Junk, garbage and trash pollute the land.
People can help keep the land clean.
They can throw trash in the right place.
They can clean up their environment.

This is a picture of a school playground that shows pollution.

What do you think people can do to make the playground clean?

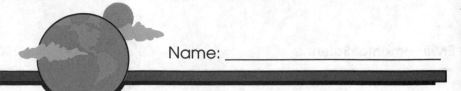

Activity 4

People Who Help

School custodians are men and women who keep schools clean. They help to get rid of the school's trash. They work to keep the environment clean.

Directions: Invite your custodian to visit your classroom. Ask your custodian to talk about ways that you can help to keep your school clean. Write two questions you will ask on the lines.

1. _____
   _____
   _____
   _____

2. _____
   _____
   _____
   _____

I Can Play A Word Game!

Directions: Finish the name of each color. Some words go down and some go across. Can you spell them by yourself?

Classifying

Directions: Look at the shapes with Mary. Then answer the questions.

How many stars ☆ ? _____

How many circles ○ ? _____

How many half-circles ◗ ? _____

How many moons ☾ ? _____

How many squares □ ? _____

How many triangles △ ? _____

How many diamonds ◇ ? _____

Skills Review: Sequencing, Classifying

Directions: 1) Write numbers by the sentences to show the order they belong in. 2) Write each word from the word box in its correct place.

Kim picks out food.

_____

Kim pays the man.

_____

Kim goes to the store.

_____

apple   ice cream   cookie   banana   orange   cake

Fruits	Sweets

Name: _____

Review

Directions: Read about cookies. Then answer the questions.

Cookies are made with many things. All cookies are made with flour. Some cookies have nuts in them. Some cookies do not. Some cookies have chips. Some cookies do not. Cookbooks give directions on how to make cookies. First turn on the oven. Then get all the things out that go in the cookies. Mix them together. Roll out, then cut the cookies. Bake the cookies. Now eat them!

1. Tell 1 way all cookies are the same.

_____

_____

_____

2. Name 2 different things in cookies. _____

_____   _____

_____   _____

_____   _____

3. Where do you find directions for making cookies?

_____

_____

_____

Name: _____

Review

Directions: Color the shapes in the picture as shown.

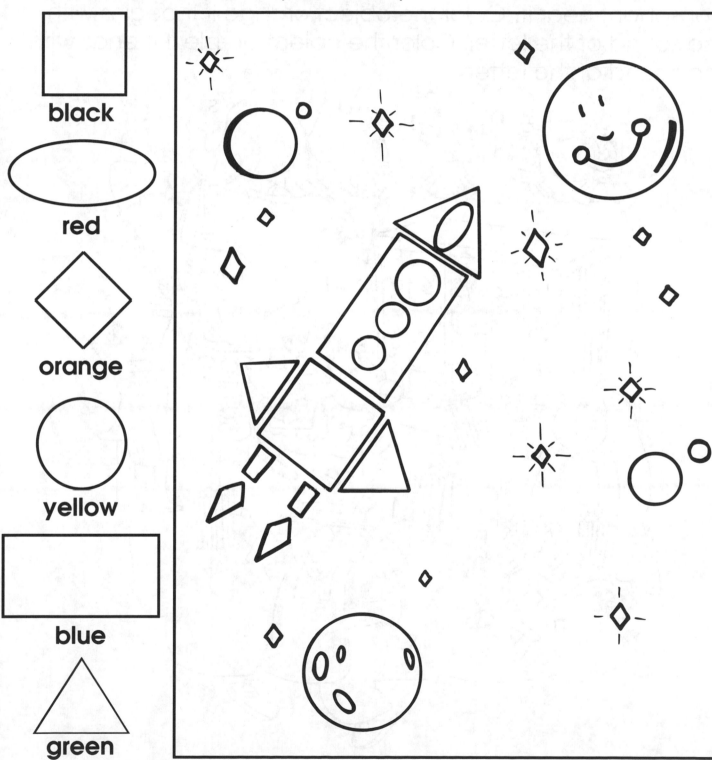

black

red

orange

yellow

blue

green

Name: _____

Review

Directions: Say the name of each object which has a consonant near it. Color the object orange if it begins with the sound of the letter. Color the object purple if it ends with the sound of the letter.

Review

Directions: 1. Write three sentences that tell about this picture. Use a color word in each one. Can you write the names of the colors and the pets by yourself now? 2. Remember to begin each sentence with a capital letter and end with a period.

Here are some more words you could use: **walks, sees, runs, flies, grows, eats, looks, jumps, sits.**

1._____

_____

2._____

_____

3._____

_____

Review

Directions: Color the stars ☆ blue.

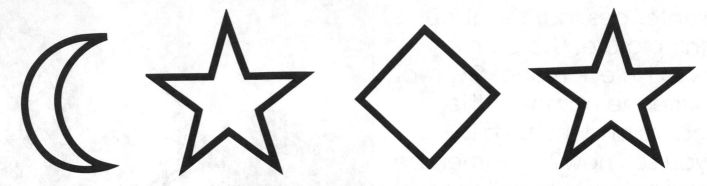

Count the moons ☾. How many moons ☾ ?_____

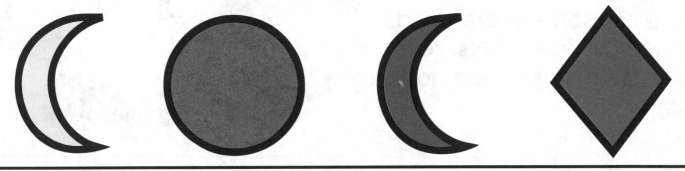

Help Bob and Mary find falling stars. Find the stars ☆ , the circles ○, and the diamonds ◇, on this page and draw a line from each to the correct baskets.

Name: _____

Rhyming Trains: Words with a

Directions: Each train has a group of pictures. Write the word that names the pictures. Read your rhyming words.

The short **a** sounds like the **a** in cat.

The long **a** sounds like the **a** in lake.

Name: _____

Find The Fruit

Directions: Fruit tastes good. It is sweet! Look at the pictures. Find the fruit. Then copy the name of each fruit in the blanks below.

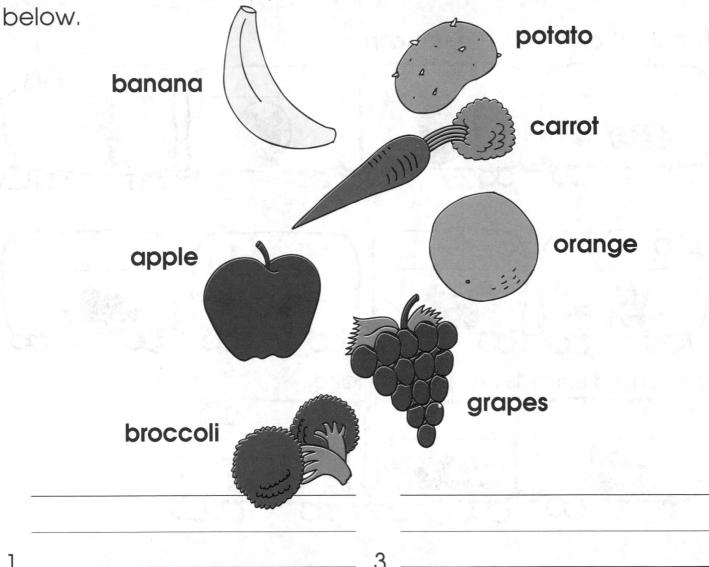

banana

potato

carrot

apple

orange

grapes

broccoli

1. _____ 3. _____

   _____   _____

   _____   _____

2. _____ 4. _____

   _____   _____

Name: _____

Addition 1, 2

Addition means "putting together" or adding two or more numbers to find the sum.

Directions: Count the cats and tell how many.

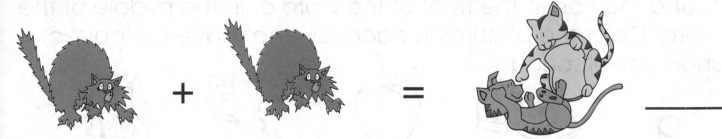

_____

_____

_____

Name: _____

Short Vowel Sounds

The short vowel sounds used in this book are found in the following words: ant, egg, igloo, on, up.

Directions: Say the name of each picture. The short vowel sound may be in the front of the word or in the middle of the word. Color the pictures in each row that have the correct short vowel sound.

a				
e				
i				
o				
u				

I Can Write The Names Of Food!

Directions: 1. Follow the lines to write the names of food.
2. Write the names by yourself. 3. Color the pictures. 4. Read the words to someone.

Like this:

bread **bread**

cookie

apple

cake

milk

egg

Name: _____

Duplicating

Directions: Look at the colored shape. Color the one beside it the same. Then draw the shape.

 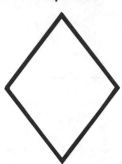

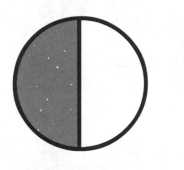 

 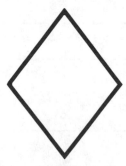

Name: _____

Words With e

Directions: Short **e** sounds like the **e** in hen. Long **e** sounds like the **e** in bee. 1) Look at the pictures. 2) If the word has a short **e** sound, draw a line to the hen. 3) If the word has a long **e** sound, draw a line to the bee.

bee

hen

Name: _____

An Animal Party

Directions: Look at the picture. Look at the word list. Then answer the questions.

bear	cat
dog	elephant
giraffe	hippo
pig	tiger

1. Which animals have on bow ties? _____

_____ _____

_____ _____

2. Which animal has on a hat? _____

_____

_____

3. Which animal has on a striped shirt? _____

_____

Name: _____

Addition 3, 4, 5, 6

Directions: Practice writing the numbers and then add.

3

4

5

6

_____
_____
_____
_____
_____
_____
_____

2
+4
———

1
+4
———

3
+2
———

1
+2
———

Long Vowel Sounds

Long vowel sounds say their own name. The following words have long vowel sounds: hay, me, pie, no, cute.

Directions: Say the name of each picture. Color the pictures in each row that have the correct long vowel sound.

a

e

i

o

u

Name: _____

I Know Which Ones Are Questions!

A question is a sentence that asks something.

Directions: 1. Write each sentence on the line. 2. Start all the sentences with capital letters. 3. Put a period at the end of the telling sentences. 4. Put a question mark at the end of the asking sentences.

Like this: do you like ice cream

Do you like ice cream?

1. milk comes from cows

_____

_____

2. is that cookie good

_____

_____

3. did you eat your apple

_____

_____

Name: _____

Duplicating

Directions: Color your circle ○ to look the same.

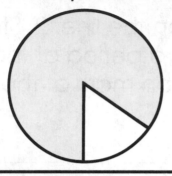 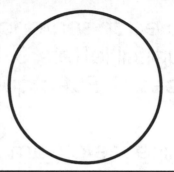

Color your square □ to look the same.

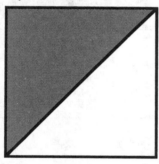 

Trace the triangle △. Color it to look the same.

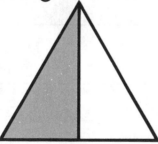 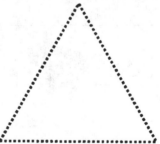

Trace the star ☆. Color it to look the same.

LESSON 5

The White House

We often hear about the White House in the news. The White House is where the President of the United States and his family live. The White House has 132 rooms. It has an indoor pool, a theater, a gym and a library.

Would you like to live in the White House? Why or why not?

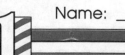

ACTIVITY 5

The White House

Directions: Pretend you have been asked to design a living room at the White House. What kinds of furniture, rugs, curtains, and lamps will your room have? What things will you include to show that the President and his family like to have fun together?

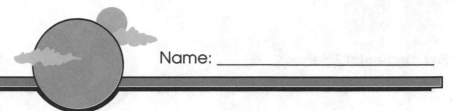

Name: _____

Start To Recycle

You know that trash pollutes the earth.
So people need to make less trash.
One way to make less trash is to recycle things.
Recycle means to save things and use them over and over.

Recycling is a way to help stop pollution.

People can recycle glass.

They can recycle paper.

People can recycle metal, too.

What is the best thing to do with your empty lunch bag?

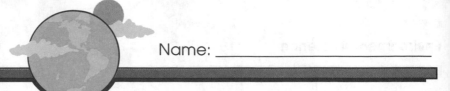

Activity 5

Let's Recycle

Look at the picture.
It is a place where people bring things to recycle.
They bring things made of paper, metal and glass.
What would you bring to recycle?

Directions: Draw something in each box that can be used over and over.

Where is the nearest place for you to recycle things?

Words With i

Directions: Short **i** sounds like the **i** in pig. Long **i** sounds like the **i** in kite. 1) Draw a circle around the words with the short **i** sound. 2) Draw an X on the words with the long **i** sound.

pin

five

pig

slide

kite

lid

tie

bib

pie

Pig Gets Ready

Directions: Look at the pictures of pig getting ready for the party. Then put them in 1-2-3-4 order.

What kind of party do you think pig is going to?

_____
_____
_____

Name: _____

Addition 4, 5, 6, 7

Directions: Practice writing the numbers and then add.

4   _____

5   _____

6   _____

7   _____

$$\begin{array}{r} 2 \\ +5 \\ \hline \end{array} \qquad \begin{array}{r} 3 \\ +1 \\ \hline \end{array}$$

$$\begin{array}{r} 4 \\ +1 \\ \hline \end{array} \qquad \begin{array}{r} 2 \\ +4 \\ \hline \end{array}$$

Discrimination Of Short And Long Aa

Directions: Say the name of each picture. If it has the short ă sound, color it red. If it has the long ā sound, color it yellow.

ă

ā

I Know Which Words Sound The Same!

Directions: Write the food words that answer the questions.

| egg | milk | ice cream | apple | cookie | cake |

1. Which food words start with the same sounds as the pictures?

_____   _____

_____   _____

_____

2. Which food word ends with the same sound as the picture?

_____

_____

3. Which food words have two letters together that are the same?

_____   _____   _____

_____   _____

Name: _____

Duplicating

Directions: Draw the triangle in the grid.

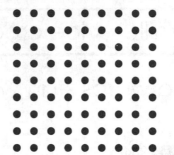

Draw this square in the grid.

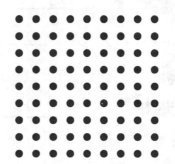

Draw this shape in the grid.

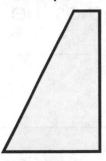
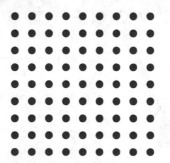

Draw this shape in the grid.

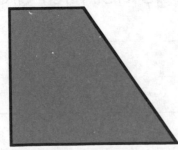

Reading

Name: _____

Words With o

Directions: The short **o** sounds like the **o** in dog. Long **o** sounds like the **o** in rope. 1) Draw a line from the picture to the word that names it. 2) Draw a circle around the word if it has a short **o** sound.

hot dog

fox

blocks

rose

boat

Name: _____

Teddy Bear, Teddy Bear

Directions: Read the teddy bear song. Then answer the questions.

Do you know this song? It is very old!

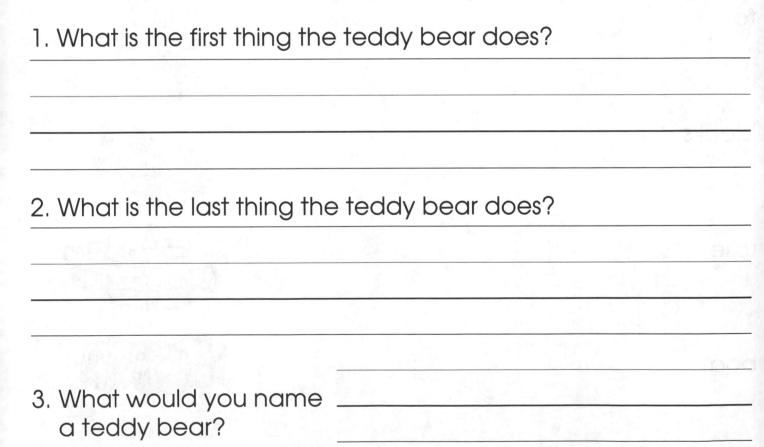

Teddy bear, teddy bear Turn around.
Teddy bear, teddy bear Touch the ground.
Teddy bear, teddy bear Climb upstairs.
Teddy bear, teddy bear Say your prayers.
Teddy bear, teddy bear Turn out the light.
Teddy bear, teddy bear Say "good night!"

1. What is the first thing the teddy bear does?

_____

_____

_____

2. What is the last thing the teddy bear does?

_____

_____

_____

3. What would you name a teddy bear? _____

_____

Name: _____

Addition 6, 7, 8

Directions: Practice writing the numbers and then add.

6 _____

7 _____

8 _____

$$\begin{array}{r} 3 \\ +4 \\ \hline \end{array}$$
$$\begin{array}{r} 5 \\ +1 \\ \hline \end{array}$$

$$\begin{array}{r} 2 \\ +6 \\ \hline \end{array}$$
$$\begin{array}{r} 4 \\ +4 \\ \hline \end{array}$$

Name: _____

Discrimination Of Short And Long Ee

Directions: Say the name of each picture. Draw a circle around the pictures which have the short ĕ sound. Draw a triangle around the pictures which have the long ē sound.

ĕ   ē

I Can Ask Questions!

Directions: Change each telling sentence into a question by moving the words around. Remember to put a question mark at the end of your question.

Like this: The girl is eating ice cream.

 Is the girl eating ice cream?

1. The boy is giving a cookie.

_____

_____

2. He is drinking milk.

_____

_____

3. She is making a cake.

_____

_____

Name: _____

Duplicating

Directions: Draw this shape in the grid.

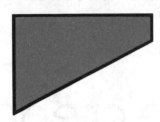
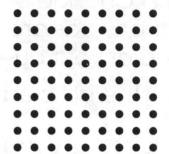

Draw this shape in the grid.

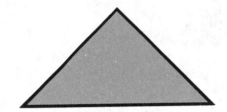

Draw this shape in the grid.

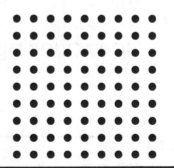

Draw this shape in the grid.

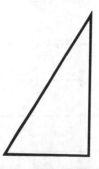
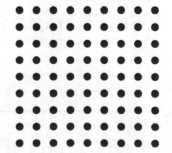

Words With u

Directions: The short **u** sounds like the **u** in bug. The long **u** sounds like the **u** in blue. 1) Draw a circle around the words with short **u**. 2) Draw an X on the words with long **u**.

rug

cup

music

tub

suit

glue

bug

puppy

gum

Name: _____

Put Teddy Bear To Bed

Directions: Re-read the story about the teddy bear. Look at the pictures. Number them in 1-2-3-4 order.

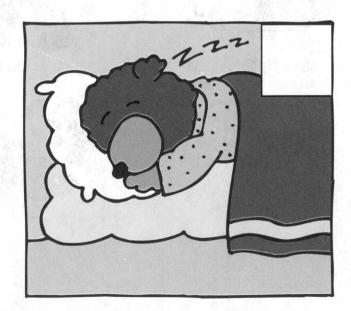

Name: _____

Addition 7, 8, 9

Directions: Practice writing the numbers and then add.

7   _____

8   _____

9   _____

$$\begin{array}{r} 8 \\ +1 \\ \hline \end{array}$$
$$\begin{array}{r} 3 \\ +5 \\ \hline \end{array}$$

$$\begin{array}{r} 2 \\ +7 \\ \hline \end{array}$$
$$\begin{array}{r} 6 \\ +1 \\ \hline \end{array}$$

Name: _____

Discrimination Of Short And Long Ii.

Directions: Say the name of each picture. Color it yellow if it has the short **i** sound. Color it red if it has the long **ī** sound.

i̅

i̲

Name: _____

I Know The Answers!

Directions: Use the food words to answer each question. The first letter is done for you. Can you write the other letters by yourself?

1. Which one can you drink?

m _____

2. Which one do you have to keep very cold?

i _____

3. Which one grows on trees?

a _____

4. Which one do you put birthday candles on?

c _____

5. Which one do people sometimes eat in the mornings?

e _____

6. Which one do you like best?

_____

Duplicating

Directions: Go outside. Look at your house. Now draw a picture of the shapes that make up your house. Name the shapes you see.

Name: _____

Short Vowel Sounds

Directions: In each box are three pictures. The words that name the pictures have missing letters. Write **a, e, i, o,** or **u** to finish the words.

p ____ n

p ____ n

p ____ n

b ____ g

b ____ g

b ____ g

c ____ t

c ____ t

c ____ t

h ____ t

h ____ t

h ____ t

Name: _____

How We Eat

Directions: Read about meals. Look at the word list. Then answer the questions.

Big kids eat with spoons and forks. They use a knife to cut their food. They use a spoon to eat soup and ice cream. They use a fork to eat peas and corn. They say "Thank you. It was good!" when they are done.

fork	ice cream	knife	soup

1. What do we use to cut food? _____

2. Name 2 things you can eat with a spoon.

_____ _____

_____

3. What do we use to eat peas and corn? _____

Subtraction 1, 2, 3

Subtraction means "taking away" or subtracting one number from another.

Directions: Practice writing the numbers and then subtract.

1

2

3

$$\begin{array}{r} 3 \\ -1 \\ \hline \end{array} \qquad \begin{array}{r} 4 \\ -3 \\ \hline \end{array}$$

$$\begin{array}{r} 2 \\ -1 \\ \hline \end{array} \qquad \begin{array}{r} 3 \\ -2 \\ \hline \end{array}$$

Name: _____

Discrimination Of Short And Long Oo

Directions: Say the name of each picture. If the picture has a long **o** sound, write a green **L** in the space. If the picture has a short **o** sound, write a red **S** in the space.

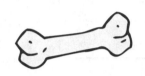

_____   _____

_____   _____   _____

_____   _____   _____

I Can Write My Own Sentences!

Directions: 1. For each sentence, write a word in the first space to tell who is doing something. Here are some words you could use: boy, girl, mother, father, baby. 2. Write one of the food words in the second space. 3. Draw a picture to show what is happening in your sentence.

Like this:

The ___**mother**___ is making ___**a cake**___ .

1. The _____ is eating _____ .

2. The _____ is buying _____ .

Name: _____

Finding Patterns

Directions: Find the hidden shape. Then color it.

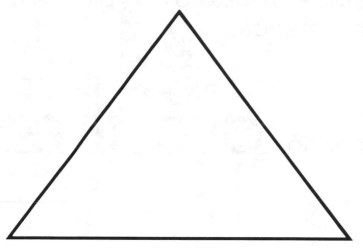

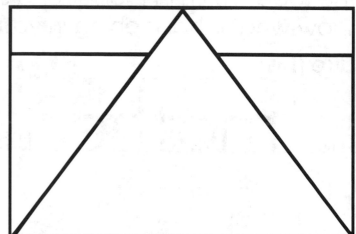

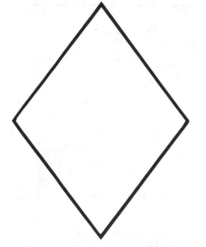

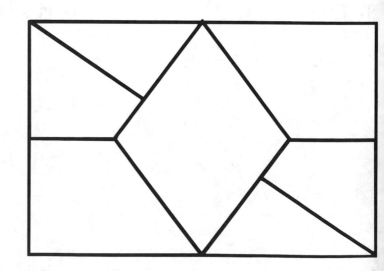

LESSON 6

Christopher Columbus

In 1492, Christopher Columbus and his sailors bravely set sail across the Atlantic Ocean from Europe. His three ships were called the *Niña*, the *Pinta*, and the *Santa Maria*.

Columbus knew that the winds would carry his three ships westward. But he did not know that after many weeks, his ships would reach a land that would later be named America.

How do you think Columbus and the sailors felt on their long trip across the ocean?

ACTIVITY 6

Christopher Columbus

Directions: Ask someone to help you make a sailing ship. You will need a toothpick, a piece of flat, recycled plastic foam, scissors, a shallow pan, and water.

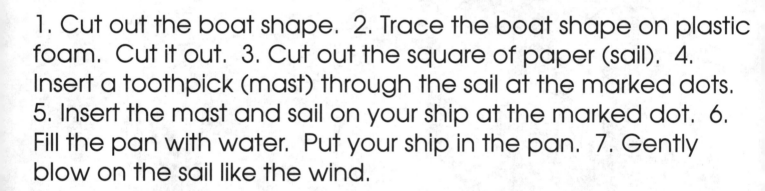

1. Cut out the boat shape. 2. Trace the boat shape on plastic foam. Cut it out. 3. Cut out the square of paper (sail). 4. Insert a toothpick (mast) through the sail at the marked dots. 5. Insert the mast and sail on your ship at the marked dot. 6. Fill the pan with water. Put your ship in the pan. 7. Gently blow on the sail like the wind.

Watch your ship sail across the water just like the *Niña*, the *Pinta*, and the *Santa Maria*!

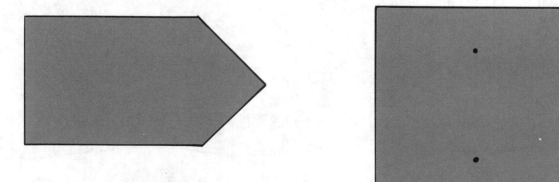

Summary

Directions: Read the sentences on this page and on page 166.

Draw a picture to go with each sentence.

Cut the pages on the dotted lines.

Put the page numbers in order.

Make a book.

Share your book with a friend.

Saving Our Planet by: _____ _____ _____ _____ 1	Our environment is everything around us. 3
Polluted air is harmful. 5	People can recycle things. 7

Name: _____

Review

Follow the directions on page 165 and complete your book.

Living things need water. · · 4	The Earth is where we live. 2
We can stop pollution! 8	Trash pollutes the land. 6

Name: _____

Long Vowel Sounds

Directions: Write **a, e, i, o,** or **u** in each blank to finish the word. Draw a line from the word to its picture.

_____

c _____ ke

r _____ se

k _____ te

f _____ t

m _____ le

Name: _____

Things That Belong

Directions: Look at the pictures in each row across. Circle the ones in each row that belong. Write the names of the pictures that do not belong.

Row 1

knife   key   fork   spoon

Row 2

orange   apple   sucker   banana

Row 3

beach ball   soccer ball   baseball   apple

These do not belong:

Row 1   Row 2   Row 3

_____   _____   _____

_____   _____   _____

_____   _____   _____

_____   _____   _____

Name: _____

Subtraction 3, 4, 5, 6

Directions: Practice writing the numbers and then subtract.

3

4

5

6

_____
_____
_____
_____
_____
_____
_____
_____
_____

$$\begin{array}{r} 5 \\ -2 \\ \hline \end{array}$$

$$\begin{array}{r} 6 \\ -1 \\ \hline \end{array}$$

$$\begin{array}{r} 6 \\ -3 \\ \hline \end{array}$$

$$\begin{array}{r} 5 \\ -1 \\ \hline \end{array}$$

Name: _____

Discrimination Of Short And Long Uu

Directions: Say the name of the picture. If it has the long **u** sound, write a **u** in the unicorn column. If it has a short **u** sound, write a **u** in the umbrella column.

_____   _____

_____   _____

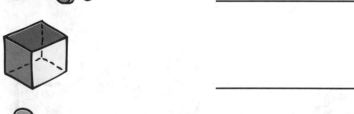

_____   _____

_____   _____

_____   _____

_____   _____

Name: _____

I Can Finish A Story!

Directions: Write the words in the story. Then read your story to someone.

Kim got up in the morning.

"Do you want an _____ ?" her mother asked.

"Yes, please," Kim said.

        "May I have some _____ , too?"

"OK," her mother said.

"How about some _____ ?" Kim asked with a smile.

Her mother laughed. "Not now," she said.

She put an _____ in Kim's lunch.

"Do you want a _____ or some

_____ today?"

"Both!" Kim said.

Name: _____

Finding Patterns

Directions: Find the hidden letter in each box. Trace it with a crayon.

1. Hidden letter: **T**

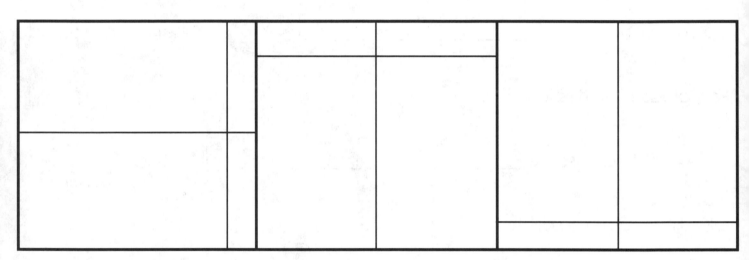

2. Hidden letter: **E**

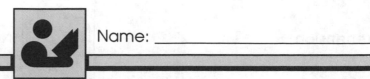

Name: _____

Skills Review: Vowel Sounds

Directions: Draw a circle around the word if it has a long vowel sound. Remember: a long vowel says its name.

feet

snake

cup

hose

tie

hat

dog

rake

bug

bone

bib

net

Name: _____

Review

Directions: Read about how to ski. Answer the questions. Then put the skiing pictures in 1-2-3-4 order.

Skiing is Fun
You need to dress warmly to ski. Two skis will fit on your boots. You wear the skis to a chair. The chair is called a ski lift. It takes you up in the air to a hill. When you get off, ski down the hill.
Be careful!
Sometimes you will fall.

1. How many skis do you need? _____

2. Skiing is classified as an   indoor sport.
                                       outdoor sport.

Name: _____

Review

Directions: Trace the numbers. Work the problems.

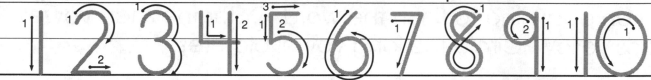

$$\begin{array}{r} 9 \\ -3 \\ \hline \end{array}$$

$$\begin{array}{r} 6 \\ +2 \\ \hline \end{array}$$

$$\begin{array}{r} 3 \\ +4 \\ \hline \end{array}$$

$$\begin{array}{r} 2 \\ -1 \\ \hline \end{array}$$

$$\begin{array}{r} 5 \\ +4 \\ \hline \end{array}$$

$$\begin{array}{r} 9 \\ -5 \\ \hline \end{array}$$

$$\begin{array}{r} 7 \\ +2 \\ \hline \end{array}$$

$$\begin{array}{r} 8 \\ -6 \\ \hline \end{array}$$

$$\begin{array}{r} 4 \\ -2 \\ \hline \end{array}$$

$$\begin{array}{r} 6 \\ +3 \\ \hline \end{array}$$

$$\begin{array}{r} 9 \\ -7 \\ \hline \end{array}$$

$$\begin{array}{r} 1 \\ +7 \\ \hline \end{array}$$

Short And Long Vowel Sounds

Directions: Say the name of the picture. Write the correct vowel on each line to finish the word. Color the short vowel pictures yellow. Circle the long vowel pictures.

  j _____ g

  t _____ pe

 l _____ af

 p _____ n

 l _____ ck

 c _____ t

 c _____ be

  b _____ ll

 k _____ te

 r _____ pe

Name: _____

Review

Directions: Write two telling sentences and one question about this picture. Be sure to use the food words you know — and the color and pet words.

Here are some more words you could use: **boy, girl, water, table, candles, finds, birthday, out, eats, jumps, helps, sees, looks, stops, falls.**

Two telling sentences:

1. _____

_____

2. _____

_____

One question: _____

_____

_____

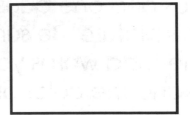

Name: _____

Review

Directions: Color your shape to look the same.

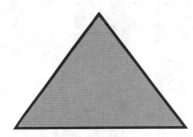

Draw the triangle in the grid. Color it to match.

Find the shape in the squares. Color it.

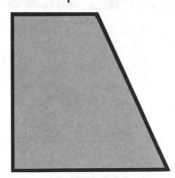

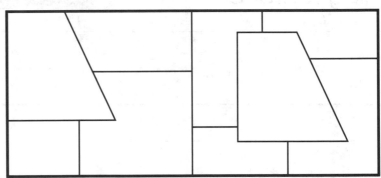

Find the letter **M** in each square. Trace it with a crayon.

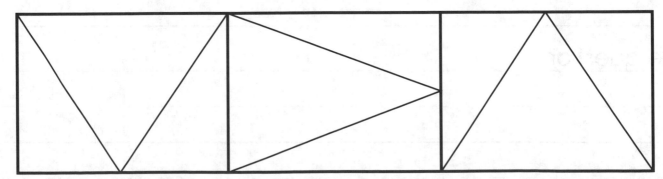

Name: _____

Consonant Blends: bl, cl, fl, gl, pl, sl

Directions: The name of each picture begins with a **blend**.
Draw a circle around the beginning blend for each picture.

bl fl cl

cl fl gl

fl bl pl

fl cl gl

pl gl cl

sl fl gl

gl fl cl

fl sl cl

cl gl sl

Name: _____

Clowns

Directions: Color the clowns. Then answer the questions. Use your crayons this way: 1 = red, 2 = blue, 3 = orange, 4 = pink.

1. What color is the clowns' hair?

_____
_____
_____
_____

2. What color are the clowns' noses?

_____
_____
_____

3. What color are the clowns' hats?

_____
_____
_____

4. What color are the clowns' clothes?

_____
_____

Name: _____

Zero

Directions: Write the number.

Example:

How many monkeys?

_3_ _____

How many monkeys?

_____ _0_

How many kites?

_____
_____
_____
_____

How many kites?

_____
_____
_____
_____

How many flowers?

_____
_____
_____

How many flowers?

_____
_____
_____

How many apples?

_____
_____
_____

How many apples?

_____
_____
_____

Name: _____

ABC Order

Use the first letter of each word to put the words in alphabetical order.

Directions: Draw a circle around the first letter of each word. Then, put the words in **ABC** order.

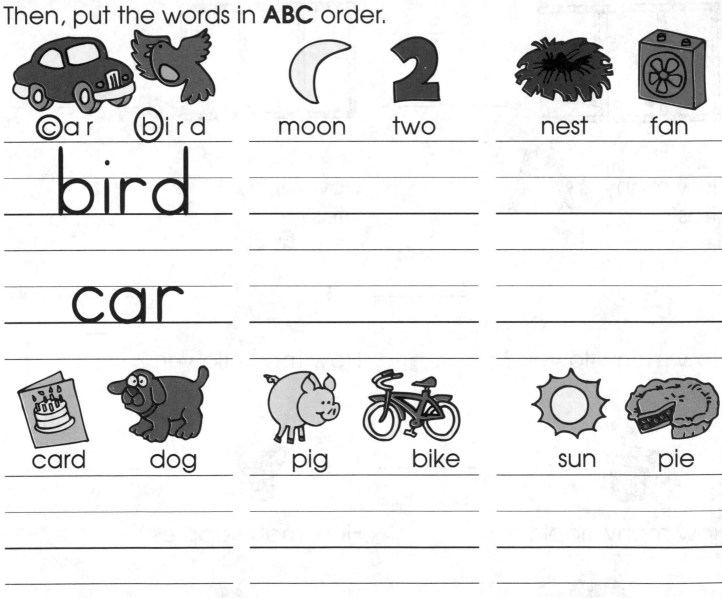

ⓒa r   ⓑi r d

bird

car

moon   two

nest   fan

card   dog

pig   bike

sun   pie

I Can Write "Doing" Words!

"Doing" words tell things we can do.

Directions: 1. Follow the lines to write the words. 2. Then write the words by yourself. 3. Read the words to someone.

Like this:

sleep   sleep

run

make

ride

play

stop

Name: _____

Finding Patterns

Directions: Draw a line from the shape on the left to the box of shapes on the right that has the same pattern.

 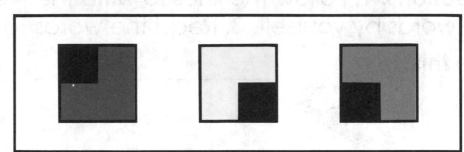

 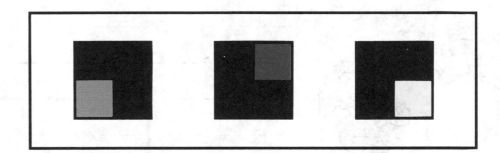

 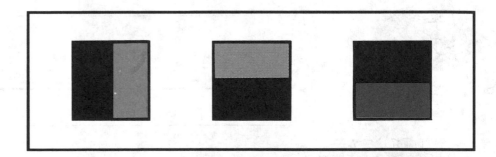

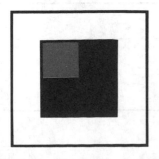 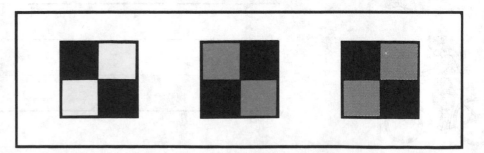

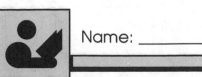

Consonant Blends: br, cr, dr, fr, pr, tr

Directions: The beginning blend for each word is missing. Using the list, fill in the correct blend to finish the word. Draw a line from the word to its picture.

_____

_____ ain

_____ og

_____ ab

_____ um

_____ ush

_____ esent

Name: _____

Simon Says

Directions: Read about how to play Simon Says. Then answer the questions.

SIMON SAYS, CLAP YOUR HANDS!

Simon Says

Here is how to play "Simon Says." One kid is Simon. Simon is the leader. Everyone must do what Simon says and does, but only if the leader says "Simon says" first. Let's try it. "Simon says pat your head." "Simon says pat your nose." "Pat your toes." Oops. You patted your toes! I did not say "Simon says" first. You are out!

_____

_____

1. Who is the leader in this game?_____

_____

_____

2. What must the leader say first each time? ———————————

_____

_____

3. What happens if you do something and the leader did not say"Simon says?" _____

_____

Name: _____

Zero

Directions: Write the number that tells how many.

How many sailboats?

 _____

How many sailboats?

_____

How many eggs?

 _____

How many eggs?

 _____

How many marshmallows?

 _____

How many marshmallows?

_____

How many candles?

 _____

How many candles?

 _____

Name: _____

ABC Order

Directions: Circle the first letter of each animal's name. Write a 1, 2, 3, 4, 5, or 6 on the line next to the animals' names to put the words in **ABC** order.

skunk _____

dog _____

butterfly _____

zebra _____

tiger _____

fish _____

Name: _____

I Know Which Word To Write!

Directions: Read each sentence and write the words in the correct spaces.

Like this:

go

sleep   I will __go__ to bed and __sleep__ all night.

1.

see

jump   The girls _____ the frogs _____ .

2.

sit

run   After the boys _____ , they _____ and rest.

3.

stop

play   They _____ at the park so they can _____ .

4.

ride

make   They will _____ a car to _____ in.

Finding Patterns

Directions: Draw a line from the letter on the left to the group of squares with the same hidden letter.

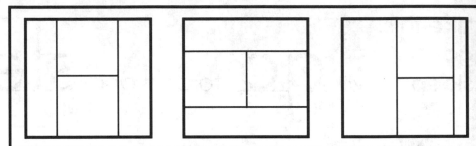

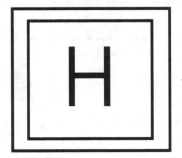

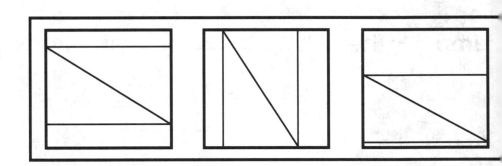

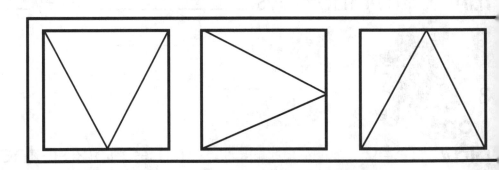

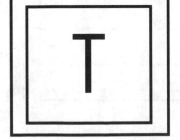

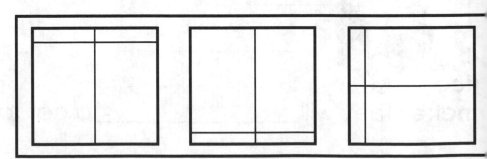

Name: _____

The Statue of Liberty

The Statue of Liberty stands on an island in New York Harbor. Over the years, millions of people came to the United States on ships from other countries. As their ships passed the Statue of Liberty, the people cheered and waved. The Statue of Liberty became a symbol of hope and freedom for these people who dreamed of becoming United States citizens.

Why do you think millions of people would leave their countries to come to the United States?

ACTIVITY 7

The Statue of Liberty

What do you think the people on the ships said as they saw the Statue of Liberty in the Harbor? Write their words in the balloons.

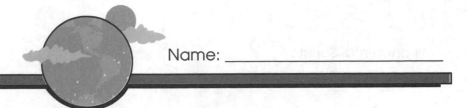

Energy To Heat Our Homes

Most of our homes use electricity to make heat.
Most electricity is made by burning gas, oil, or coal.
Gas, oil, and coal are sources of energy.
Now new kinds of houses are being built.
These homes use solar energy, or energy from the sun.
They are called solar homes.

A solar home has glass sheets on its roof.
There are black plates under the glass sheets.
The glass sheets and black plates collect sunlight.
On sunny days, the plates and sheets help turn sunlight into heat.

Solar homes do not cost much to heat because sunlight is free.
They do not use up gas, oil, or coal.
They do not make the air dirty.
Solar homes do not pollute the environment.

How is your home heated?

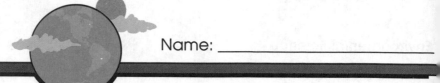

Name: _____

Activity 6

Would You Build A Solar Home?

Directions: Think about what you
know about solar homes.
Read each question.
Write your answer on the
lines.

1. Why might a person build a solar home?

_____

_____

2. Why would people not build solar homes in some places?

_____

_____

3. Would you like to live in a solar home? Tell why you think as you do.

_____

_____

_____

_____

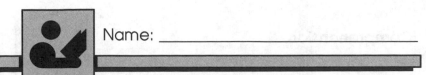
Consonant Blends: sk, sl, sm, sp, st, sw

Directions: Draw a line from the picture to the blend that begins its word.

sk

sl

sm

sn

sp

st

sw

Name: _____

Same/Different: Look At Simon

Directions: Look at both pictures. Find 4 things in picture #2 that are not in picture #1. Look at the word list to see how to spell the word. Write your answers in the numbered spaces.

hat	head	socks	bare feet
feather	watch	untied shoes	tied shoes

1. _____

2. _____

3. _____

4. _____

Name: _____

Addition 1, 2, 3, 4, 5

Directions: Add the numbers. Put your answers in the nests.

Example: $2 + 3 =$  5

$1 + 2 =$

$1 + 3 =$

$4 + 1 =$

$1 + 1 =$

The Super E

When you add an **e** to some words, the vowel changes from a short vowel sound to a long vowel sound.

Example: rip + **e** = ripe.

Directions: Say the word under the first picture in each pair. Then, add an **e** to the word under the matching picture. Say the new word.

pet _____

tub _____

man _____

kit _____

pin _____

cap _____

Name: _____

I Know Which Words Sound The Same!

Directions: Write the "doing" words that answer the questions.

| sit | run | make | see | jump | stop | play | ride |

1. Which three words start the same as ?

_____ _____ _____

_____ _____ _____

_____ _____ _____

2. Which two words start the same as  ?

_____ _____

_____ _____

3. Which words start the same as each of these words?

 _____   _____   _____

_____ _____ _____

4. Which words end the same as these?

 _____  _____  _____

_____ _____ _____

_____ _____ _____

Name: _____

Tracking

Directions: Trace the lines to connect the shapes. Then color the matching shapes the same color.

circle   **square**   **half-circle**   **star**   **triangle**

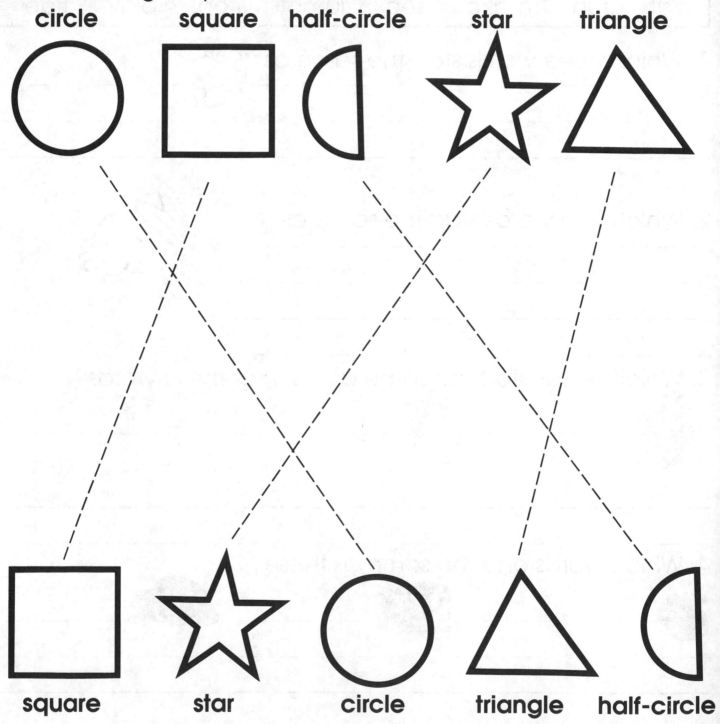

square   **star**   **circle**   **triangle**   **half-circle**

Name: _____

Consonant Digraphs: ch, sh, th, wh

Directions: Look at the first picture in each row. Circle the pictures in the row that start with the same sound.

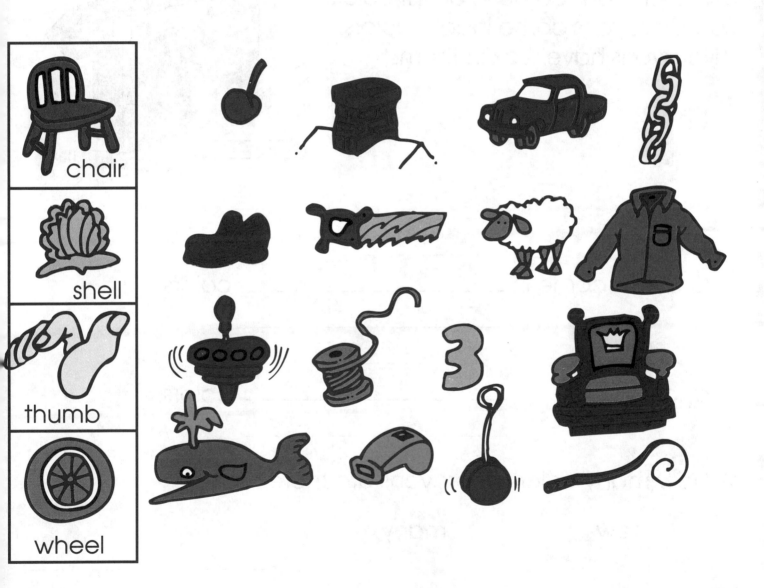

chair

shell

thumb

wheel

Comprehension: Do You Like Crayons?

Directions: Read about crayons. Then answer the questions.

There are many colors of crayons
Some crayons come in bright colors.
Some crayons come in light colors.
All crayons have wax in them.

_____

_____

1. Crayons come in _____ colors

_____

_____

and _____ colors.

_____

2. How many colors of crayons are there?

few   many

_____

_____

3. What do all crayons have in them? _____

_____

Name: _____

Addition 6, 7, 8, 9, 10

Directions: Add the numbers. Put your answers in the doghouses.

Example: 4 + 2 =  6

2 + 6 =

7 + 3 =

6 + 1 =

4 + 5 =

6 + 2 =

7 + 2 =

Name: _____

Compound Words

Compound words are two words that are put together to make one word.

Directions: Look at the pictures and read the two words that are next to each other. Now, put the words together to make a new word. Write the new word.

Example:

house   **boat**

houseboat

_____

_____

side   **walk**

_____

_____

lip   **stick**

_____

_____

sand   **box**

_____

_____

lunch   **box**

_____

Name: _____

I Can Show Two Of Something!

To show two or more of something, most of the time we add "s" to the end of the word.

Like this:

one cat    two cats

Directions: For each sentence, add "s" to show two or more. Then write in the "doing" word that finishes the sentence.

| sit | jump | stop | ride |

Like this:

The frog __s__ __sleep__ in the sun.

_____

1. The boy ____ _____ on the fence.

_____

2. The car ____ _____ at the sign.

_____

3. The girl ____ _____ in the water.

_____

4. The dog ____ _____ in the wagon.

_____

Name: _____

Tracking

Directions: Connect the letter on the left with the same letter on the right. Use a different color crayon for each line.

O

Q

S

D

G

N

D

Q

N

O

S

G

Consonant Blends: ft, lt

Directions: Write **lt** or **ft** to complete the words.

be _____

ra _____

sa _____

qui _____

ki _____

Name: _____

Can You Find Me?

Directions: To find the hidden picture, color only the shapes with a number inside. Do not color the shapes with a letter inside.

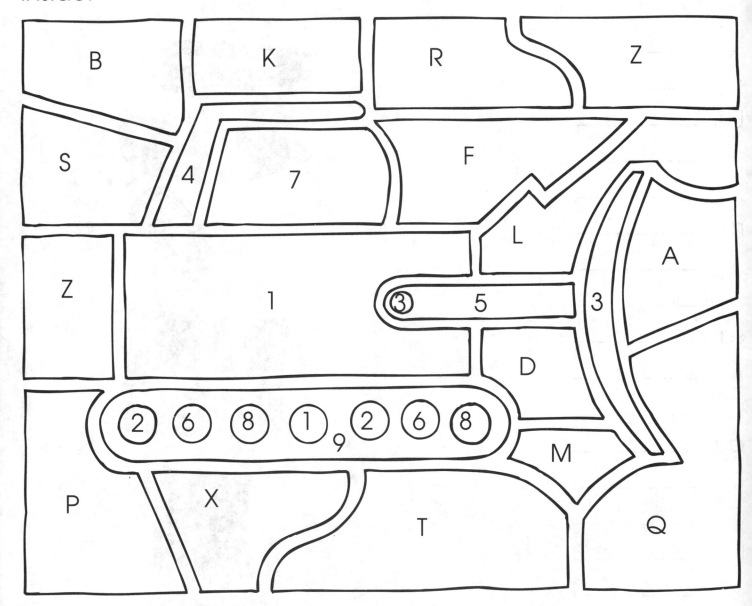

Name: _____

Subtraction 1, 2, 3, 4, 5

Directions: Count the fruit in each bowl. Write your answers on the blanks. Circle the problem that matches your answer.

4

5
-1

4
-2

___

3
-0

4
-2

___

5
-1

4
-3

___

3
-2

5
-0

Name: _____

Synonyms

Synonyms are words that mean the same thing. **Start** and **begin** are synonyms.

Directions: Find the two words that describe each picture. Write the words in the boxes below the picture.

small	funny	large	sad	silly	little	big	unhappy

I Know Which Spelling Is Right!

Directions: Circle the word that is spelled right. Then write the word the right way.

Like this:

seep
(sleep)
slep

sleep

paly
pay
play

seee
cee
see

rum
run
runn

jump
jumb
junp

mack
maek
make

Name: _____

Tracking

Directions: Draw a straight line from **A** to **B**. Use a different color crayon for each line.

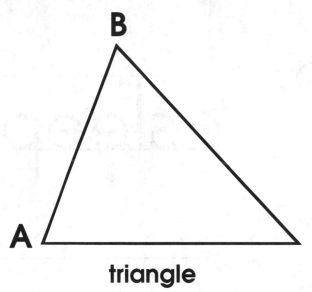

triangle

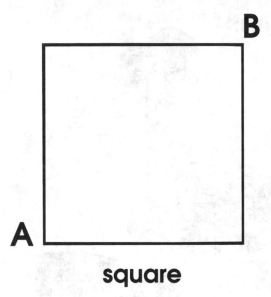

square

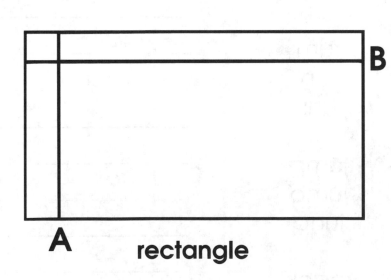

rectangle

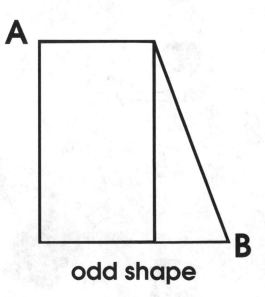

odd shape

Name: _____

Consonant Blends: lf, lk, sk, sp, st

Directions: Draw a line from the picture to the blend that ends its word.

lf

lk

sk

sp

st

Name: _____

Rhyme Time

Directions: Read about words that rhyme. Then answer the questions.

Words that rhyme have the same end sounds. "Wing" and "sing" rhyme. "Boy" and "toy" rhyme. "Rhyme" and "time" rhyme. Can you think of other words that rhyme?

1. Words that rhyme have the same   end sounds
                                          end letters

2. Tell the words that rhyme with these words.

Wing	Boy	Rhyme
_____	_____	_____
_____	_____	_____
_____	_____	_____
		_____
		_____

3. Can you think of a word on your _____
   own that rhymes with "pink?" _____

Name: _____

Subtraction 6, 7, 8, 9, 10

Directions: Count the flowers. Write your answers on the blanks. Circle the problems with the same answer.

$$\begin{array}{r} 10 \\ -1 \\ \hline \end{array}$$ $$\begin{array}{r} 9 \\ -1 \\ \hline \end{array}$$ $$\begin{array}{r} 7 \\ -2 \\ \hline \end{array}$$ $$\begin{array}{r} 9 \\ -3 \\ \hline \end{array}$$

$$\begin{array}{r} 9 \\ -6 \\ \hline \end{array}$$ $$\begin{array}{r} 8 \\ -0 \\ \hline \end{array}$$ $$\begin{array}{r} 10 \\ -2 \\ \hline \end{array}$$ $$\begin{array}{r} 8 \\ -1 \\ \hline \end{array}$$

Name: _____

Antonyms

Antonyms are words that are opposites. **Hot** and **cold** are antonyms.

Directions: Draw a line between the words that are opposites. Can you think of other words that are opposites?

closed

below

full

empty

above

old

new

open

Name: _____

I Can Ask Questions!

Directions: Write a question about each picture. Start with "can." Add a "doing" word. Remember that a question starts with a capital letter and ends with a question mark.

Like this:

I with you can

Can I sit with you?

cookies she can _____

_____

_____

_____

with you can I  _____

_____

_____

_____

I can in the box  _____

_____

_____

_____

Name: _____

Tracking

Directions: Trace 3 paths from **A** to **B**.

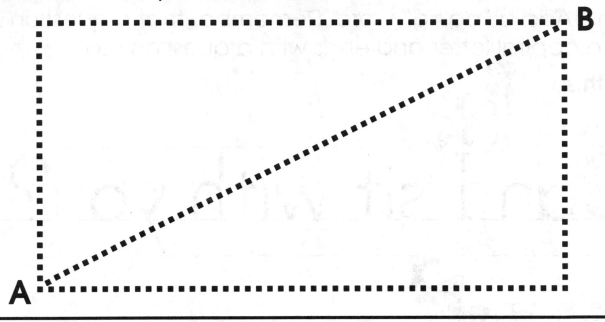

Trace the path from **A** to **B**.

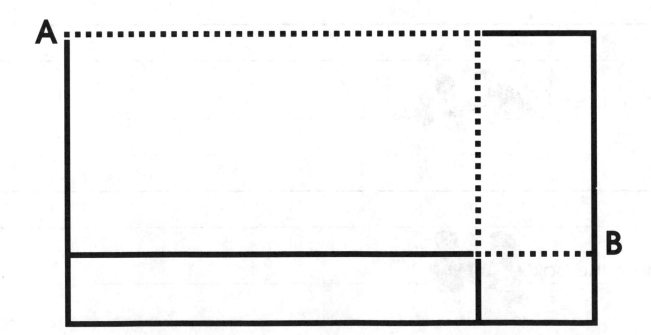

How many corners did you turn? _____

LESSON 8

The Liberty Bell

The Liberty Bell is a symbol of our country. It stands for America's independence.

On July 8, 1776, the Liberty Bell rang out to announce that the United States had become a new country. Later, the Liberty Bell cracked, so it could no longer be rung.

Today, people can see the Liberty Bell in Philadelphia. Visitors can look at the bell and think about when it rang to declare freedom.

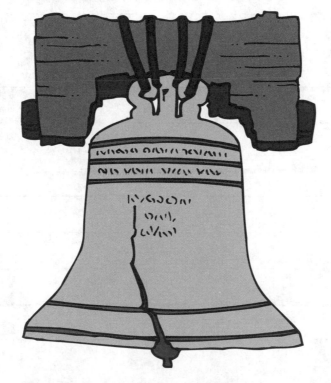

Suppose you heard the Liberty Bell ringing on July 8, 1776. What might you say? How would you feel?

Name: _____

ACTIVITY 8

The Liberty Bell

Directions: A newspaper headline tells about something important. Think about the day the Liberty Bell rang to tell people that the United States had become a new country. What would the newspaper headline say about the new country? What would it say about the bell? Write the headline on the lines.

★EARLY TIMES NEWSPAPER★

July 8, 1776

Name: _____

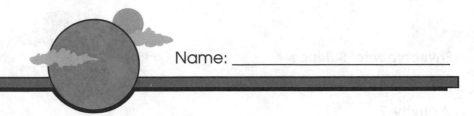

Rain Forests

Trees need a lot of water and warm weather to grow.
It is always hot in a rain forest.
There is always plenty of rain.
Trees grow and grow in a rain forest.

Now people have started to chop down trees in rain forests.
This chopping harms the environment.
It hurts the many animals that live in rain forests.
It may change the weather all around the world.
It may even change the air we breathe.
People must stop cutting down the trees in rain forests.

How does cutting down the trees in rain forests hurt animals?

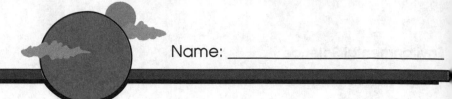

Activity 7

Save The Trees

Directions: Look at the picture. People are chopping down trees in a rain forest. They do not understand what will happen. Pretend you are in this rain forest. What will you say to the people? Write your words on the lines above the picture.

If you cut down the trees, then

_____

_____

_____

_____

_____

Color the picture.

Get some drawing paper.

Draw what will happen after you talk to the people.

Name: _____

Consonant Blends: mp, nd, nk, ng

Directions: In every box is a word ending and a list of letters. Add each of the letters to the word ending to make rhyming words.

____ and
b _____
h _____
l _____
s _____

____ ent
b _____
d _____
t _____
w _____

____ ump
b _____
d _____
j _____
p _____

____ ink
p _____
s _____
l _____
th _____

____ ing
r _____
s _____
st _____
k _____

____ ank
b _____
r _____
s _____
t _____

Name: _____

I Can Find A Rhyme

Directions: Look at the pictures in each row across. Circle the ones that rhyme. Then write the names of the ones that do not rhyme in the blanks below.

Row 1

Row 2

Row 3

These words do not rhyme with the others in the row.

Row 1	Row 2	Row 3
_____	_____	_____
_____	_____	_____
_____	_____	_____
_____	_____	_____

Name: _____

Addition And Subtraction

Directions: Work the problems. Remember, addition means "putting together" or adding two or more numbers to find the sum. Subtraction means "taking away" or subtracting one number from another.

1 + 3 = _____   4 - 3 = _____   4 + 5 = _____

6 + 1 = _____   7 - 2 = _____   8 - 4 = _____

9 - 1 = _____   10 - 3 = _____

5 - 2 = _____   6 + 3 = _____

8 + 2 = _____   5 + 5 = _____

Name: _____

Homonyms

Homonyms are words that sound the same but are spelled differently and mean something different. **Blew** and **blue** are homonyms.

Directions: Look at the word pairs. Choose the word that describes the picture. Write the word on the line next to the picture.

1. sew   so   _____

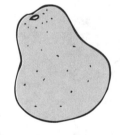

2. pair   pear   _____

3. eye   I   _____

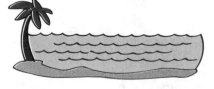

4. see   sea   _____

Name: _____

I Can Finish A Story!

Directions: Write in the "doing" words to finish the story. The first letter of each "doing" word is done for you.

One day Mom said I could __r_____ the school bus

home with Pat.   We watched Pat's

__p_____ with a ⬤ .   Then Pat told me, "My

mother said she would __m_____ some 🍪🍪 .

I will get us some."

Pat went inside to get the 🍪🍪 .   Just then I saw a

__r_____ into the yard.   Oh, no!   He might

chase Pat's 🐱🐱 .   I have to __S_____ him!

Pat came back with the 🍪🍪 .   The 🐕 began

to __j_____ on Pat and lick Pat's face.   Then he ran off

with the 🍪🍪 .

Name: _____

Tracking

Directions: Help Megan find Randy. How many paths can she follow to reach him? _____

Name: _____

Skills Review: Consonant Reviews

Directions: Finish each sentence with a word from the word box.

| sting | shelf | drank | plant | stamp |

_____
_____
1. Tom _____ his milk.

_____
_____
2. A bee can _____ you.

_____
_____
3. I put a _____ on my letter.

_____
_____
4. The _____ is green.

5. The book is on the _____ .

_____

Review

Directions: Read about words that tell about how you move. Circle the right answer on 1. Then answer the other questions.

   You can move in many ways. There are many words that tell how. You can run. When you run, one foot hits the ground at a time. You can jump. When you jump, you land on two feet. You can hop. To hop, first stand on one leg. Then jump up and down.

1. Running and jumping are different because

   A) One foot hits the ground at a time when you run. Two feet hit the ground at a time when you jump.

   OR

   B) Two feet at a time hit the ground when you run. One foot hits the ground at a time when you jump.

2. Fill in the missing directions on how to hop.

_____

1) _____

_____

2) _____

_____

Review

Directions: Work the problems. Color the picture.

9
- 4

5
+3

3
- 2

8
+1

4
+5

10
- 6

7
- 2

6
+4

10
- 7

8
- 3

6
+3

9
+1

5
+2

8
- 9

5 - 4 =

9 + 1 =

Name: _____

Review

Directions: Read the sentences below. Fill in the blanks with the correct word. Then circle the first letter of each word and write them in **ABC** order on the lines below.

| sunglasses | Pete | rock | cold | eight |

1. Sun + glasses = _____.

2. Another word for stone is _____.

3. The opposite word for hot is _____.

4. A word that sounds like the word ate _____.

5. Add an "e" to the word pet _____.

ABC Order: _____ _____ _____

_____ _____ _____

_____ _____ _____

_____ _____ _____

_____ _____ _____

Review

Directions: 1. Write three telling sentences and one question about this picture. Put a "doing" word in each sentence. 2. Read your sentences to someone.

Here are some more words you could use: **boys, girls, mothers, fathers, people, they, sand, bikes, tree**.

_____

1. _____

_____

_____

2. _____

_____

_____

3. _____

_____

One question: _____

_____

_____

_____

Name: _____

Review

Directions: Circle the boxes that have **P** in them.

 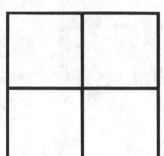  

Color the triangles.

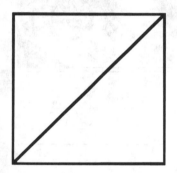 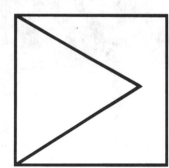 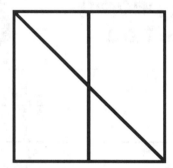 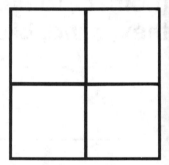

Trace all the paths from **A** to **B** with different colors.

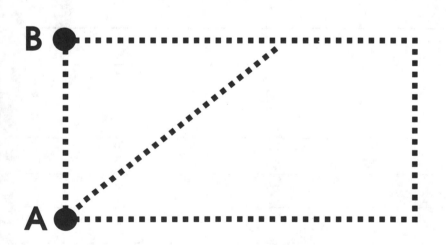 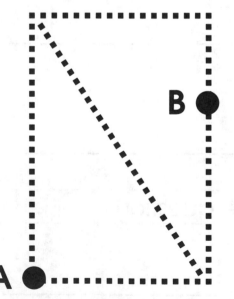

How many paths?_____   How many paths? _____

Name: _____

Picture Clues

Directions: 1) Look at the big picture. 2) Now read the sentences. 3) Draw a line from each little picture to the word that tells about it.

I see the  .   tree

I see the .   boy

I see the .   swing

I see the .   dog

I see the .   sun

Name: _____

These Don't Belong

Directions: Look at the pictures in each row across. Circle the ones that go together. Then write the names of the ones that do not belong in the blanks below.

Row 1   cookies   cake   beans   ice cream

Row 2   apple   banana   orange   cookies

Row 3   kite   dice   checkers   chess

Row 1 _____   Row 2 _____   Row 3 _____

Name: _____

Place Value: Tens And Ones

The place value of a digit, or numeral, is shown by where it is in the number. For example, in the number **123**, **1** has the place value of **hundreds**, **2** is **tens**, and **3** is **ones**.

Directions: Count the groups of ten crayons and write the number by the word **tens**. Count the other crayons and write the number by the word **ones**.

Example: + = __|__ ten + __|__ one

  + = ____ tens + ____ ones

  +  = ____ tens + ____ ones

 + = ____ tens + ____ ones

---

6 tens + 3 ones = ____   5 tens + 1 one = ____

3 tens + 8 ones = ____   9 tens + 7 ones = ____

4 tens + 5 ones = ____   2 tens + 8 ones = ____

Nouns Are Naming Words

Nouns tell the name of a person, place, or thing.

Directions: Look at each picture. Color it red if it names a person. Color it blue if it names a place. Color it green if it names a thing.

I Can Write "Weather" Words!

Directions: 1. Follow the lines to write the words. 2. Write the words by yourself. 3. Color the pictures. 4. Read the words to someone.

Like this:

sun   **sun**

snow

hot

rain

wet

cold

Name: _____

Finding Similarities

Directions: Circle the picture in each row that is most like the first picture.

Example:

maple

rose

tomato

oak

shirt

mittens

boots

jacket

bluejay

robin

cat

monkey

tiger

giraffe

lion

zebra

Vocabulary Building with Visual Clues

Directions: Draw a line from the sentence to its picture.

The ducks like to swim.

The bear eats honey.

The cat is under a table.

The bee is on a flower.

Name: _____

Babies

Directions: Read about babies. Then answer the questions.

Babies are small. Some babies cry a lot. They cry when they are wet. They cry when they are hungry. They smile when they are dry. They smile when they are fed.

1. Name 2 reasons babies cry.

_____ _____

_____ _____

2. Name 2 reasons babies smile.

_____ _____

_____ _____

3. Write a baby's name you like.

_____

_____

_____

Name: _____

Place Value: Tens And Ones

Directions: Write the answers in the correct spaces.

	tens	ones		
3 tens, 2 ones	_3_	_2_	=	_32_
3 tens, 7 ones	___	___	=	___
9 tens, 1 one	___	___	=	___
5 tens, 6 ones	___	___	=	___
6 tens, 5 ones	___	___	=	___
6 tens, 8 ones	___	___	=	___
2 tens, 8 ones	___	___	=	___
4 tens, 9 ones	___	___	=	___
1 ten, 4 ones	___	___	=	___
8 tens, 2 ones	___	___	=	___
4 tens, 2 ones	___	___	=	___

28 = _____ tens, _____ ones

64 = _____ tens, _____ ones

56 = _____ tens, _____ ones

72 = _____ tens, _____ ones

38 = _____ tens, _____ ones

17 = _____ tens, _____ ones

63 = _____ tens, _____ ones

12 = _____ tens, _____ ones

Nouns Are Naming Words

Directions: Write these naming words in the correct box.

store	zoo	child	baby	teacher	table
cat	park	gym	woman	sock	horse

Person

_____ _____

_____ _____

Place

_____ _____

_____ _____

Thing

_____ _____

_____ _____

I Can Finish Sentences!

Directions: 1. Write the word that completes each sentence. Use each word only one time. 2. Put a period at the end of the telling sentences. 3. Put a question mark at the end of the asking sentences.

Like this:

Do flowers grow in the _____ **sun** _____ **?**

rain	water	wet	hot

1. The sun makes me _____ ☐

2. When it rains, the grass gets_____ ☐

3. Do you think it will _____ on our

picnic ☐

4. Should you drink the _____ from

the rain ☐

Name: _____

Finding Similarities

Directions: Circle the picture in each row that is most like the first picture.

Example:

carrot marbles bread celery

baseball sneakers basketball bat

store school home bakery

kitten dog bear cat

Citizenship

Name: _____

LESSON 9

The Bald Eagle

The bald eagle became the national bird of the United States in 1782. Bald eagles have great strength and power, just as the United States is a great and powerful nation.

Pictures of the bald eagle can be found on many things in the United States. Draw some of the places where you have seen pictures of bald eagles.

Why do you think pictures of the bald eagle are found on so many things in the United States?

Name: _____

ACTIVITY 9

The Bald Eagle

Directions: Pretend your _____ team needs a symbol. You want the bald eagle because it is the symbol of your country too. Design a T-shirt for your team that has our national bird on it.

Refuges

Many wild animals are in trouble.
They have a hard time getting food.
They can not find safe places to live.
Some are in danger of disappearing from the earth.

Many people are trying to help these animals.
One way to help an animal is to protect its home.
People save homes for wild animals in places called refuges.
Refuges are safe places for wild animals.
People protect the animals in refuges.

How do refuges help wild animals?

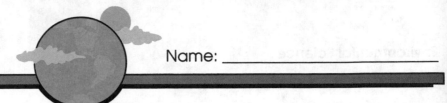

Name: _____

Activity 8

Bison

Bison are the largest land animals in our country.
Bison may be as tall as six feet.
They may weigh up to 2000 pounds.

Long ago there were many bison in the United States.
But people started to hunt them for food and sport.
Soon there was only one tiny herd left.

Some people knew the bison were in trouble.
They passed laws to end bison hunting.
They made a refuge for the tiny herd that was left.
Now there are more bison in the United States.
The bison was saved because people helped.

Directions: This bison is lost from its herd. Follow the maze to help him find his refuge.

Name: _____

More Than One

Directions: An **s** at the end of a word often means there is more than one. 1) Look at each picture. 2) Draw a circle around the right word. 3) Write the word on the line.

two

dog   dogs

_____

_____

_____

four

flower   flowers

_____

_____

_____

one

bikes   bike

_____

_____

_____

three

toys   toy

_____

_____

_____

a

lamb   lambs

_____

_____

_____

two

cat   cats

_____

_____

_____

Name: _____

All About Ann And Ben

Directions: Read the story. Look at the pictures of Ben and Ann. Then use the word list to spell the answers to the questions.

Ben and Ann are twin babies. They were born at the same time. They have the same mama. Ben is a boy baby. Ann is a girl.

bow	boy	girl	hat	twins

1. Tell 1 way Ann and Ben are the same.

_____

_____

_____

2. Tell 2 ways Ann and Ben are different.

1) Ann is a _____. Ben is a _____.

2) Ann is wearing a _____. Ben is wearing a _____.

Ordinal Numbers

Ordinal numbers are used to indicate order in a series, such as **first**, **second**, or **third**.

Directions: Draw a line to the picture that corresponds to the ordinal number in the left column.

eighth

third

sixth

ninth

seventh

second

fourth

first

fifth

tenth

1st

7th

10th

2nd

4th

6th

8th

9th

3rd

5th

Name: _____

More Than One

Some nouns name more than one person, place or thing.

Directions: Add an "s" to make the words tell about the picture.

frog___

pan ___

boy ___

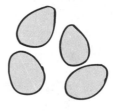

egg___

horn ___

girl ___

Name: _____

I Know Which Letters Are The Same!

Directions: 1. Read the letter that starts each row. 2. Find the two pictures in each row that start with that letter. 3. Write the letter under those pictures.

Like this:

s

_____   S   S   _____

w

_____   _____   _____   _____

c

_____   _____   _____   _____

p

_____   _____   _____   _____

s

_____   _____   _____   _____

r

_____   _____   _____   _____

Name: _____

Finding Similarities

Directions: Randy and Megan are looking for sea shells. They only want the shells that look similar to this . Color the shells that Randy and Megan take home.

Name: _____

Going For A Ride

Directions: 1) Read the sentence. 2) Draw a circle around the word that tells about the picture. 3) Write the word.

I ride on a _____ .

   bike   hike

I ride on a _____ .

   train   tree

I ride in a _____ .

   car   can

I ride on a _____ .

   bus   bug

I ride in a _____ .

   jar   jet

I ride in a _____ .

   took   truck

Name: _____

Hats

Directions: Read about hats. Then answer the questions.

There are many kinds of hats. Some hats have brims. Some hats have feathers. Some knit hats pull down over your ears. Some straw hats set on top of your head. Do you like hats?

1. Name 4 kinds of hats.
   _____

1) _____

2) _____

3) _____ 4) _____

2. What kind of hats pull down over your ears?   straw hats
                                                  knit hats

3. What kind of hats set on top of your head?   straw hats
                                                 knit hats

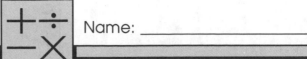

Name: _____

Counting By Tens

Directions: Count in order by tens to draw the path the boy takes to the store.

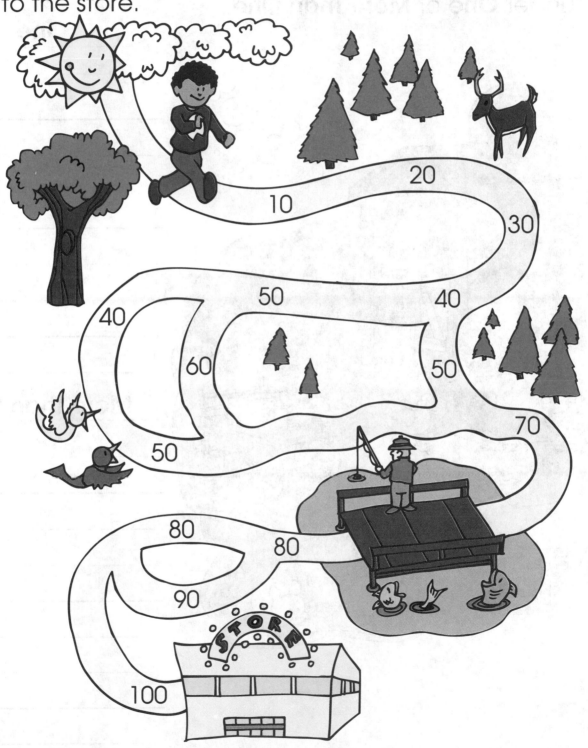

Name: _____

More Than One

Directions: Read the nouns under the pictures. Then, write the noun under **One** or **More Than One**.

One

_____

_____

_____

_____

_____

barn

cows

ducks

wagon

pigs

horse

More Than One

_____

_____

_____

_____

_____

Name: _____

I Know Where The Sentences Stop!

Directions: 1. Read the two sentences on each line. 2. Draw a line between them. 3. Write them again. 4. Remember to begin each sentence with a capital letter. Put a period or a question mark at the end of each one.

Like this: will it rain/the sky is dark

Will it rain? The sky is dark.

1. she jumped in the water she got wet

_____

_____

_____

_____

2. do you like my snowman does he need a hat

_____

_____

_____

_____

Name: _____

Finding Similarities

Directions: Circle the word in each row that is most like the first word in the row.

Example:

grin (smile) frown mad

bag jar sack box

frown angry joke laugh

apple rot cookie fruit

around circle square dot

brown tan black red

bird dog cat duck

bee fish ant snake

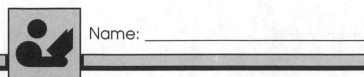
Sentences With "Not"

Directions: 1) Say the word. 2) Write the word. 3) Read the sentences. 4) Look at the picture. 5) Draw a circle around the sentence that tells about the picture.

n o t   not _____

The baby is happy.

The baby is not happy.

The car can go.

The car can not go.

The girl can jump.

The girl can not jump.

Name: _____

I Like Hats

Directions: Look at the pictures. Then number them in 1-2-3-4 order.

Counting By Fives

Directions: Count by fives to draw the path to the playground.

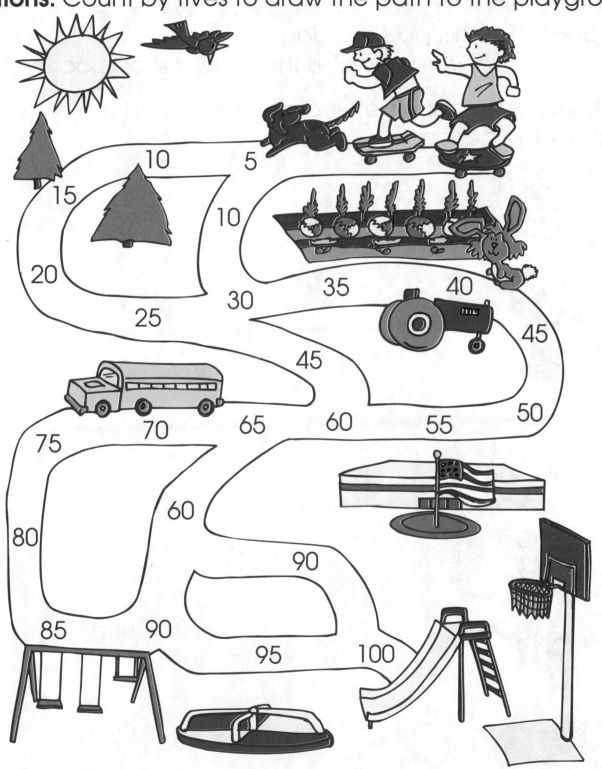

10   5

15

10

20

25   30   35   40

45

45

50

75   70   65   60   55

60

80

90

85   90   95   100

Name: _____

Verbs Are Action Words

Verbs are words that tell what a person or a thing can do.

Example: The girl pats the dog.
The word "pats" is the verb. It shows action.

Directions: Draw a line between the verbs and the pictures that show the action.

eat

run

sleep

swim

sing

hop

Name: _____

I Know How The Letters Go!

Directions: Put the letters in the right order.

Like this:

t e w

w o s n

a e t w r

n s u

d c o l

t h o

sun

_____

_____

_____

_____

_____

_____

_____

_____

Name: _____

Finding Opposites

Directions: Find and circle the picture in each row that is the opposite of the first picture.

up

down

over

across

cold

frozen

hot

warm

in

beside

out

over

cloud

rain

storm

sun

My House

Directions: 1) Read the word. 2) Write the word. 3) Write the word to finish the sentences. 4) Draw a picture of your house.

house house _____

Here is my _____ .   I like my _____ .

Name: _____

Name The Cats

Directions: Look at the pictures of the cats. Read about the cats. Then write the correct name beside each cat.

Fluffy, Blackie and Tiger are playing. Tom is sleeping. Blackie has spots. Tiger has stripes.

_____   _____

_____   _____

_____

Z Z Z

_____   _____

_____   _____

_____   _____

Name: _____

Fractions: Whole And Half

Directions: Color half of each object.

Example:

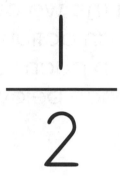

Whole apple   **Half an apple**

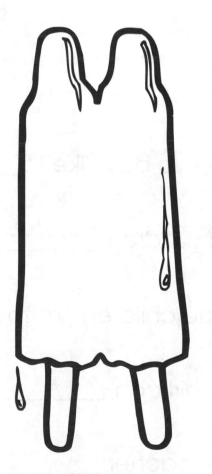

Name: _____

Verbs Are Action Words.

Directions:
Look at the pictures.
Read the words.
Write an action
word in each
sentence below.

swing   rings   kick   run   talk

1. The two boys like to _____ together.

2. The children_____ the soccer ball.

3. Some children like to _____ on the swings.

4. The girl can_____ very fast.

5. The teacher_____ the bell.

Name: _____

I Know Which Ending Makes Sense!

Directions: 1. Read the words carefully. 2. Draw a line from the first part of the sentence to the words that finish it.

Like this:

When I'm cold ——————— I put on my coat.

I take off my shoes.

1. When it rains,

we ride our bikes to the park.

we play games inside.

2. I like snow

because I can eat lunch.

because I can make a snowman.

3. When the sun comes out,

the grass grows fast.

the grass gets wet.

4. At night the rain

makes ice on my window.

helps me go to sleep.

Name: _____

Finding Opposites

Directions: Color the things that are the opposite of "up" in this picture.

LESSON 10

The Fourth of July

Americans celebrate the birthday of the United States on the Fourth of July. On this day, citizens remember that long ago other Americans worked and fought so that America would be free.

Color the Fourth of July celebration. What colors will you use the most? Add your family to the picture.

How do Americans show that the Fourth of July is a special holiday for all citizens?

Name: _____

ACTIVITY 10

The Fourth of July

Directions: It's your lucky day! You have been given the honor of carrying the United States flag in your community's Fourth of July parade. First, follow the maze to get to the front of the parade line. Then draw yourself proudly holding the United States flag.

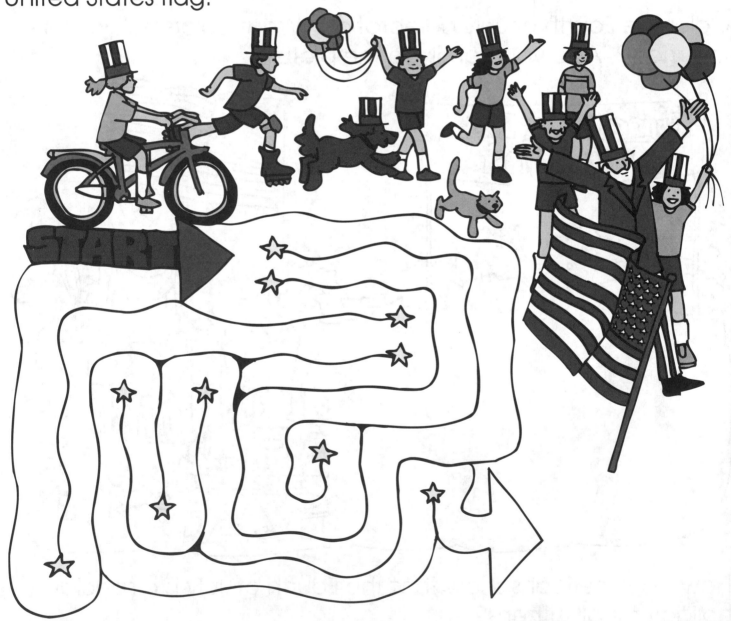

Conservation

Conservation of plants, animals and energy protect the environment.
Theodore Roosevelt was the 26th President of the United States.
President Roosevelt was a conservationist, too.
Conservationists are people who take care of the environment.

Roosevelt helped start a refuge for wild animals in Florida.
He built a dam to save the plants in the dry land of Arizona.
He looked for ways to save the forests in our country.
He set aside land for nature studies.
Theodore Roosevelt worked hard to protect our environment.

Why is Theodore Roosevelt called a conservationist?

Name: _____

Activity 9

President For Today

Directions: Pretend you are the President of the United States...and a conservationist, too! You are going to speak on TV. What will you tell the people of our country about the environment?

Name: _____

You And Me

Directions: 1) Read the word. 2) Write the word. 3) Draw a circle around the right word to finish each sentence. 4) Write the word on the lines.

you and me _you and me_

I will play with _____ .   you   me

You can go with _____ .   you   me

Can you run with _____ ?   you   me

Name: _____

See The Cats!

Directions: Look at the pictures of Tom, Fluffy, Tiger and Blackie on page 270. In picture 2, one thing about each cat is different. Look at the word list. Then write your answers.

ball	bow	brush	collar

What's different about each cat?

1. Tom is wearing a
_____
_____
_____

2. Fluffy is wearing a
_____
_____
_____

3. Blackie has a
_____
_____
_____

4. Tiger has a
_____
_____
_____

Fractions: Thirds And Fourths

A fraction is a number that names part of a whole, such as **1/2** or **3/4**.

Directions: Each object has 3 equal parts. Color one section.

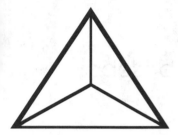

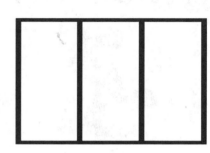

Directions: Each object has 4 equal parts. Color one section.

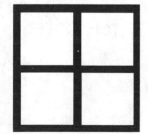

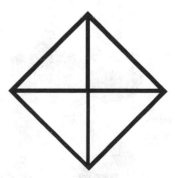

Name: _____

Is And Are Are Special Words

Use "is" when talking about one person or one thing. Use "are" when talking about more than one person or thing.

Example: The dog is barking.
The dogs are barking.

Directions: Write "is" or "are" in the sentences below.

1. Jim_____ playing baseball.

2. Fred and Sam _____ good friends.

3. Cupcakes _____ my favorite treat.

4. Lisa _____ a good soccer player.

I Can Finish A Story!

Directions: Write the missing words in the story. The first letter of each word is there. Can you write the other letters by yourself?

"Please may I go outside?" I asked again.

"It's too _C_____," my father told

me again. "Maybe later the sun will come

out."   Later, the sun did come out.

Then it began to _r_____.

"May I go out now?" I asked again.

Dad looked out the window.   "You will get _W_____,"

he said.

"But I want to see if the _r_____ helped our flowers

grow," I said.

"You mean you want to play in the _W_____," Dad

said with a smile.

How did Dad know that?

Name: _____

Finding Opposites

Directions: Draw a line between the words that are opposites.

up	**wet**
over	**down**
dry	**dirty**
clean	**under**

Name: _____

Skills Review: Vocabulary

Directions: Write the word from the word box that finishes the sentences.

house	me	you	not	ride

1. Will you play with _____ ?

2. I live in a big, red _____ .

3. _____ are my friend.

4. I like to _____ my bike.

5. A flower is _____ a tree.

Review

Directions: Read the story. Look at the pictures. Then answer the questions.

Some clothes are for winter. Some clothes are for summer. Winter clothes keep us warm. Summer clothes keep us cool. In summer, I first put on shorts. Then a shirt. Then sandals. These clothes keep me cool!

1. Tell the order of clothes I put on in summer.

_____ _____ _____

_____ _____ _____

1) _____ 2) _____ 3) _____

_____ _____ _____

2. List the winter clothes pictured.

_____ _____

_____ _____

_____ _____

3. How are summer and winter clothes different?
   Summer clothes keep us _____   Winter clothes keep us _____

_____ _____

_____ _____

_____ . _____

Name: _____

Review

Directions: Write the missing numbers by counting by tens and fives.

_____ , 20, _____ , _____ , _____ , _____ , 70, _____ , _____ , 100

5, _____ , 15, _____ , _____ , 30, _____ , _____ , _____ , _____

Directions: Color the object with thirds red. Color the object with halves blue. Color the object with fourths green.

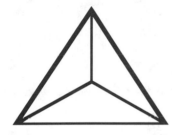  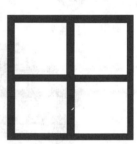

Directions: Draw a line to the correct equal part.

 $\frac{1}{3}$

 $\frac{1}{4}$

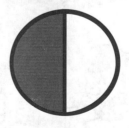

$\frac{1}{2}$

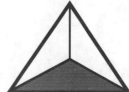

Nouns And Verbs

Directions: Read the sentences below. Draw a red circle around the nouns. Draw a blue line under the verbs.

1. The boy runs fast.

2. The turtle eats leaves.

3. The fish swim in the tank.

4. The girl hits the ball.

Name: _____

Review

Directions: Write a telling sentence about each of these pictures. Then write an asking sentence about one of the pictures. Use the weather words and the other words you know how to write.

Here are some more words you could use: **people, coats, hats, bikes, puddles**.

Telling sentences:

_____

1. _____

_____

2. _____

_____

Asking sentence:

_____

_____

_____

Review

Directions: Color the picture in the row that is similar to the first picture.

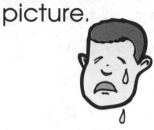   

cry   laugh   smile   sad

Color the picture in the row that is **not** similar to the first picture.

pear   apple   turnip   orange

Circle the opposite of day.

black   night   sunrise   sunset

Circle the opposite of first.

second   middle   last   end

Name: _____

Compound Words

Directions: Draw lines to make compound words. Write the six new words on the lines.

Example: song + bird = songbird.

dog	room
foot	box
bed	house
mail	light
some	ball
moon	thing

_____ _____

_____ _____

_____ _____

_____ _____

_____ _____

_____ _____

_____ _____

_____ _____

Name: _____

The Zoo And The Farm

Directions: Read the story about the zoo and the farm. Then fill in the the puzzle with the right answers about the animals.

The zoo is for wild animals. Tigers live at the zoo. Snakes live at the zoo. The farm is for tame animals. Ducks and donkeys live on farms.

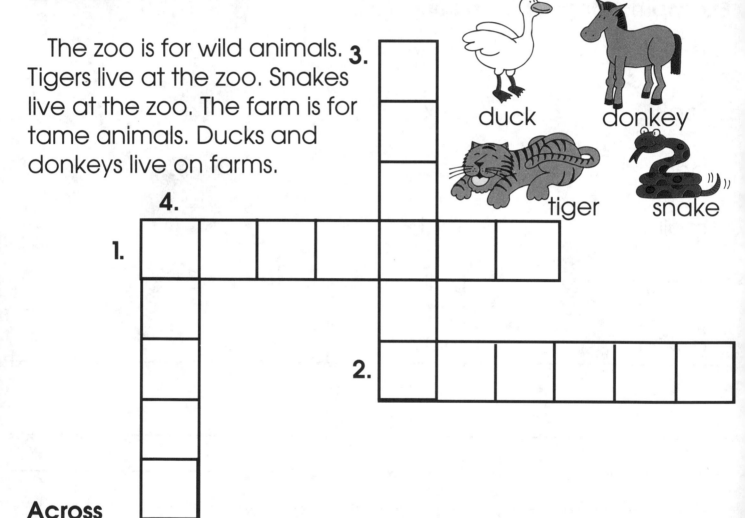

duck   donkey

tiger   snake

Across
1. These animals say "hee-haw." They live on the farm.
2. These animals are long and thin. They live in the zoo.

Down
3. These animals have stripes. They live in the zoo.
4. These animals say "quack." They live on the farm.

Name: _____

Addition: 10 - 15

Directions: Circle groups of ten crayons. Add the remaining ones to make the correct number.

		tens	ones
+ =		3	9
+ =		___	___
+ =		___	___
+ =		___	___
+ =		___	___
+ =		___	___

6 + 6 = _____   8 + 4 = _____   9 + 5 = _____

Words That Describe

Describing words tell us more about a person, place, or thing.

Directions: Read the words in the box. Choose a word that describes the picture. Write it next to the picture.

happy	round	sick	cold	long

_____

_____

_____

_____

_____

_____

_____

_____

_____

_____

_____

_____

_____

_____

I Can Write "Opposite" Words!

Some words are opposites. "Big" and "little" are opposites. Today you will write more opposite words.

Directions: Follow the lines to write the words. Then write the words by yourself.

Like this:

new   new

old

big

little

lost

found

Name: _____

Sequencing

Directions: Look at each group of pictures. Write 1, 2 or 3 under the picture to show where it should be. The first one is done for you.

tallest __3__   tall __1__   taller __2__

small _____   smallest _____   smaller _____

biggest _____   big _____ bigger _____

wider _____   wide _____   widest _____

Name: _____

Compound Words

Directions: Draw a circle around the compound word to finish each sentence. Write the words on the lines.

1. The _____ brings us letters.

mailman   snowman

2. A _____ grows tall.

sunlight   sunflower

3. The snow falls _____ .

outside   inside

4. A _____ fell on my head.

raindrop   rainbow

5. I put the letter in a _____ .

mailbox   shoebox

Name: _____

Week Days

Directions: Read about the days of the week. Then answer the questions.

Do you know the names of the 7 days of the week? Here they are: Monday, Tuesday, Wednesday, Thursday, Friday, Saturday, Sunday. Each name has a meaning. Thursday is "Thor's day." Long ago, some people thought a man named Thor was in charge of wars.

1. What day is "Thor's day?"

_____

_____

_____

2. What was Thor in charge of?

_____

_____

_____

3. How many days are in each week?

_____

_____

_____

I AM IN CHARGE OF WAR!

Name: _____

Subtraction: 10 - 15

Directions: Count the crayons in each group. Put an **X** through the number of crayons being subtracted. How many are left?

		- 5	= __10__
		- 4	= ____
		- 7	= ____
		- 6	= ____
		- 5	= ____
		- 8	= ____

13 - 8 = ____   11 - 5 = ____   12 - 9 = ____

14 - 7 = ____   10 - 7 = ____   13 - 3 = ____

15 - 9 = ____   11 - 8 = ____   12 - 10 = ____

Words That Describe

Directions: Read the words in the box. Choose the word that describes the picture. Write it on the line below.

wet	round	funny	soft	sad	tall

_____

_____

_____

_____

_____

_____

Name: _____

I Can Write About A Picture!

Directions: 1. Read the sentence about the first picture.
2. Write another sentence about the picture beside it. Use the "opposite" words. 3. Start your sentences with a capital and end with a period.

Like this: This apple is little.

 This apple is big

| dark | old | first | new | light | last |

1. This coat is light green.

_____
_____

2. This woman is first in line.

_____
_____

3. This is Mike's old friend.

_____
_____

Name: _____

Sequencing

Directions: Look at the pictures in each row. Put a number next to the word to show whether it comes 1, 2 or 3 in the row.

shortest _____   shorter _____   short _____

longer _____   longest _____   long _____

happy _____   happier _____   happiest _____

hotter _____   hot _____   hottest _____

LESSON 11

The Bill of Rights

The Constitution of the United States is the law that tells how our government works. The Bill of Rights is part of the Constitution. It protects the rights of all Americans.

The Bill of Rights says Americans may worship as they want. It says citizens may write and speak openly. It also says Americans may meet and talk about ways to make their government better.

Why do you think it is important for people to be able to speak and write freely?

Name: _____

The Bill of Rights

Directions: A *right* is the freedom to act or behave in a certain way. On the lines below, list the rights you have at school.

_____ School's Bill of Rights

_____

_____

_____

_____

_____

_____

_____

_____

_____

_____

_____

_____

Name: _____

Summary

Directions: Draw a under the pictures that show people or things that help the environment.
Draw a under the pictures that show people or things that hurt the environment.

REMEMBER: Help 😊   Hurt 😠

Name: _____

Review

Directions: Unscramble the words. Use the clues to help. The first one is done for you.

bison   refuges   rain forest   solar homes   conservationist

1. **nair esroft**

   Clue: A wet, warm place where many trees grow

   rain forest

2. **noverncstistoia**

   Clue: President Theodore Roosevelt

3. **sbion**

   Clue: A wild animal that was in trouble

4. **guferse**

   Clue: Safe places for wild animals

5. **larso mohse**

   Clue: Homes heated with heat from the sun

Name: _____

How Do I Work?

Directions: 1) Read the word. 2) Write the word. 3) Write the word to finish the sentences. 4) Draw a picture of how you work.

work _work_____

_____

I can _____ .

_____

I like to _____ .

_____

How do I _____ ?

_____

Name: _____

I Like Calendars

Directions: Read about the days of the week. Put the first letter of the days of the week in the correct order on the calendar. (Use "Th" for Thursday and "Su" for Sunday.)

Calendars show the days of the week in order. Sunday comes first. Saturday comes last. There are 5 days in between.

DAY 1	DAY 2	DAY 3

DAY 4	DAY 5	DAY 6

DAY 7

Name: _____

Addition And Subtraction

Remember, addition means "putting together" or adding two or more numbers to find the sum. Subtraction means "taking away" or subtracting one number from another.

Directions: Work the problems. From your answers, use the code to color the quilt.

Color:

6 = blue
7 = yellow
8 = green
9 = red
10 = orange

$$9 + 1$$

$$6 + 3$$

$$10 - 2 =$$

$$12 - 6 =$$

$$10 - 4$$

$$4 + 6$$

$$11 - 2$$

$$5 + 5$$

$$12 - 6$$

$$10 - 1$$

$$3 + 4$$

$$12 - 5$$

$$10 - 3$$

$$6 + 1$$

$$11 - 5$$

$$3 + 5$$

$$11 - 1$$

$$4 + 4$$

$$6 + 2$$

$$6 + 3$$

$$1 + 5 =$$

$$9 - 2 =$$

$$6 + 2 =$$

Name: _____

Words That Describe

Directions: Circle the describing word in each sentence. Draw a line from the word to the picture.

1. The hungry dog is eating.

2. The tiny bird is flying.

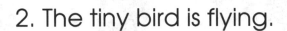

3. Horses have long legs.

4. She is a fast runner.

5. The little boy was lost.

Name: _____

I Know Which Words Sound The Same!

Directions: Write the "opposite" words that answer the questions.

dark found old light new first lost last

1. Which three words start the same as 🪜 ?

_____ _____

_____ _____

_____ _____

2. Which two words start the same as 🪶 ?

_____ _____

_____ _____

_____ _____

3. Which words start the same as each of these words?

_____ _____

_____ _____

_____ _____

4. Which two words end the same as 🐦 ?

_____ _____

_____ _____

_____ _____

Sequencing

Directions: These children are waiting to see a movie. Look at the group and follow the instructions.

1. Color the person who is first in line yellow.
2. Color the person who is last in line brown.
3. Color the person who is second in line pink.
4. Circle the person who is at the end of the line.

Name: _____

How Do I Play?

Directions: 1) Read the word. 2) Write the word. 3) Write the word to finish the sentences. 4) Draw a picture of how you play.

p l a y

play

_____

I can _____ .

I like to _____ .

How do I _____ ?

Name: _____

See The Boats

Directions: Read about boats. Then answer the questions.

See the boats! They float on water. Some boats have sails. The wind moves the sails. It makes the boats go. Many people name their sailboats. They paint the name on the side of the boat.

1. What makes sailboats move?

2. Where do sailboats float?

3. What would you name a sailboat?

Name: _____

Time: Hour

The short hand of the clock tells the hour. The long hand tells how many minutes after the hour. When the minute hand is on the **12**, it is the beginning of the hour.

Directions: Look at each clock. Write the time.

Example:

__3__ o'clock

_____ o'clock

_____ o'clock

_____ o'clock

_____ o'clock

_____ o'clock

_____ o'clock

_____ o'clock

_____ o'clock

Name: _____

Names Of People

The names of people begin with a capital letter.

Directions: Choose a name from the box to go with each child. Write the name on the line. Start each name with a capital letter.

Sam	Fred
Jack	Lisa
Ann	Jenny

1   2   3   4   5   6

1. _____ 4. _____

2. _____ 5. _____

3. _____ 6. _____

I Can Tell What Happens Next!

Directions: Read the sentence under the first picture. Then look at the next picture. Write a sentence that tells about it.

Like this: The little dog eats.

The dog grows big.

found	new	first	lost	old	last

1. His book is lost.

_____
_____
_____

2. She feeds her dog first.

_____
_____

_____
3. I like my old shirt.

_____
_____

Sequencing

Directions: Look at each group of shapes. Figure out the order. Fill in the missing shape. Color it.

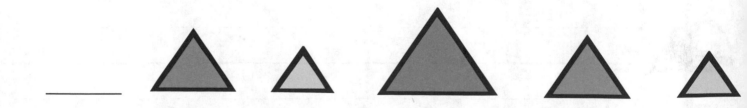

Name: _____

Over or Under?

Directions: 1) Read the words. 2) Write the words. 3) Draw a circle around the correct word to finish each sentence. 4) Write it on the line.

o v e r   _over_____

u n d e r   _under_____

The kite is
over under   _____ the tree.

The kite is
over under   _____ the tree.

Name: _____

Boats That Are The Same

Directions: Look carefully at the picture. Find the boats that are the same. Color them all the same. Only 1 boat is different. Color it a different color.

Name: _____

Time: Hour, Half-Hour

The short hand of the clock tells the hour. The long hand tells how many minutes after the hour. When the minute hand is on the **6**, it is on the half-hour. A half-hour is thirty minutes. It is written **:30**, such as **5:30**.

Directions: Look at each clock. Write the time.

Example:

hour   half-hour

__1__ : __30__

___ : ___   ___ : ___   ___ : ___   ___ : ___

___ : ___   ___ : ___   ___ : ___   ___ : ___

Name That Cat

The name of a pet begins with a capital letter.

Directions: Read the names in the box. Choose one name for each cat. Write the name in the space under the cat.

Fritz	Fuzzy	Boots	King	Queenie	Lola

I Can Find The Spelling Mistakes!

Directions: Circle any words that are not spelled right. Then write the word correctly.

dark	found	old	first	lost

Like this:

The house is (litle.)

little

1. Are those your olde shoes?

2. I fond your book.

3. He is frist in line.

4. She losst her lunch.

5. I am afraid of the drak.

Sequencing

Directions: Draw red flowers in holes 1 and 2. Draw yellow flowers in holes 3 and 4. Draw blue flowers in holes 5 and 6.

1

3

5

2

4

6

Name: _____

Day Or Night?

Directions: 1) Read the words. 2) Write the words. 3) Look at each picture. 4) Write day or night on the lines to show if they happen at day or night.

d a y

n i g h t

   _____

   _____

   _____

   _____

Name: _____

Let's Go On A Trip!

Directions: Read about going on trips. Then answer the questions.

   Pack your bag. Shall we go by car, plane or train? Shall we go to the sea? When we get there, let's go on a sailboat.

1. Name 3 ways to travel.

_____ _____ _____

_____ _____ _____

_____

_____

2. Where will we go? _____

_____

3. What will we do when
   we get there? _____

_____

 Name: _____

Time: Hour, Half-Hour

Directions: Draw the hands on each clock to show the correct time.

 **2:30**

 **9:00**

 **7:00**

 **4:30**

 **3:00**

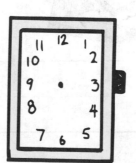 **1:30**

Holidays

Holidays begin with capital letters.

Directions: Choose the words from the box to match the holiday. Write the words under the picture. Be sure to start with capital letters.

| Fourth of July | Valentine's Day |
| President's Day | Thanksgiving |

_____

_____

_____

_____

_____

_____

_____

_____

_____

_____

_____

_____

I Can Write The Answer!

Directions: Look at each picture. Write the answer to the question.

Like this: Is the cookie big?

No, the cookie is little.

1. Has the boy found   his boat?

_____

_____

2. Is she eating her apple last?

_____

_____

dark blue

3. Is the book light brown?

_____

_____

Sequencing

Directions: Put the following groups in **ABC** order. Then number them in **1, 2, 3** order.

Example:

cold	**w**arm	**h**ot
1	3	2

small	**b**ig	**c**ute
___	___	___

baby	**m**other	**f**amily
___	___	___

doll	**t**ruck	**b**all
___	___	___

man	**b**oy	**g**randma
___	___	___

Name: _____

LESSON 12

Mary McLeod Bethune

Mary McLeod Bethune wanted to learn how to read, but there were no schools for black children in her South Carolina town.

Finally, when Mary was eleven, she attended a new school for black children. Mary loved learning, and she eventually became a teacher. She even opened her own school for black students. Mary taught her students how to be good citizens. She told them always to be aware of their rights as citizens.

Mary McLeod Bethune believed that all people are important and should have equal chances to do their best. She spent her whole life working for people's rights.

Why do you think Mary McLeod Bethune worked so that all people would have equal chances?

Name: _____

ACTIVITY 12

Mary McLeod Bethune

Directions: Make up a song about Mary McLeod Bethune's school. Sing it to the tune of "Mary Had a Little Lamb."

Mary had a little school, little school, little school.

Mary had a little school where

_____

_____

_____

_____

_____

_____

_____

_____

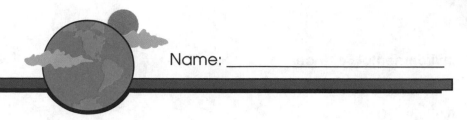

Using Paper at School

Say this tongue twister:

Patty packed the place with piles of paper.

Look around your classroom. Where do you see paper?
Think about other ways you use paper at school.
Would all of the paper make a big pile?
Write the ways you use paper at school on the map.

_____

_____

_____

_____

_____

_____

_____

_____

_____

_____

_____

Using too much paper hurts the environment.
What are some ways you can help?
How can you make the pile of paper smaller?

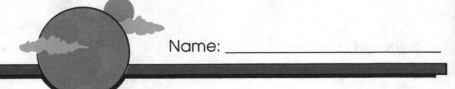

Name: _____

Perry Paper

Directions: Perry is a happy sheet of paper. Read what happens when he goes back to school. Write what Perry might say on the lines.

Perry Paper was very happy. Sally used him on both sides. Then she remembered to save him. She took him to be recycled. Perry came out like a new sheet of paper.

Now Perry was in school again. He was very excited.
Perry was on a big table. He knew someone would write on him soon.

Val sat in front of Perry. She started to write. But Val only wrote a few words. Then she scrunched Perry. She threw him in the trashcan.

"_____

_____"

yelled Perry from inside the can.

Just then Luis walked by the trash can. He took Perry out of the can. "I will fix this paper," said Luis. "I will write on both sides," he thought.

"_____

_____"

said Perry.

Name: _____

Bo Bo The Clown

Directions: 1) Read the story. 2) Write a word from the story to finish the following sentences. 3) Draw a circle around Yes or No.

Bo Bo is a clown. He works at the circus. Bo Bo plays with a seal.

Bo Bo is a _____. Bo Bo plays with a _____.

Does Bo Bo work at the zoo?   Yes   No

Let's Go To The Beach!

Directions: Look at the picture. Use your crayon to draw the way to the beach. On the way, you will stop for (1) food and (2) gas. Then you will (3) cross a bridge. Finally, you will be at the sea (4)! Write the correct number 1, 2, 3 or 4 in the box before each of your stops.

Name: _____

Money: Penny And Nickel

A penny is worth one cent. It is written **1¢** or **$.01**. A nickel is worth five cents. It is written **5¢** or **$.05**.

Directions: Count the money and write the answers.

penny   1 penny = 1¢

nickel   1 nickel = 5¢

   = ___3___ ¢

   = ___15___ ¢

   = _____ ¢

   = _____ ¢

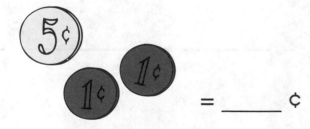   = _____ ¢

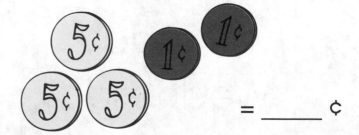   = _____ ¢

337

Name: _____

Days of the Week

The days of the week begin with capital letters.

Directions: Write the days of the week in the spaces below. Put them in order. Be sure to start with capital letters.

Tuesday

Saturday

Monday

Friday

Thursday

Sunday

Wednesday

Name: _____

I Know Which Word To Write!

Directions: Write the opposite words that finish these sentences. Can you spell them all by yourself?

Like this:

The rain made my **little** flower grow **big** .

dark	first	found	last	light	lost

1. Kim opened the box and ate the _____ candy. The

next day she ate the _____ candy.

2. All day John looked for his _____

shoe.   Then his father called, "John, come here!

_____ your shoe."

3. When I get up, it is _____ outside.

By the time I go to school, it is _____ .

Sequencing

Directions: Follow the instructions under each glass. Use crayons to draw your favorite drink in the ones that are full and half-full.

full

half-full

empty

empty

half-full

full

Name: _____

Skills Review: Vocabulary

Directions: 1) Look at each picture. 2) Draw a circle around the correct word to finish the sentence. 3) Write it on the line.

_____

_____

1. Mike can make a _____ .

snowman   snowball   _____

_____

2. Beth can _____ outside.

play   work   _____

_____

3. The cat is _____ the chair.

over   under   _____

_____

4. I sleep in the _____ .

day   night   _____

Name: _____

Review

Directions: Read about coins. Look at the pictures of coins. Then answer the questions.

You can use all coins to buy things. Some coins are worth more than others. Do you know the names of coins? A penny is worth 1 cent. A nickel is worth 5 cents. A dime is worth 10 cents.

1. What can you use all coins to do?

_____

_____

_____

2. How are coins different?

_____

_____

_____

3. Number the coins in order, from the coin that is worth the least to the coin that is worth the most. Under each picture, write how many pennies each coin is worth.

_____ pennies   _____ penny   _____ pennies

Name: _____

Review

Directions: What time is it?

_____ o'clock

Directions: Draw the hands on each clock.

2:30

7:30

11:00

Directions: How much money?

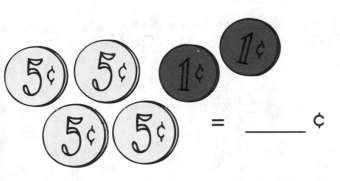

= _____ ¢

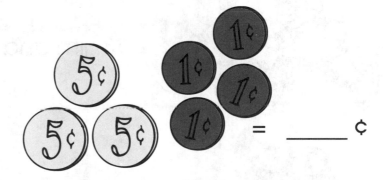

= _____ ¢

Directions: Add or Subtract.

9 + 3 = _____   6 + 8 = _____   15 - 9 = _____

13 - 8 = _____   12 + 2 = _____   7 + 6 = _____

Name: _____

Review

Directions: Circle the letters that should be capital letters. Underline the describing words.

1. jan has red flowers for mother's day.

2. We eat a hot lunch on monday.

3. jim and fred are fast runners.

4. spot is a small dog.

5. We go to the big store on friday.

Review

Directions: 1. Look at all three pictures in each row. 2. Write one sentence about the last picture in each row. 3. Start each sentence with a capital letter and end with a period.

_____

_____

_____

_____

_____

_____

Review

Directions: Put the boys in **1, 2, 3** order from shortest to tallest.

tallest _____   tall _____   taller _____

Color the person who is last in line.
Circle the person who is first.

Finish the sequence.

Put the words in **ABC** order.

dog _____   **c**at _____   **b**ear _____

Name: _____

Find The Synonyms

Directions: 1) Look at the underlined word in each sentence.
2) Draw a circle around the word that means the same thing.
3) Write the new words.

1. The <u>little</u> dog ran   tall   funny   small

2. The <u>happy</u> girl smiled.   glad   sad   good

3. The bird is in the <u>big</u> tree.   green   pretty   tall

4. He was <u>nice</u> to me.   kind   mad   bad

5. The baby is <u>tired</u>.   sleepy   sad   little

_____   _____   _____

_____   _____   _____

_____   _____   _____

_____   _____   _____

_____   _____   _____

_____   _____   _____

Name: _____

Things To Drink

Directions: Look at the pictures. Find the pictures of things you can drink. Write the names of those things in the blanks.

milk

ice

soup

juice

pop

ice cream bar

_____ _____ _____

_____ _____ _____

Name: _____

Picture Problems: Addition 0 - 9

Directions: Work the number problem under each picture.

6 + 2 = _____

3 + 1 = _____

5 + 3 = _____

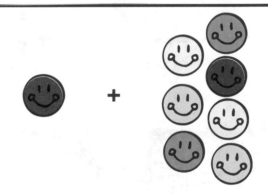

1 + 7 = _____

4 + 5 = _____

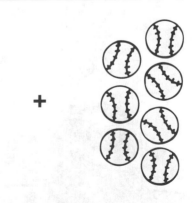

0 + 7 = _____

Name: _____

Telling Sentences

Sentences can tell us something. Telling sentences begin with a capital letter. They end with a period.

Directions: Read the sentences. Draw a yellow circle around the capital letter at the beginning of the sentence. Draw a purple circle around the period at the end of the sentence.

1. I am seven years old.

2. The bird is pretty.

3. The boy likes to dance.

4. Turtles like to swim.

Name: _____

I Can Write More "Doing" Words!

Directions: 1. Follow the lines to write the words. 2. Write the words by yourself. 3. Read the words to someone.

catch

color

eat

grow

fly

buy

Classifying

Directions: Color the clothes Scott should wear outside to build a snowman.

Getting The Main Idea

Directions: 1) Look at each picture. 2) Read the sentences.
3) Draw a circle around Yes or No.

Jack has two shoes.
Yes   No

Jill likes to jump rope.
Yes   No

The hat is too big.
Yes   No

The dog has a bone.
Yes   No

It is Jill's birthday.
Yes   No

Jack is in school.
Yes   No

Name: _____

Ticking Clocks

Directions: Read about clocks. Then answer the questions.

Many clocks make 2 sounds. The sounds are "tick tock". Big clocks often make loud tick tocks. Little clocks often make small tick tocks. Sometimes people put little clocks in the box with a new puppy. The puppy likes the sound. The tick tock makes the puppy feel safe.

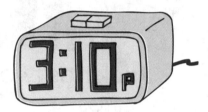

1. What 2 sounds do many clocks make?

_____ _____

_____ _____

_____

2. What kind of tick tocks do big clocks make?

_____

_____

3. What kind of clocks make a new puppy feel safe?

_____

_____

Name: ____________________

Picture Problems: Addition 0 - 9

Directions: Work the number problem under each picture.

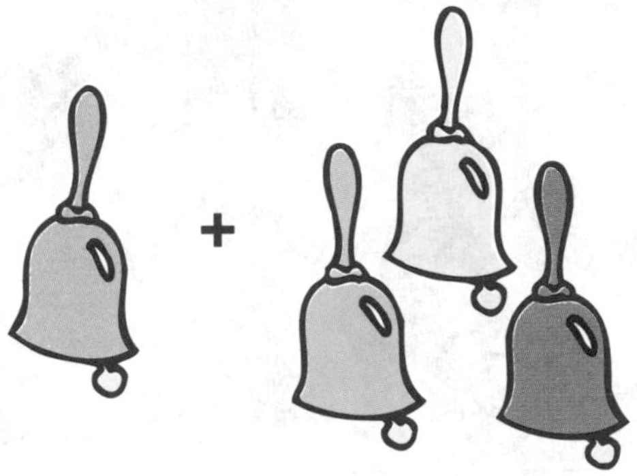

1 + 3 = ____

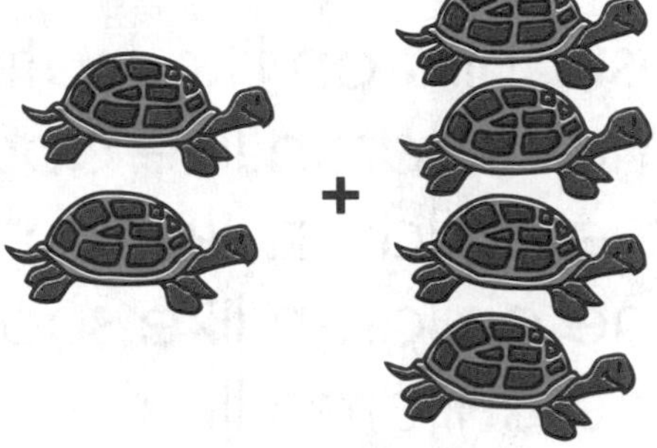

2 + 4 = ____

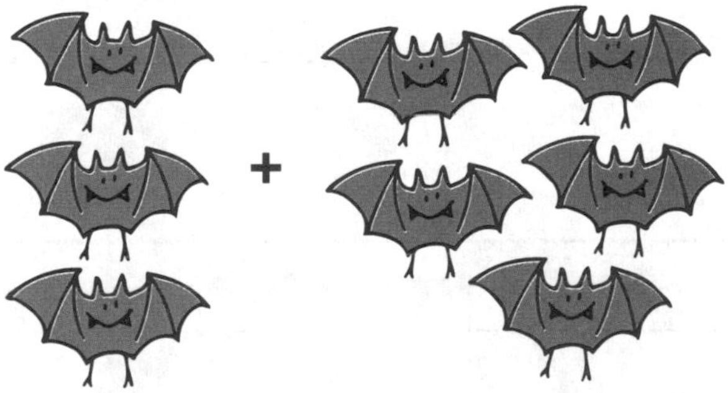

3 + 5 = ____

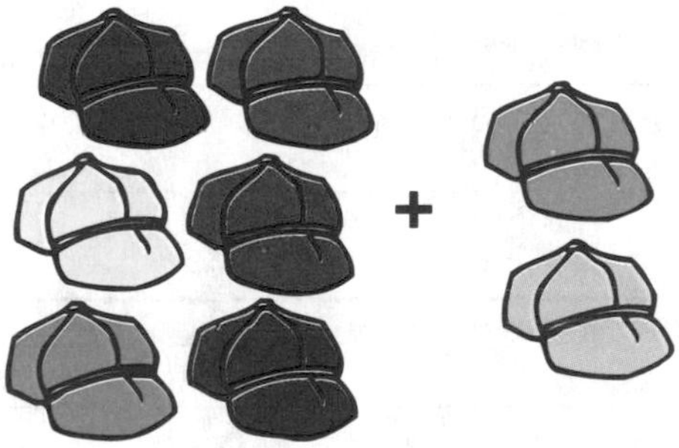

6 + 2 = ____

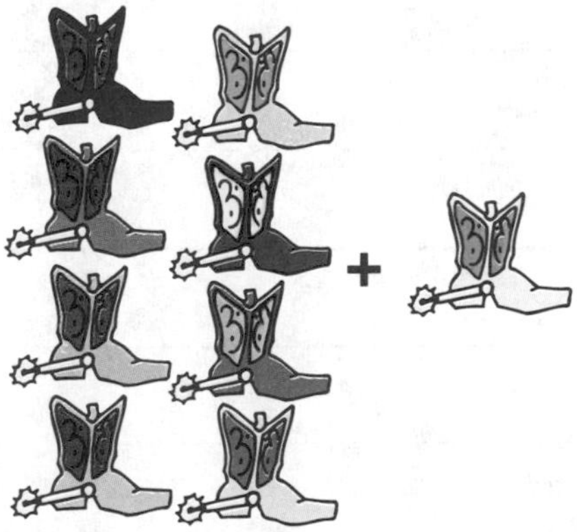

8 + 1 = ____

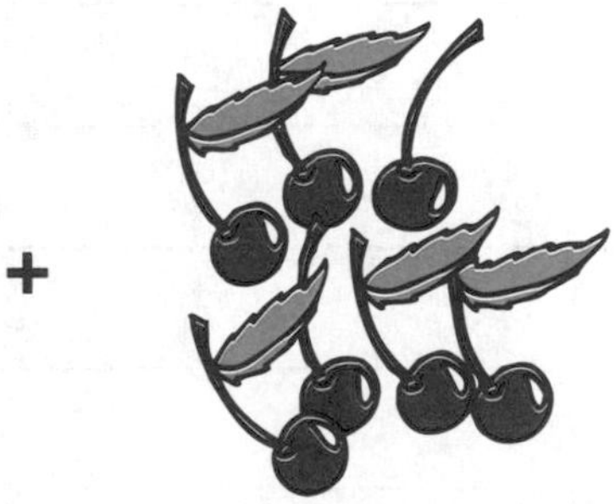

0 + 7 = ____

Name: _____

Telling Sentences

Directions: Read the sentences. Write the sentences on the lines below. Begin each sentence with a capital letter. End each sentence with a period.

1. most children like pets
2. some children like dogs
3. some children like cats
4. some children like snakes
5. some children like all animals

1. _____

_____

_____

2. _____

_____

_____

3. _____

_____

_____

4. _____

_____

_____

5. _____

_____

Name: _____

I Know How To Make A Sentence!

Directions: Write a sentence that tells about the picture. Use the words next to the picture. Remember to begin with a capital letter and end with a period.

Like this: likes boy to paint the

The boy likes to paint.

1. tall he grow will

_____

_____

_____

2. bird this can fly

_____

_____

_____

3. color she wants to

_____

_____

_____

Name: _____

Classifying

Directions: Put an **X** on the picture that does not go in each group.

fruit

apple   peach   corn   melon

wild animals

bear   kitten   gorilla   lion

pets

cat   fish   elephant   dog

flowers

grass   rose   daisy   tulip

LESSON 13

Pioneer Children

In the early 1800s, many citizens left their homes in the East to travel to unsettled lands in the West. If you lived at this time, there would be a chance of your family going on this long trip in a covered wagon.

As a pioneer child, you would be a big help to your family. You might gather dead sagebrush for fires, milk cows, or fetch water from rivers. Often you would help skin animals, cook the food, and wash the dishes. You and the other pioneer children would be an important part of helping your families to settle America.

Would you like to be a pioneer child? Tell why or why not.

ACTIVITY 13

Pioneer Children

Directions: Draw a picture of yourself doing a chore a pioneer child might have had to do.

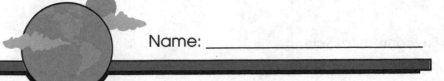

Name: _____

Conserve Heat Energy

People use heat in many ways.

On cold days, heat is used to warm homes.

Heat is one kind of energy.

People must learn not to waste energy.

They must find ways to conserve energy.

One way to conserve energy Is to use less heat.

Read how you can conserve energy in your home.

1. Thermostats should be set no higher than 68.

2. Do not turn up the heat. Dress warmly instead.

3. Help your parents change the air filters in your furnace.

4. Pull down window shades and close curtains at night.

Can you add another way to conserve energy to the list?

Help At Home

Directions: It is winter. Snow is falling all around. Look at the pictures in the first row. Energy is being wasted. Think about ways to conserve energy. Draw ways to conserve in the second row. The first one is done for you.

WASTE

CONSERVE

Matching Pictures And Sentences

Directions: Draw a line from the picture to the sentence that tells about it.

Kelly has flowers in her basket.

A red apple is on the green tree.

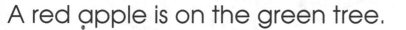

Four ducks swim in the lake.

The toy train goes fast!

The brown bear is eating honey.

Name: _____

Help The Puppy Feel Safe

Directions: Re-read the story about the clocks on page 354. Look at the pictures. Then number them in 1-2-3-4 order.

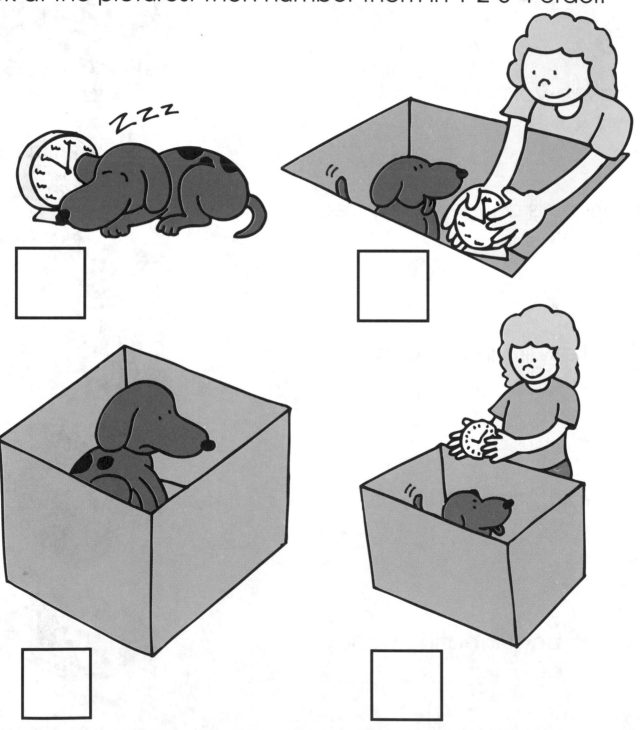

Name: _____

Picture Problems: Subtraction

Directions: Work the number problem under each picture.

5 - 2 = _____

6 - 1 = _____

7 - 4 = _____

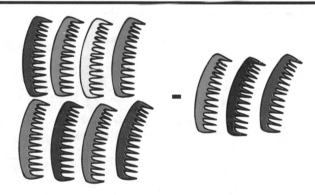

8 - 3 = _____

9 - 2 = _____

4 - 4 = _____

Telling Sentences

Directions: Read the sentences. Write the sentences below. Start each sentence with a capital letter and end with a period.

1. i like to go to the store with Mom
2. we go on Friday
3. i get to push the cart
4. i get to buy the cookies
5. i like to help Mom

1. _____

_____

_____

2. _____

_____

_____

3. _____

_____

_____

4. _____

_____

_____

5. _____

_____

Name: _____

I Know Which Words Sound The Same!

Directions: Write the words that answer the questions.

catch	fly	eat	grow	buy	color

1. Which words start the same as  ?

_____   _____

_____   _____

_____   _____

2. Which word starts the same as each of these pictures?

_____   _____

_____   _____

_____   _____

3. Which words rhyme with ?

_____   _____

_____   _____

_____   _____

4. Which "doing" word rhymes with these?

_____   _____

_____   _____

_____   _____

Name: _____

Classifying

Directions: Help Ben clean up the park. Circle the litter. Underline the coins. Put a box around the balls.

Name: _____

What Do You See?

Directions: 1) Look at the picture. 2) Read the sentences.
3) Draw a circle around Yes or No.

1. The clown has five balloons.	Yes	No
2. The girl has a hat on.	Yes	No
3. There are three children.	Yes	No
4. Two children are sad.	Yes	No
5. The clown has no shoes.	Yes	No
6. The clown has a big nose.	Yes	No
7. One child is waving.	Yes	No

Name: _____

I Like Soup

Directions: Read about soup. Then answer the questions.

Soup is good! It is good for you, too. We eat most kinds of soup hot. Some people eat cold soup in the summer. Carrotsand beans are in some soups. Do you like crackers with soup?

1. Name 2 ways people eat soup.

_____   _____

_____   _____

_____

2. Tell 2 things that are in some soups.

_____   _____

_____   _____

_____

_____

3. Name the soup   _____
   you like best.   _____

Name: _____

Picture Problems: Subtraction

Directions: Work the number problem under each picture.

6 - 2 = _____

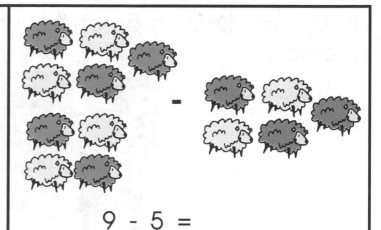

9 - 5 = _____

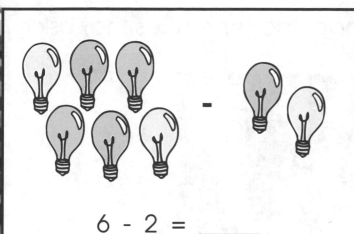

7 - 2 = _____

4 - 1 = _____

8 - 1 = _____

4 - 0 = _____

Asking Sentences

Asking sentences ask a question. An asking sentence begins with a capital letter. It ends with a question mark.

Directions: Draw a green line under the sentences that ask a question.

1. Does your room look like this?

2. Are the walls yellow?

3. There are many children.

4. Do you sit at desks or tables?

5. The teacher likes her job.

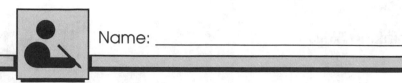

I Can Write My Own Sentences!

Directions: You will write five sentences with the "doing" words. Read your sentences to someone.

Words to start your sentences: **I, we, they, boys, girls, people, birds, dogs, airplanes, flowers, apples, cats**.

Words to end your sentences: **balls, frogs, ice cream, cookies, pictures, bigger, in my house, in the sky, in a tree, in the rain, in a bed, at school, at home**.

1._____ catch _____

2._____ color _____

3._____ eat _____

4._____ grow _____

5._____ fly _____

Name: _____

Classifying

Directions: Write each word in the correct row at the bottom of the page.

car　　pencil　chalk　　radio　　boat　　fork　　plate　　friend

airplane　　drum　　television　　crayon

Things we ride in:

_____　_____　_____

_____　_____　_____

_____　_____　_____

Things we eat with:

_____　_____　_____

_____　_____　_____

_____　_____　_____

Things we draw with:

_____　_____　_____

_____　_____　_____

_____　_____　_____

Things we listen to:

_____　_____　_____

_____　_____　_____

_____　_____　_____

What Am I?

Directions: 1) Read the word. 2) Write the word. 3) Read each riddle. 4) Draw a line to the picture it tells about.

house
_____
_____
_____

I like to play.
I am little. I am soft.
What am I?

house

kitten
_____
_____
_____

I am big.
You live in me.
What am I?

kitten

flower
_____
_____
_____

I am pretty.
I am green and
yellow.
What am I?

flower

pony
_____
_____
_____

I can jump. I can run.
I am brown.
What am I?

pony

Name: _____

Eating Soup

Directions: 1) Look at both pictures. 2) Find 4 things in picture #1 that are not in picture #2. 3) Say your answers aloud. 4) Draw a circle around them.

#1   #2

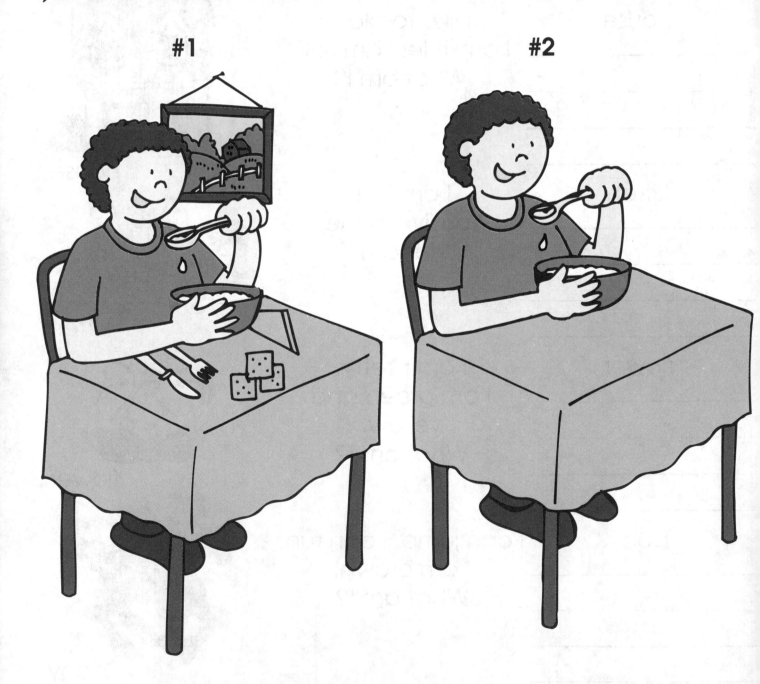

Name: _____

Picture Problems: Addition And Subtraction

Directions: Work the number problem under each picture.

7 - 4 = ____

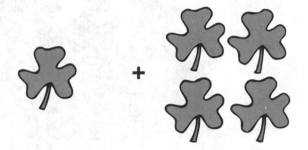

1 + 4 = ____

3 + 5 = ____

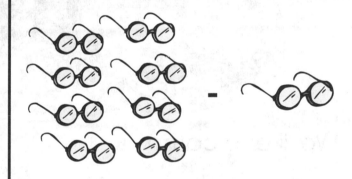

8 - 1 = ____

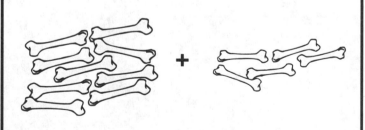

9 + 5 = ____

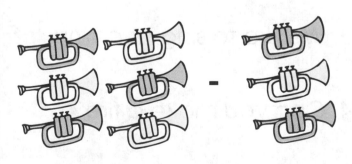

6 - 3 = ____

Asking Sentences

Directions: Draw a blue line under the sentences that ask a question.

1. We like to camp.

2. Do you like to camp?

3. We like to sing at camp.

4. Can you make a fire?

5. We like to cook hot dogs.

I Know Which Letters Are Missing!

Directions: Write in the missing letters. Can you spell the words by yourself now?

Like this:

paint   paint

ca ch   cat

c lor   co

ea   e t

gro   g w

f y   ly

Classifying

There are four food groups: meat, fruit and vegetables, breads, and dairy (milk and cheese).

Directions: Color the meats brown. Color the fruits and vegetables green. Color the breads tan. Color the dairy items yellow.

hotdog

bread

apple

cheese

rolls

celery

orange

hamburger

steak

pear

milk

butter

ice cream

chicken

potato

muffin

Animal Riddles

Directions: 1) Read the word. 2) Write the word. 3) Draw a line from the sentences to the animal they tell about.

l o n g _long_____

I am very big.
I lived a long, long time ago.
What am I?

giraffe

My neck is very long.
I eat leaves from trees.
What am I?

rabbit

I have long ears.
I hop very fast.
What am I?

dinosaur

Name: _____

Put The 3 Bears To Bed

Directions: Read about the 3 bears. Then match the bears with their beds. Put # 1 beside Papa Bear's bed. Put # 2 beside Mama Bear's bed. Put # 3 beside Baby Bear's Bed.

Do you know the story of the 3 bears? Papa Bear was the biggest bear. He had the biggest bed. Mama Bear was a middle-size bear. She had the middle-size bed. Baby Bear was the little bear. He had the baby bed.

1   # 2   # 3

Picture Problems: Addition and Subtraction

Directions: Work the number problem under each picture.
Write **+** or **-** to show if you should add or subtract.

How many 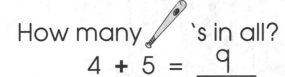's in all?
4 **+** 5 = __9__

How many 's in all?
7   5 = ____

How many 's are left?
12   3 = ____

How many 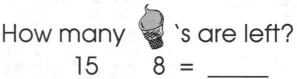's are left?
15   8 = ____

 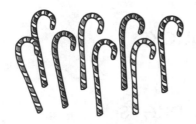

How many 's in all?
5   8 = ____

How many 's are left?
11   4 = ____

Asking Sentences

Directions: Write the first word of each asking sentence. Be sure to start each question with a capital letter. End each question with a question mark.

1. _____ you like the zoo   **do**

2. _____ much does it cost   **how**

3. _____ you feed the ducks   **can**

4. _____ you see the monkeys   **will**

5. _____ time will you eat lunch   **what**

Name: _____

I Can Make Two Sentences Into One!

Directions: Make two sentences into one.

Like this: The ball is red. The ball is blue.

The ball is red and blue.

1. I eat apples. I eat cookies.

_____

_____

2. We buy milk. We buy eggs.

_____

_____

3. I color a horse. I color a cow.

_____

_____

4. Flowers grow. Trees grow.

_____

_____

Name: _____

Classifying

Directions: Draw food you like to eat. Draw one meat, one fruit or vegetable, one bread and something with milk in it. Then answer the questions.

What is your meat?_____

What is your fruit or vegetable?_____

What is your bread?_____

What is your milk food?_____

Name: _____

LESSON 14

Samantha Smith

In 1989, a ten-year-old girl named Samantha Smith was worried that the United States would go to war with the country that used to be called the Soviet Union. She wrote a letter to the leader of the Soviet Union and asked him to work for peace.

The Soviet leader wrote back to Samantha. He invited her to the Soviet Union to see that his people wanted peace too.

Samantha's famous trip made people think about working together for world peace. She helped Americans realize how important one person's efforts can be.

Do you think Samantha thought that her letter would make a difference in the way people thought about peace? Explain.

Name: _____

ACTIVITY 14

Samantha Smith

When Samantha visited a children's camp in the Soviet Union, she and the other campers wrote messages. They put their messages in bottles and threw them into the Black Sea for others to find and read.

Directions: Write what you think Samantha's message said.

Name: _____

Your Community

Think about the wild animals and birds that live in your environment. Write the names on the the lines.

WILD ANIMALS   **BIRDS**

_____   _____

_____   _____

_____   _____

_____   _____

_____   _____

_____   _____

_____   _____

_____   _____

_____   _____

_____   _____

Is your community a good place for wild animals and birds to live?

Activity 12

Plan A Refuge

Directions: You know that wild animals and birds need safe places to
live. Help the leaders of your
community. Plan a refuge for your
community.

What will the animals and birds eat?
What will their homes look like?

Draw your refuge.

Write a name for the community refuge.

_____

_____

_____

Name: _____

More Riddles

Directions: Write a word from the word box to answer each riddle.

| ice cream | book | chair | sun |

There are many words in me.
I am fun to read.
What am I?

_____
_____
_____

I have four legs.
I am made of wood.
You can sit on me.
What am I?

_____
_____
_____

I am in the sky in the day.
I am hot. I am yellow.
What am I?

_____
_____
_____

I am cold. I am sweet.
You like to eat me.
What am I?

_____
_____
_____

Name: _____

3 Bears Puzzle

Directions: Re-read the story of the 3 bears on page 382. Then fill in the puzzle with the right answers about the bears.

Across

1. Papa Bear was the _____ bear.
3. All the bears slept in _____.

Down

1. This bear was the little bear.
2. Mama Bear was middle - _____.

Name: _____

Picture Problems: Addition and Subtraction

Directions: Work the number problem under each picture.
Write **+** or **-** to show if you should add or subtract.

How many 's in all?

7 + 5 = __12__

How many 's are left?

8   3 = _____

How many 's are left?

9   4 = _____

How many 's in all?

14   1 = _____

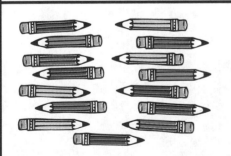

How many 's are left?

15   6 = _____

How many 's in all?

9   5 = _____

Name: _____

Periods And Question Marks

Use a period at the end of a telling sentence. Use a question mark at the end of an asking sentence.

Directions: Put a period or a question mark at the end of each sentence below.

1. Do you like a parade

2. The clowns lead the parade

3. Can you hear the band

4. The balloons are big

5. Can you see the horses

Name: _____

I Can Finish A Story!

Directions: Write in the missing "doing" words. The first letter of each word is there. Another word you know is missing, too. Write it by its picture.

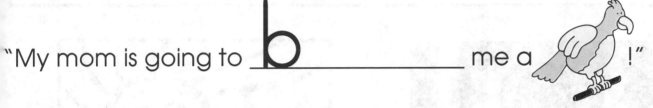

"My mom is going to __b_____ me a !"

I told my teacher.   "I saw it in the pet store! It is a

baby _____, but it will __g_____ bigger."

"Can it __f_____ ?" she asked. "If it gets away, how

will you __c_____ it?"

"I will hold up some food," I said. "When my _____ comes to

__e_____ , I can __c_____ him."

Name: _____

Classifying

Directions: Put the words from the list under the pictures they describe.

| stars | sun | moon | rays | dark | light | night | day |

_____   _____

_____   _____

_____   _____

_____   _____

_____   _____

_____   _____

Skills Review:
Understanding Sentences: Riddles

Directions: Read the riddle. Draw a picture of the answer.

I am a big toy.
I am fun to ride.
I have two wheels.
What am I?

Name: _____

Review

Directions: Read how to make no-cook candy. Then answer the questions.

Some candy neds to be cooked on a stove. But you do not need to cook this candy. It is an easy candy for kids to make. You will need a large bowl to mix the things in. You will need 5 things to make this candy.

No-Cook Candy
1/2 cup peanut butter
4 cups powdered sugar
1 cup cocoa
pinch of salt
4 tablespoons milk
A pinch of salt is just a tiny bit!
Mix everything in the bowl. Roll it into small balls.

1. What is # 3 on the list of cooking? _____

_____

2. What is different about no-cook candy?

_____

_____

_____

3. First mix everything in a bowl. Then

_____

_____

_____

Review

Directions: Work the number problem under each picture.
Write **+** or **-** to show if you should add or subtract.

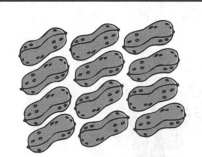

How many 's are left?

12   4 = _____

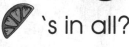

How many 's in all?

6   8 = _____

How many 's are left?

4   4 = _____

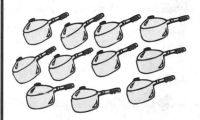 

How many 's are left?

11   7 = _____

How many 's in all?

9   3 = _____

How many 's in all?

10   0 = _____

Name: _____

Review

Directions: Look at the picture. In the space below, write one telling sentence about the picture. Then, write one asking sentence about the picture.

A telling sentence.

_____

_____

_____

An asking sentence.

_____

_____

_____

Name: _____

Review

Directions: Use the words you know to write sentences that tell about these pictures. Write a question about the last picture.

Here are some more words you could use in your sentences: **boys, girls, he, she, they**.

Like this:

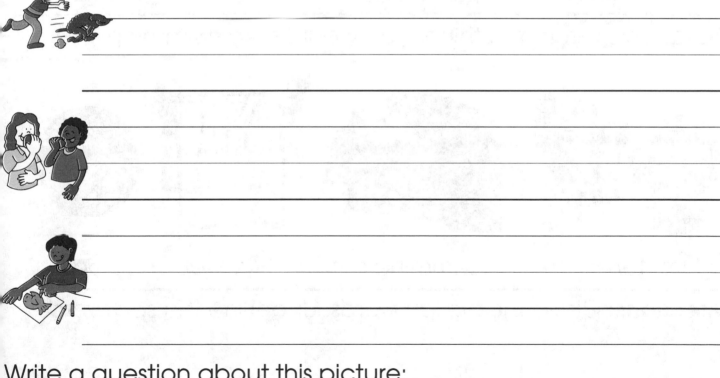

Rain makes flowers grow.

Write a question about this picture:

Name: _____

Review

Directions: Color the item that does **not** belong in the group.

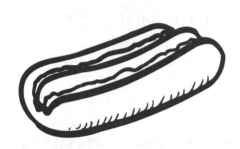   

| hotdog | hamburger | pear | bacon |

Directions: Circle the things you would take swimming.

mittens   swimming suit   towel   ball

Directions: Circle the happy words. Underline the sad words.

grin   laugh   funny   cry   happy   frown

yawn   tear   upset   dark   fun   glad

Name: _____

A Poem

Directions: Read the poem. Write the correct words in the blanks.

A Poem
The hat was on a mat.
A cat sat on the hat.
And now the hat is flat.

_____
_____

The hat was on _____ .

_____

_____

Who sat on the hat? _____

_____

_____

Now the hat is _____ .

_____

Name: _____

See The Barnyards

Directions: Look at the 2 pictures of the barnyard. Find 5 things that are different in the 2 pictures. Color only the things that are different.

Money: Penny, Nickel, Dime

A penny is worth one cent. It is written **1¢** or **$.01**. A nickel is worth five cents. It is written **5¢** or **$.05**. A dime is worth ten cents. It is written **10¢** or **$.10**.

Directions: Add the coins pictured and write the total amounts in the blanks.

Example:

dime   **nickel**   **nickel**   **pennies**

10¢   =   5¢   +   5¢   =   10¢

10¢   +   1¢   =   ____ ¢   10¢   +   ____ ¢ =   ____ ¢

____ + ____ + ____ =   ____ ¢

____ ¢ =   ____ ¢   =   ____ ¢

Name: _____

Word Order

Word order is the logical order of words in a sentence.

Directions: Put the words in each sentence in order. Write the sentence on the lines.

1. We made lemonade. some
2. good. It was
3. We the sold lemonade.
4. cost It five cents.
5. <u>fun. We had</u>

1. _____

2. _____

3. _____

4. _____

5. _____

Name: _____

I Can Write "People" Words!

Directions: 1. Follow the lines to write the words. 2. Then write the words again by yourself. 3. Read the words to someone.

girl

boy

man

woman

people

children

Name: _____

Predicting Outcome

Directions: Finish the story by drawing a picture in the last box.

Dan likes to paint.   **He likes to help his dad.**

He is tired when he's finished.

Draw A Picture

Directions: Read the sentences. Draw the picture the sentences tell about.

A boy and a girl play ball.
The girl has a hat on.
See the yellow sun!

The ball is red.
There is a big, green tree.
The dog can run.

Hey Diddle Diddle

Directions: Read "Hey Diddle Diddle." Then answer the questions.

Hey diddle diddle
The cat and the fiddle
The cow jumped over the moon.
The little dog laughed
To see such sport
And the dish ran away with the spoon!

1. Who jumped over the moon?

_____

_____

_____

2. Who laughed?

_____

_____

_____

3. Who ran away?

_____ _____

_____ and _____

_____ _____

Time: Hour, Half-Hour

Directions: Tell what time it is on the clocks.

 _____

 _____

 _____

 _____

 _____

 _____

Name: _____

Word Order

Directions: Look at the picture. Put the words in the correct order. Write the sentences on the lines below.

1. a Jan starfish. has
2. and Bill to Peg swim. like
3. The shining. sun is
4. sand. the in Jack likes play to
5. cold. water The is

1. _____

2. _____

3. _____

4. _____

5. _____

Name: _____

I Can Finish Sentences!

Directions: Find the sentence that goes with each picture. Then write in the word that finishes the sentence.

people	man	girl	children	boy	woman

1. The _____ feeds the cat.

2. The _____ are buying dessert.

3. What is the _____ painting?

4. The _____ will grow corn.

5. The dog runs to the _____ .

6. There are long lines of _____ .

Name: _____

Predicting Outcome

Directions: Read the story. Fill in the first and last box. How do you think the story will end?

Susan is new at school.

Hello, I'm Amy.

Do you like to jump rope?

Name: _____

LESSON 15

Labor Day

Labor Day is a holiday that honors all working people. On Labor Day citizens are reminded that all jobs are important. Americans remember that all citizens working together help to keep our country strong.

Read the names of the places where people work. Then complete the chart with the names of workers.

PLACE	NAME OF WORKER	
airport	pilot	
sports stadium		baseball player
factory	engineer	
movie theater		ticket seller
space lab		scientist

Which of the jobs on the chart would you like to do? Tell why.

Name: _____

ACTIVITY 15

Labor Day

Directions: Think of a place where people do their jobs or pick one of these places:

Grocery Store   Restaurant   Hospital

Write the name of the place on the sign. Inside the building, draw pictures of the workers who do their jobs in this place.

Your drawing will show **Citizens Now** working together to make America great.

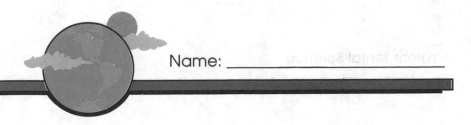

Name: _____

Summary

Directions: Play tic-tac-toe with a friend. Mark an X or an O in the box.
Tell if the picture shows something that hurts or helps the environment.
Use pencils so you can erase and play again.

Name: _____

Review

Directions: Everyone must work to protect the environment. Look back in this book. Think about what you have learned. You know there are many ways to help. Draw what you will do to save our earth.

Name: _____

Fill In The Blanks

Directions: Look at the picture. Write the words from the word box to finish the sentences.

frog	log	bird	fish	ducks

_____

The turtle is on a _____.

_____

The _____ can jump.

_____

The boy wants a _____.

A _____ is in the tree.

_____

I see three _____.

_____

Name: _____

Hey Diddle Diddle, Again!

Directions: Re-read the story of "Hey Diddle Diddle" on page 410. Then put the pictures of the story in 1-2-3-4 order.

Name: _____

Shapes: Square, Circle, Rectangle, Triangle

Directions: Use the code to color the shapes.

Squares - Orange
Circles - Red
Rectangles - Blue
Triangles - Green

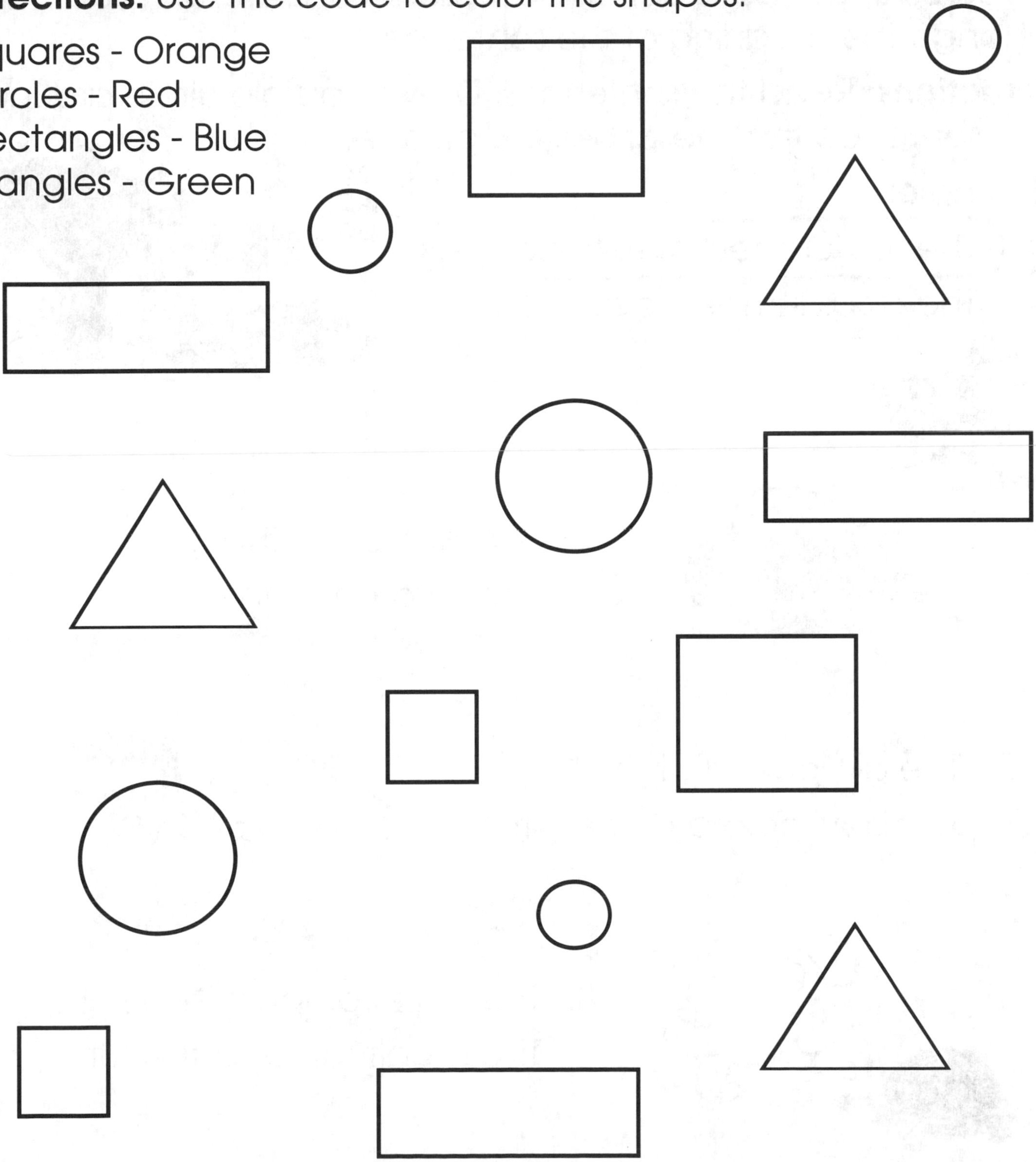

Word Order Can Change Meaning

If you change the order of the words in a sentence, you can change the meaning of the sentence.

Directions: Read the sentences. Draw a purple circle around the sentence that describes the picture.

Example:

(The fox jumped over the dogs.)

The dogs jumped over the fox.

1. The cat watched the bird.
   The bird watched the cat.

2. The girl looked at the boy.
   The boy looked at the girl.

3. The turtle ran past the rabbit.
   The rabbit ran past the turtle.

Name: _____

I Can Play A Word Game!

Directions: Find each of the "people" words. Put circles around them, like the circle around "baby."

people	boy	woman	girl	children	man
u	a	w	r	c	a
c	f	d	k	h	n
s	r	b	h	i	y
p	e	o	p	l	e
n	l	y	j	d	o
k	c	g	i	r	l
x	b	h	s	e	b
w	o	m	a	n	m
r	b	a	b	y	e
t	o	n	d	k	m

Name: _____

Predicting Outcome

Directions: Read the story. Fill in the last box.

That's my ball!

I got it first.

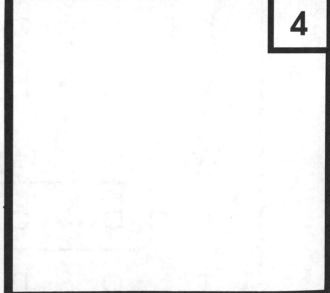

It's mine!

Name: _____

A Short Story

Directions: Read the story. Write the word from the story that completes each sentence.

Ben and Sue have a bug.
It is red with black spots.
They call it Spot.
Spot likes to eat green
leaves and grass.
The children keep him in a box.

_____

_____

Ben and Sue have a _____.

_____

It is _____ with black spots.

_____

The bug's name is _____.

_____

The bug eats _____.

Name: _____

Bluebird

Directions: Read about the bluebird. Look at the word list. Choose the words that tell what blue things the bluebird sees.

Bluebird, bluebird
Up in the tree
How many blue things
Do you see?

book	flowers
girl	grass
hat	sky
shoes	tree

Here are the blue things
the bluebird sees:
_____

1. _____

2. _____   3. _____

4. _____   5. _____

Name: _____

Place Value: Tens, Ones And One Hundred

The place value of each digit, or numeral, is shown by where it is in the number. For example, in the number **123**, **1** has the place value of **hundreds**, **2** is **tens**, and **3** is **ones**.

Directions: Count the groups of crayons and add.

Example:

 + +

Hundreds	Tens	Ones
1	1	3

1 Hundred + **1 Ten** + **3 Ones**

 = ___ ___ ___

 = ___ ___ ___

I Can Write Sentences

A story has more than one sentence.

Directions: Use the words from the pictures to write a story.

girl

boy

play

books

swing

school

I am a happy _____ . I go to _____ .

I like to read _____ . I like to _____

on the playground. I like to _____ on the swings.

I Know Other Words For People!

Sometimes we use other words to mean people: For boy or man, we can use "he." For girl or woman, we can use "she." For two or more people, we can use "they."

Directions: Write "he," "she," or "they" in these sentences.

Like this:

The boy likes cookies.

He _____ likes cookies.

1. The girl is running fast.

_____ is running fast.

2. The man reads the paper. _____ reads the paper.

3. The woman has a cold.

_____ has a cold.

4. Two children came to school.

_____ came to school.

Name: _____

Making Inferences

Dave likes baseball. He likes to win. He hits the ball hard. Dave's team does not win.

Directions: Circle the right answers.

1. Dave likes

football soccer baseball

2. Dave likes to win.

  lose.

3. Dave uses a bat. Yes

  No

4. Dave is

  happy  sad

A Rainy Day Story

Directions: Read the story. Write the words from the story in the blanks to finish the sentences.

Jane and Bill like to play in the rain. They take off their shoes and socks. They splash in the puddles. It feels cold! It is fun to splash!

_____

_____

Jane and Bill like to _____ .

_____

_____

They take off their _____ .

_____

_____

They splash in _____ .

Do you like to splash in puddles?   Yes   No

Name: _____

Inside And Outside

Directions: 1) Read about inside animals and outside animals. 2) Look at the pictures. 3) Circle the animals that can live inside. 4) Write the names of the ones that belong outside.

Some animals belong inside. Some animals belong outside. Wild animals belong outside. Large animals belong outside. Small, tame animals can live inside.

Animals that belong outside:

1. _____

2. _____

3. _____

4. _____

cat

tiger

bird

bird

cow

horse

Name: _____

Fractions: Half, Third, Fourth

Directions: Count the equal parts, then write the fraction.

Example:

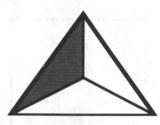

Shaded part = __1__   Write $\dfrac{1}{3}$

Equal parts = __3__

Shaded part = __1__   Write

Equal parts = ____   __—__

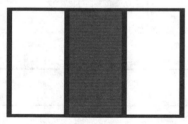

Shaded part = __1__   Write

Equal parts = ____   __—__

Shaded part = __1__   Write

Equal parts = ____   __—__

I Can Write Sentences

Directions: Draw a picture of yourself in the box marked **Me**. Then write three sentences about yourself on the lines.

Me

1. _____

2. _____

3. _____

Name: _____

I Can Spell By Myself!

Directions: 1. Write a "people" word in each sentence to tell who is doing something. The first letter is there. Can you spell the rest of the word by yourself? 2. Then, on your own paper, draw a picture to show what is happening.

1. The b_____ was last in line at the toy store.

2. The c_____ took a walk in the woods.

3. The g_____ had to help her father.

4. The w_____ had a surprise for the children.

5. Some p_____ like to eat outside.

6. Something came out of the box when the m_____ opened it.

Making Inferences

Lynn looks at the stars. She sings a song about them. She makes a wish on them. The stars help Lynn sleep.

Directions: Answer the questions about Lynn.

1. Lynn likes the:

moon   sun   stars

2. What song do you think she sings?

Row, Row, Row Your Boat

Twinkle, Twinkle Little Star

Happy Birthday to You

3. What does Lynn "make" on the stars?

_____

_____

_____

_____

Skills Review:
Understanding What Is Read

Directions: Read the story. Draw a picture about the story.

Dee and Duke are at the zoo. They like to feed the animals. They like the giraffe. The giraffe eats leaves. Dee and Duke give leaves to the giraffe.

Name: _____

Review

Directions: Read about the ways we can play with balls. Then answer the questions.

Some balls are soft. A beach ball is soft. Some balls are hard. We play baseball with a hard ball. Basketballs bounce. Can you throw a basketball through a hoop? First bounce it 3 times. Then hold the basketball high. Now, throw it toward the hoop. Did you make a basket?

1. Tell how to throw a basketball.

1) First bounce it 3 times.

_____

2) _____ .

_____

_____

3) _____ .

_____

2. How is a beach ball different from a hard ball?

_____

_____

_____

Review

Directions: Follow the instructions.

1. How much money?

_____ ¢

	Tens	**Ones**			**Hundreds**	**Tens**	**Ones**
2. 57 =	_____	_____		128 =	_____	_____	_____

3. What is this shape? Circle the answer.

Square

Triangle

Circle

What is this shape? _____

4.

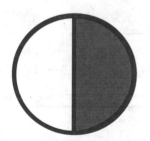

Shaded part = _____   Write

Equal parts = _____   ___

Shaded part = _____   Write

Equal parts = _____   ___

5.   12 + 3 = _____   9 + 6 = _____   15 - 7 = _____

Name: _____

Review

Directions: Put the words in the right order to make a sentence. The sentences will tell a story.

1. a gerbil. has Ann
2. is The Mike. named gerbil
3. likes eat. Mike to
4. play. to Mike likes
5. happy a is gerbil. Mike

1. _____

_____

2. _____

_____

3. _____

_____

4. _____

_____

5. _____

_____

Name: _____

Look What I Can Write!

Here are all the words you know now - **Pets:** dog, fish, cat, bird. **Colors:** blue, yellow, red, green, black, brown. **Food:** cake, apple, milk, egg, ice cream, cookie. **"Doing" Words:** ride, sit, stop, color, make, eat, run, grow, play, fly, see, catch, jump, buy. **Weather:** rain, snow, cold, hot, wet, water. **Opposites:** new, old, first, last, lost, found, light, dark. **People:** girl, boy, man, woman, people, children.

Directions: 1. Write three telling sentences below. Use three or more of these words in each one. Remember to start with a capital letter and end with a period. 2. Write one question. Remember to end with a question mark. 3. Read your sentences to someone.

_____

1. _____

_____

2. _____

_____

3. _____

_____

A question: _____

_____

_____

Name: _____

Review

Directions: Read each story. Follow the instructions.

Complete this story.

1. **Ed's dog runs away.**
2. **Ed chases it.**
3. **The dog runs into a store.**
   _____
   _____

4. _____
   _____
   _____
   _____
   _____

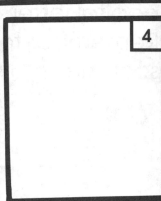

Liz plays games with her little sister. Sometimes she hides from her. Her sister calls her name over and over. Liz does not answer. Liz thinks it is funny.

1. Is Liz being nice or mean to her sister? _____

2. Do you think her sister likes Liz to hide?   Yes   No

3. What would you do if you were Liz's sister?
   _____
   _____
   _____

Glossary

Reading Glossary

Alphabetical Order.   Putting words in a-b-c order.

Auditory Discrimination. The skill of identifying sounds in words.

Beginning Sounds.   The sounds made by the first letters of words.

Blends. Two consonant sounds put together.

Classifying. Putting similar things into categories.

Compound Words. When two words are put together to make one.

Consonants. Letters that are not vowels (a, e, i, o, and u).

Digraphs. Two consonants that make one special sound at the beginning of a word.

Ending Sounds. The sounds made by the last letters of words.

Following Directions. Doing what the directions say to do.

Opposites. Things that are different in every way.

Phonics. Using the sounds letters make to decode unknown words.

Plural. More than one.

Rhymes. Words with the same ending sounds.

Riddles. A puzzling question.

Sequencing. Putting things in logical order.

Visual Clues. Looking at the pictures to figure out meaning.

Vowels. The letters a, e, i, o, and u.

Comprehension Glossary

Classifying. Putting things that are alike into categories.

Comprehension. Understanding what is seen, heard or read.

Following Directions. Doing what the directions say to do.

Same/Different. Being able to tell how things are the same and different.

Sequencing. Putting things in order.

Math Glossary

Addition. "Putting together" or adding two or more numbers to find the sum.
For example, $3 + 5 = 8$

Glossary continued on next page

Math Glossary continued

Circle. A figure that is round. It looks like this: ◯

Diamond. A figure with four sides of the same length. Its corners form points at the top, sides, and bottom. It looks like this: ◇

Digit. The symbols used to write numbers: 1, 2, 3, 4, 5, 6, 7, 8, and 9.

Dime. Ten cents. It is written **10¢** or **$.10**.

Fraction. A number that names part of a whole, such as **1/2** or **1/3**.

Half-hour. Thirty minutes. When the long hand of the clock is pointing to the six, the time is on the half-hour. It is written **:30**, such as **5:30**.

Hour. Sixty minutes. The short hand of a clock tells the hour.

Nickel. Five cents. It is written **5¢** or **$.05**.

Ordinal number. Numbers that indicate order in a series, such as first, second, or third.

Oval. A figure that is egg shaped. I looks like this: ⬯

Penny. One cent. It is written **1¢** or **$.01**.

Place Value. The value of a digit, or numeral, shown by where it is in the number. For example, in the number **123**, **1** has the place value of **hundreds**, **2** is **tens**, and **3** is **ones**.

Rectangle. A figure with four corners and four sides. Sides opposite each other are the same length. It looks like this: ▭

Sequencing. Putting numbers in the correct order, such as 7, 8, 9.

Square. A figure with four corners and four sides of the same length. It looks like this: ☐

Subtraction. "Taking away" or subtracting one number from another.
For example, 10 - 3 = 7.

Triangle. A figure with three corners and three sides. It looks like this: △

English Glossary

ABC Order. Putting objects or words in the same order in which they appear in the alphabet.

Antonyms. Words that are opposites.

Asking Sentences. An asking sentence begins with a capital letter, ends with a question mark and asks a question.

Beginning Consonants. Sounds that come at the beginning of words that are not vowel sounds. (Vowels are the letters a, e, i, o, u and sometimes y.)

Glossary continued on next page

English Glossary continued

Capital Letters. Letters that are used at the beginning of names of people and places. They are also used at the beginning of sentences. These letters (**A B C D E F G H I J K L M N O P Q R S T U V W X Y Z**) are sometimes called the "big" letters.

Compound Words. When two words are put together to make one word. Example: house + boat = houseboat

Describing Words. Words that tell us more about a person, place or thing.

Ending Consonants. Sounds, which are not vowel sounds, that come at the end of words.

Homonyms. Words that sound the same but are spelled differently and mean different things. Example: blue and blew.

Nouns. Words that tell the name of persons, places or things.

Sound Discrimination. Being able to identify the differences between sounds.

Super E. When you add an e to some words and the vowel changes from a short vowel sound to a long vowel sound. Example: rip + e = ripe.

Synonyms. Words that mean the same thing. Example: small and little.

Telling Sentences. These sentences begin with a capital letter, end with a period and tell us something.

Verbs. Words that tell what a person or thing can do.

Words Order. The logical order of words in sentences.

Thinking Skills Glossary

Classifying. Putting things that are alike into categories.

Duplicating. Copying.

Opposites. Things that are different in every way.

Finding Patterns. Recognizing similar shapes.

Finding Similarities. Finding items that are almost the same.

Following Directions. Doing what the directions say to do.

Inference. Using logic to figure out what is unspoken but evident.

Predicting Outcome. Telling what is likely to happen based on available facts.

Same/Different. Being able to tell how things are the same and different.

Sequencing. Putting things in order.

Tracking. Following a path.

Glossary continued on next page

Environmental Science Glossary

Conservationist. A person who takes care of the environment.

Conserve. To keep from being wasted or used up.

Earth. The planet we live on.

Environment. Everything around you.

Polluted. Air, land or water that is very dirty.

Pollution. Things that make the environment unclean.

Recycle. Saving things and using them over and over.

Refuge. A safe place for wild animals.

School Custodians. Men and women who keep the school clean.

NOTES

NOTES

ANSWER KEY

COMPREHENSIVE CURRICULUM

OF BASIC SKILLS

1

Name: _____

Color Code

Directions: Color the B words orange. Color the M words yellow. Color the L words blue. Color the S words black.

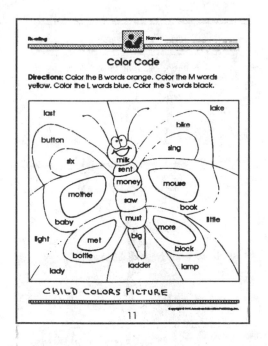

CHILD COLORS PICTURE

11

Math Name: _____

Number Recognition

Directions: Write the numbers 1-10. Color the bear.

13

Comprehension Name: _____

Things I Know About

Directions: 1. Say each of the 4 words aloud. 2. Write each word where it belongs in the blanks. 3. Now write each word beside its picture in the puzzle.

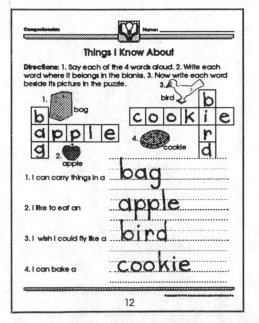

1. I can carry things in a **bag**

2. I like to eat an **apple**

3. I wish I could fly like a **bird**

4. I can bake a **cookie**

12

English Name: _____

ABC Order

Directions: Draw a line to connect the dots. Follow the letters in ABC order.

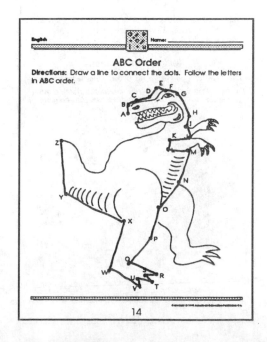

14

I Can Write The Names Of Pets!

Directions: 1. Follow the lines to write the name of each pet.
2. Write each name again by yourself. 3. Color the pictures.
4. Read the words to someone.
Like this:

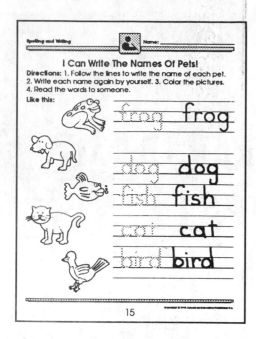

frog   frog

dog   dog

fish   fish

cat   cat

bird   bird

15

Snow Is Cold!

Directions: Read about snow. Then answer the questions.

When you play in snow, dress warmly. Wear a coat. Wear a hat. Wear gloves. Do you wear these when you play in snow?

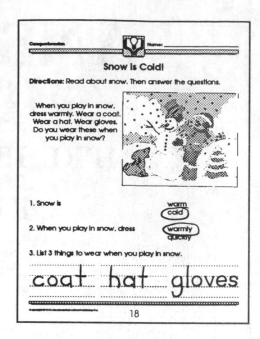

1. Snow is   warm / (cold)

2. When you play in snow, dress   (warmly) / quickly

3. List 3 things to wear when you play in snow.

coat   hat   gloves

18

Following Directions

Directions: Put a box around the circle ○.

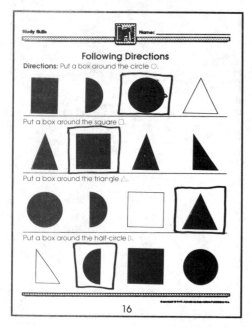

Put a box around the square □.

Put a box around the triangle △.

Put a box around the half-circle D.

16

Number Recognition 1, 2, 3, 4, 5

Directions: Use the color code to color the parrot.

Color:
1's red
2's blue
3's yellow
4's green
5's orange

19

Building A Snowman

Directions: Read the sentences. Do what they tell you to do.

Bob is making a snowman. He needs your help. Draw a black hat on the snowman. Draw red buttons. Now, draw a green scarf. Draw a happy face on the snowman.

CHILD ADDS ELEMENTS TO COMPLETE PICTURE

17

abc order

Directions: Draw a line to connect the dots. Follow the letters in abc order.

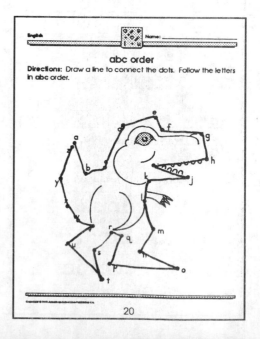

20

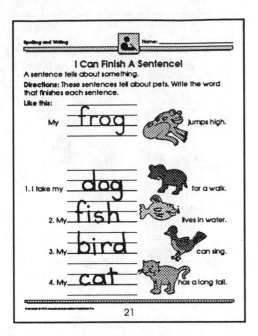

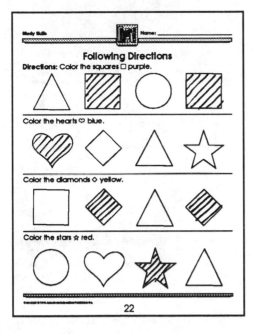

Citizenship

Children Are
Citizens Now Activity

Refer to page **522**
for Answer Key

Environmental Science

Your Environment

Refer to page **537**
for Answer Key

Citizenship

Children Are
Citizens Now

Refer to page **522**
for Answer Key

Environmental Science

Your Environment
Activity

Refer to page **537**
for Answer Key

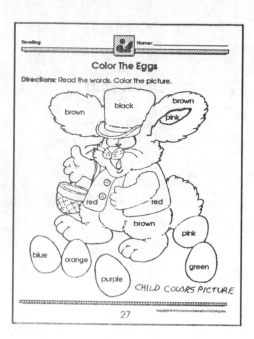

Color The Eggs

Directions: Read the words. Color the picture.

brown   black   brown
                  pink

red   red

brown

pink

blue   orange

purple   green

CHILD COLORS PICTURE

27

Look And See

Directions: 1. Look at both pictures. 2. Find five things in picture # 1 that are not in picture # 2. 3. Say your answers aloud. 4. Draw a circle around them.

#1

#2

28

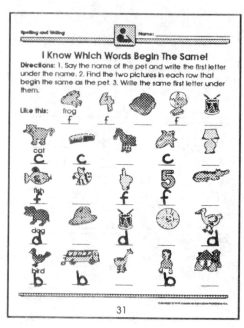

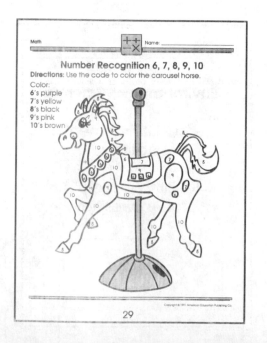

Number Recognition 6, 7, 8, 9, 10

Directions: Use the code to color the carousel horse.

Color:
6's purple
7's yellow
8's black
9's pink
10's brown

29

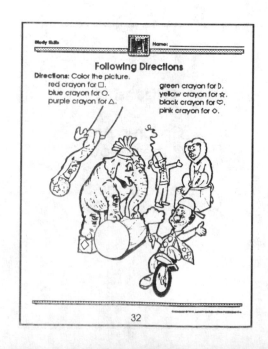

452

Color The Pictures

Directions: Color each picture the correct colors. Draw and color another picture like the first one.

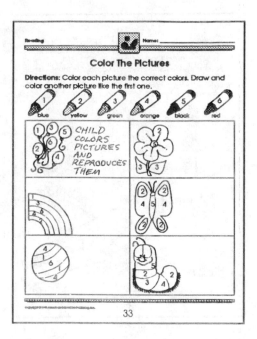

blue   yellow   green   orange   black   red

CHILD COLORS PICTURES AND REPRODUCES THEM

33

I Like Apples

Directions: Read about apples. Then answer the questions.

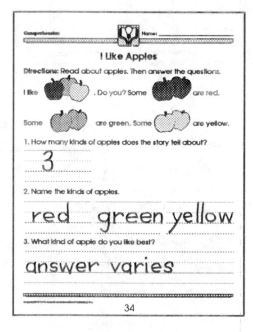

I like ___ . Do you? Some ___ are red.

Some ___ are green. Some ___ are yellow.

1. How many kinds of apples does the story tell about?

     3

2. Name the kinds of apples.

red   green   yellow

3. What kind of apple do you like best?

answer varies

34

Number Recognition

Directions: Count the number of objects in each group. Draw a line to the correct number.

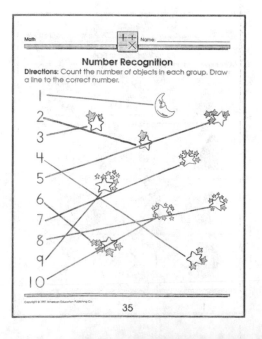

1
2
3
4
5
6
7
8
9
10

35

Beginning Consonants Gg, Hh, Jj, Kk

Directions: Say the name of each letter. Say the sound that each letter makes. Then, trace the letter that makes the beginning sound in the picture. After you finish, look around the room. Name the things that start with the letters Gg, Hh, Jj, and Kk.

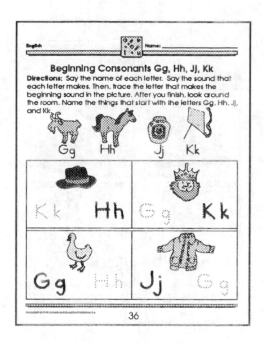

Gg   Hh   Jj   Kk

Kk   Hh   Gg   Kk

Gg   Hh   Jj   Gg

36

I Can Write A Whole Sentence!

A telling sentence ends with a period.

Directions: 1. Write the name of the pet on the line with the same number. 2. Find a picture that shows the pet doing something. 3. Write that word on the line to make a whole sentence. 4. Put a period at the end of each sentence.

Like this:

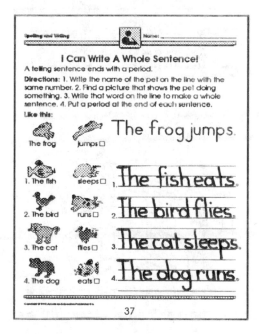

The frog   jumps ☐   The frog jumps.

1. The fish   sleeps ☐   1. The fish eats.

2. The bird   runs ☐   2. The bird flies.

3. The cat   flies ☐   3. The cat sleeps.

4. The dog   eats ☐   4. The dog runs.

37

Following Directions

Directions: Trace a circle ○, a square ☐, a triangle △, and a half-circle D. Color each one. Draw other shapes. Color them.

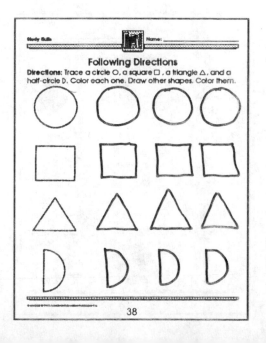

38

Following Directions

Directions: Look at the pictures. Follow the directions in each box.

Draw a circle around the caterpillar. Draw a line under the stick.

Put an X on the mother bird. Draw a triangle around the baby birds.

Put a box around the rabbit.

Color the flowers. Count the bees.

39

These Keep Me Warm

Directions: Look at the pictures. Color only the things that keep you warm.

40

Sequencing Numbers

Sequencing is putting numbers in the correct order.
Directions: Write the missing numbers.

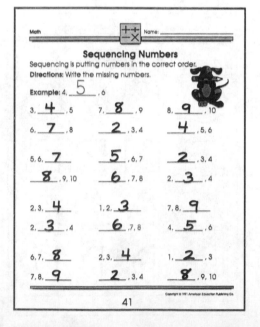

Example: 4, 5 , 6

3, 4 , 5   7, 8 , 9   8, 9 , 10

6, 7 , 8   2 , 3, 4   4 , 5, 6

5, 6, 7   5 , 6, 7   2 , 3, 4

8 , 9, 10   6 , 7, 8   2, 3 , 4

2, 3, 4   1, 2, 3   7, 8, 9

2, 3 , 4   6 , 7, 8   4, 5 , 6

6, 7, 8   2, 3, 4   1, 2 , 3

7, 8, 9   2 , 3, 4   8 , 9, 10

41

454

Beginning Consonants Ll, Mm, Nn, Pp

Directions: Say the name of each letter. Say the sound each letter makes. Then, trace the letters. Now, draw a line from each letter to the picture which begins with the letter. After you finish, say the letters Ll, Mm, Nn, Pp again.

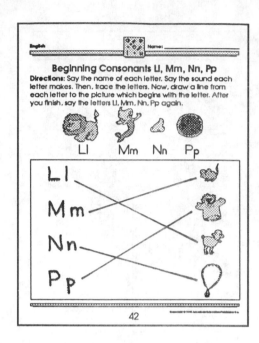

Ll   Mm   Nn   Pp

42

I Know Which Letters Are Missing!

Directions: Fill in the missing letters for each word. Then write the word by yourself.
Like this:

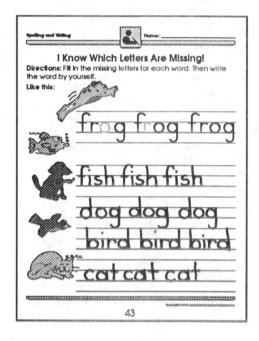

frog frog frog

fish fish fish

dog dog dog

bird bird bird

cat cat cat

43

Same/Different

Directions: Color the shape next to it that looks the same as the first shape in each row.

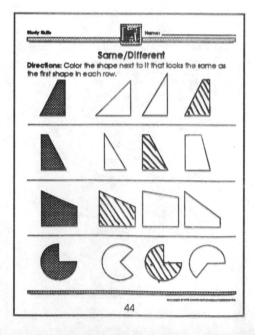

44

Finish The Pictures

Directions: Read the words. Finish the pictures.

RED — a red ball
BLACK — a black hat
YELLOW — a yellow sun
PINK — a pink kite
ORANGE — an orange balloon
BLUE — a blue umbrella

45

Beginning Consonants Qq, Rr, Ss, Tt

Directions: Say the name of each letter. Say the sound that each letter makes. Then, trace each letter in the boxes. Color the picture which begins with the sound of the letter.

Qq   Rr   Ss   Tt

T t   Q q
R r   S s

48

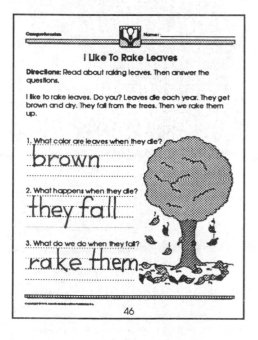

I Like To Rake Leaves

Directions: Read about raking leaves. Then answer the questions.

I like to rake leaves. Do you? Leaves die each year. They get brown and dry. They fall from the trees. Then we rake them up.

1. What color are leaves when they die?

brown

2. What happens when they die?

they fall

3. What do we do when they fall?

rake them

46

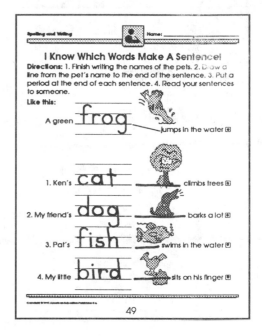

I Know Which Words Make A Sentence!

Directions: 1. Finish writing the names of the pets. 2. Draw a line from the pet's name to the end of the sentence. 3. Put a period at the end of each sentence. 4. Read your sentences to someone.

Like this:

A green **frog** → jumps in the water ⊡

1. Ken's **cat** → climbs trees ⊡
2. My friend's **dog** → barks a lot ⊡
3. Pat's **fish** → swims in the water ⊡
4. My little **bird** → sits on his finger ⊡

49

Counting

Directions: How many are there of each? Write the answers in the boxes. The first one is done for you.

| ☀ | 1 | ☁ | 7 | 🕊 | 6 |
| 🎈 | 10 | 🦁 | 3 | 🦒 | 2 |

47

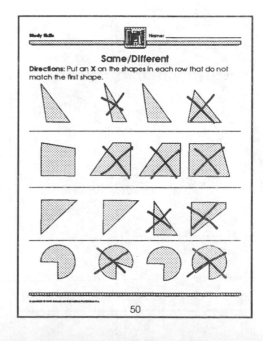

Same/Different

Directions: Put an X on the shapes in each row that do not match the first shape.

50

455

Citizenship

America 2000

Refer to page **523**
for Answer Key

51

Citizenship

America 2000
Activity

Refer to page **523**
for Answer Key

52

Environmental Science

Water

Refer to page **538**
for Answer Key

53

Environmental Science

Water
Activity

Refer to page **538**
for Answer Key

54

55

56

Counting

Directions: How many are there of each? Write the answers in the boxes. The first one is done for you.

7
4
10
5
3

57

Same/Different

Directions: Color the shape that does not belong in each group.

Example:

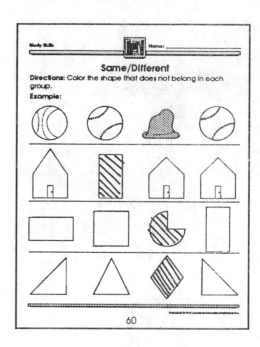

60

Beginning Consonants Vv, Ww, Xx, Yy, Zz

Directions: Say the name of each letter. Say the sound the letter makes. Then, trace the letters. Now, draw a line from the letters that match the beginning sound in each picture.

Vv   Ww   Xx   Yy   Zz

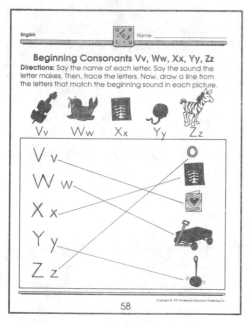

58

Skills Review: Following Directions, Color Word Vocabulary

Directions: Read the sentences. Follow the directions.

CHILD COLORS PICTURE

1. Color one house red.
2. Color two cars green.
3. Color two jets blue.
4. Color a big truck orange.
5. Color a bus yellow.

61

I Know How The Letters Go!

Directions: The letters in the name of each pet are mixed up. Write them the way they should be.

Like this:

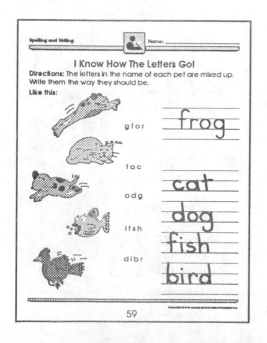

g f o r   frog

t a c   cat

o d g   dog

l f s h   fish

d l b r   bird

59

Do You Like To Bake?

Directions: Read the story. Then follow the instructions.

Some things used in baking are dry. Some things used in baking are wet. To bake a cake, first mix the salt, sugar and flour. Then add the egg. Now add the milk. Stir. Put the cake in the oven.

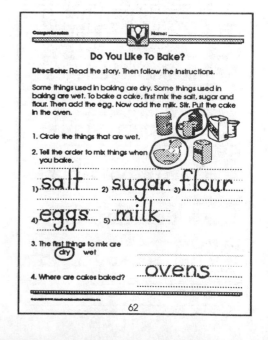

1. Circle the things that are wet.

2. Tell the order to mix things when you bake.

1) salt   2) sugar   3) flour

4) eggs   5) milk

3. The first things to mix are
(dry)   wet

4. Where are cakes baked?   ovens

62

457

Review

Directions: Count the shapes and write the answers.

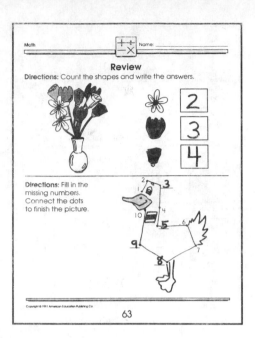

2
3
4

Directions: Fill in the missing numbers. Connect the dots to finish the picture.

63

Review

Directions: Color the circles O red.

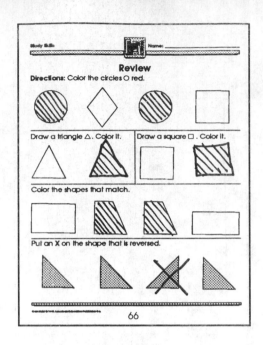

Draw a triangle △. Color it.   Draw a square □. Color it.

Color the shapes that match.

Put an X on the shape that is reversed.

66

Review

Directions: Help Meg and Kent and their dog, Sam, get to the magic castle. Trace all of the letters of the alphabet. Then, write the lower case consonant next to the matching upper case letter on the road to the magic castle. Make the sound for each consonant. After you finish, draw a picture on another paper of what you think Meg and Sam will find in the magic castle.

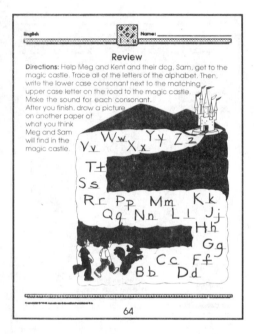

64

Which Are Opposites?

Directions: Draw a line between the opposites.

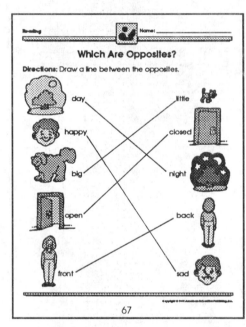

day — little
happy — closed
big — night
open — back
front — sad

67

Review

Directions: Use the words in the pictures to write a sentence about each pet. Can you spell the name of the pet by yourself? Put a period at the end of each sentence.

Like this:

The 🐸 eats bugs   The frog eats bugs.

The 🐱 drinks milk

The cat drinks milk.

The 🐦 eats an apple

The bird eats an apple.

The 🐶 jumps out

The dog jumps out.

The 🐟 sees a friend

The fish sees a friend.

65

I Like Cats

Directions: Read the story. Then answer the questions.

Do you like cats? I do. To pet a cat, move slowly. Hold out your hand. The cat will come to you. Then pet its head. Do not grab a cat. It will run away.

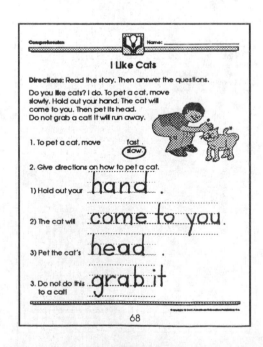

1. To pet a cat, move   fast / (slow)

2. Give directions on how to pet a cat.

1) Hold out your   hand .

2) The cat will   come to you .

3) Pet the cat's   head .

3. Do not do this to a cat   grab it

68

458

Number Words

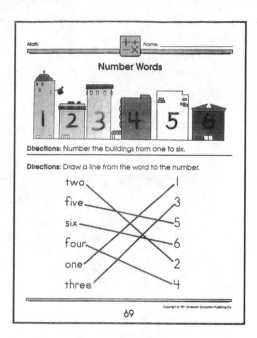

Directions: Number the buildings from one to six.

Directions: Draw a line from the word to the number.

two   1
five   3
six   5
four   6
one   2
three   4

69

Ending Consonants b, d, f

Ending consonants are the sounds that come at the end of the words that are not the vowel sounds.

Directions: Say the name of each picture. Then, write b, d, or f to name the ending sound for each picture.

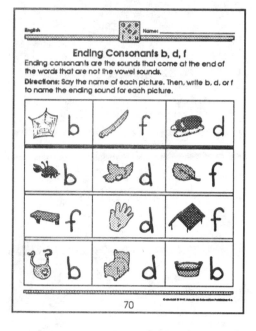

70

I Can Write The Names Of Colors!

Directions: Follow the lines to print the name of each color. Then print the name again by yourself.
Like this:

orange   orange
blue   blue
green   green
yellow   yellow
red   red
brown   brown

71

Classifying

Directions: Bob is looking for stars. Help him find them. Color all the stars blue.

How many stars did Bob find? __10__

72

Game Of Opposites

Directions: Write each word from the word box under its opposite.

| no | bad | hot | up | in | went | go | off |

good	came
bad	**went**

yes	stop
no	**go**

down	on
up	**off**

out	cold
in	**hot**

73

Where Flowers Grow

Directions: Read about flowers. Then answer the questions.

Some flowers grow in pots. Many flowers grow in flower beds. Others grow beside the road. Some flowers begin from seeds. They grow into small buds. Then they open wide and bloom. Flowers are pretty!

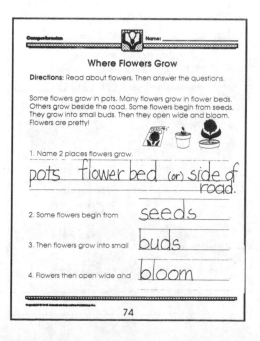

1. Name 2 places flowers grow.

pots   flower bed (or) side of road.

2. Some flowers begin from   seeds

3. Then flowers grow into small   buds

4. Flowers then open wide and   bloom

74

Number Words

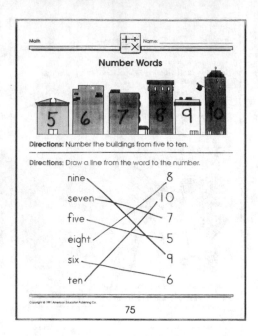

Directions: Number the buildings from five to ten.

Directions: Draw a line from the word to the number.

nine   8

seven   10

five   7

eight   5

six   9

ten   6

75

Ending Consonants g, m, n

Directions: Say the name of the picture. Draw a line from each letter to a picture which ends with the sound of that letter.

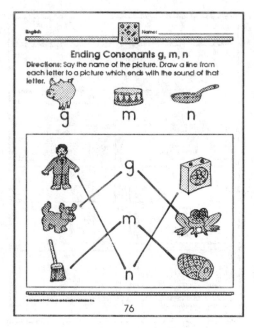

g   m   n

76

I Can Finish A Sentence!

Directions: Use the color words to finish these sentences. Then put a period at the end.

Like this: My new ___ are **orange** .

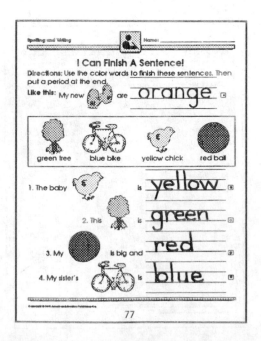

green tree   blue bike   yellow chick   red ball

1. The baby ___ is **yellow** .

2. This ___ is **green** .

3. My ___ is big and **red** .

4. My sister's ___ is **blue** .

77

Classifying

Directions: Color the stars ☆.   How many stars? **2**

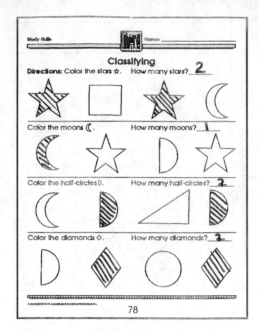

Color the moons ☾.   How many moons? **1**

Color the half-circles ◖.   How many half-circles? **2**

Color the diamonds ◇.   How many diamonds? **2**

78

Citizenship

The United States Flag

Refer to page **524**
for Answer Key

79

Citizenship

The United States Flag
Activity

Refer to page **524**
for Answer Key

80

460

Environmental Science

Air

Refer to page **538**
for Answer Key

Environmental Science

Air
Activity

Refer to page **538**
for Answer Key

Classifying

Directions: Draw a circle around the correct pictures.

What Can Swim?

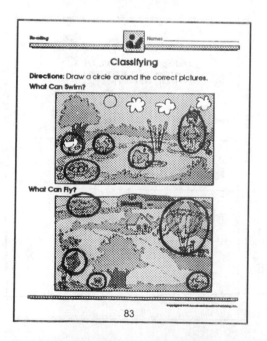

What Can Fly?

Flower Puzzle

Directions: Re-read the story about flowers on page 10. Then fill in the puzzle with the right answers about flowers.

Across
1. Flowers do this when they open wide.
2. Some flowers grow from these.

Down
1. Before it blooms, a flower grows a ___.
3. A flower can grow in a flower bed or a ___.

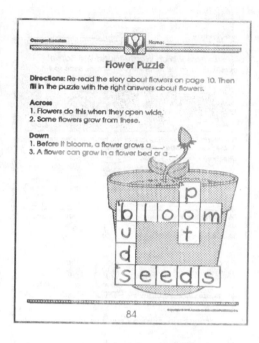

Shapes: Square

A square is a figure with four corners and four sides of the same length. This is a square □.

Directions: Find the squares and circle them.

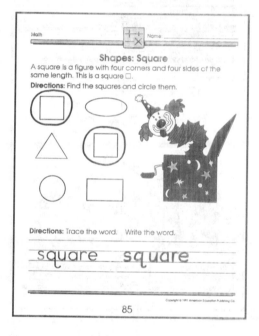

Directions: Trace the word.   Write the word.

square   square

Ending Consonants k, l, p

Directions: Say the name of the pictures. Color the pictures in each row that end with the sound of the letter at the beginning of the row. Trace the letters.

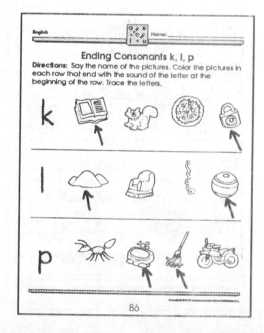

k

l

p

I Know Which Words Sound The Same!

Directions: Circle the words that start with the same sound.
Like this:

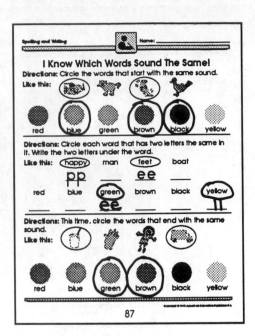

red　blue　green　brown　black　yellow

Directions: Circle each word that has two letters the same in it. Write the two letters under the word.
Like this: (happy)　man　(feet)　boat
pp　＿　ee　＿

red　blue　(green)　brown　black　(yellow)
ee　　　　　　　　　　　　　ll

Directions: This time, circle the words that end with the same sound.
Like this:

red　blue　green　brown　black　yellow

87

Balloons

Directions: Read about balloons. Then answer the questions.

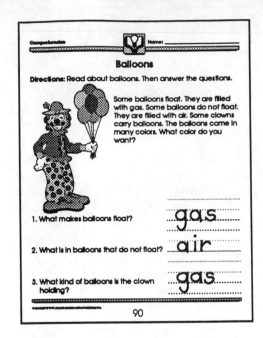

Some balloons float. They are filled with gas. Some balloons do not float. They are filled with air. Some clowns carry balloons. The balloons come in many colors. What color do you want?

1. What makes balloons float?　_gas_

2. What is in balloons that do not float?　_air_

3. What kind of balloons is the clown holding?　_gas_

90

Classifying

Directions: Mary and Bob are taking a trip into space. Help them find the stars ☆, moons ☾, circles ○, and diamonds ◇.

Color them:
Use yellow for ☆.　Use blue for ☾.
Use red for ○.　Use purple for ◇.

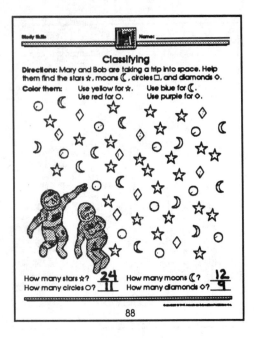

How many stars ☆?　24
How many circles ○?　11
How many moons ☾?　12
How many diamonds ◇?　9

88

Shapes: Circle

A circle is a figure that is round. This is a circle ○.
Directions: Find the circles and put a square around them.

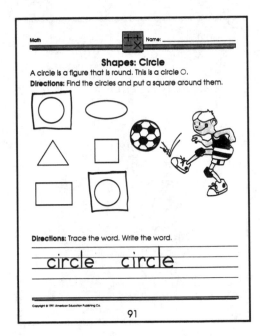

Directions: Trace the word. Write the word.

circle　circle

Copyright © 1991 American Education Publishing Co.

91

What Are They?

Directions: Read the words in the boxes. Put each word in its correct place.

Joe	cat	blue	Tim
two	dog	red	ten
Sue	green	pig	six

Name Words　Joe Sue Tim

Number Words　Two Ten Six

Animal Words　Cat Dog Pig

Color Words　Blue Red Green

89

Ending Consonants r, s, t, x

Directions: Say the name of the picture. Then circle the ending sound for each picture.

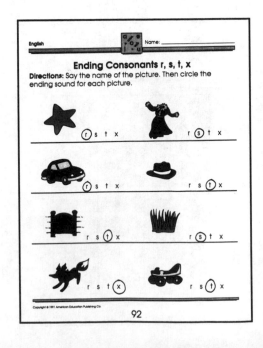

r (s) t x　　r (s) t x

r (s) t x　　r s (t) x

r s (t) x　　r (s) t x

r s t (x)　　r s (t) x

Copyright © 1991 American Education Publishing Co.

92

462

Name: _____

I Know Which Ones Are Sentences!

Directions: Some of these sentences tell the whole idea. Others have something missing. If you think something is missing, draw a line to a word that would finish that sentence. Remember to put a period after the last word in the sentence.

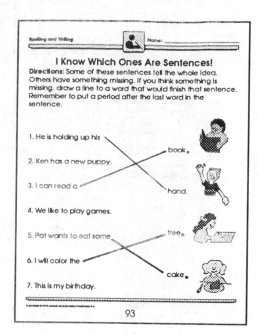

1. He is holding up his
2. Ken has a new puppy.
3. I can read a
4. We like to play games.
5. Pat wants to eat some
6. I will color the
7. This is my birthday.

book.
hand.
tree.
cake.

93

Name: _____

Clowning Around

Directions: Look at the pictures of the clowns. Find 4 things that are different in picture 2. Color the things that are different.

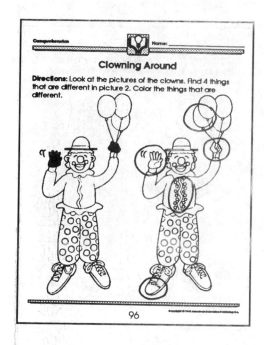

96

Name: _____

Classifying

Directions: Help Mary and Bob sort their shapes. Draw a line from each shape to the basket it should go in.

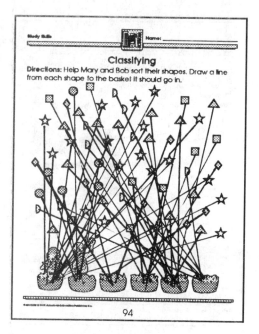

94

Name: _____

Shapes: Triangle

A triangle is a figure with three corners and three sides. This is a triangle △.

Directions: Find the triangles and put a circle around them.

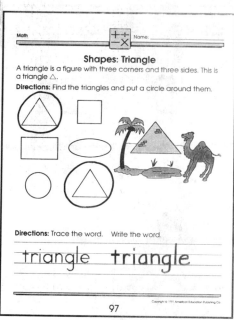

Directions: Trace the word. Write the word.

triangle   triangle

97

Name: _____

Alphabetical Order

Directions: Look at the words in each box. Circle the word that comes first in a-b-c order.

A-B-C Order

duck	chair	peach
four	apple	this
rock	yellow	walk
game	light	mouse
boy	come	ten
pink	one	orange
angel	zebra	foot
table	watch	boat
hair	five	mine
look	who	book
blue	dog	tan
rope	black	six

95

Name: _____

Beginning and Ending Sounds Discrimination

Directions: Say the name of the picture. Draw a blue circle around the picture if it begins with the sound of the letter. Draw a green triangle around the picture if it ends with the sound of the letter.

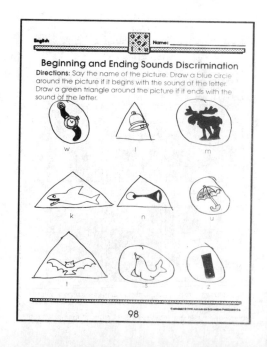

w   l   m

k   n   u

t   s   z

98

463

I Know Which Words Begin The Same!

Directions: Say the name of the color and the picture beside it. If they begin with the same sound, write an X in the box.

Like this:

red ☒

blue ☒

yellow ☐

black ☒

green ☒

brown ☐

99

Classifying

Directions: Look at the shapes. Answer the questions.

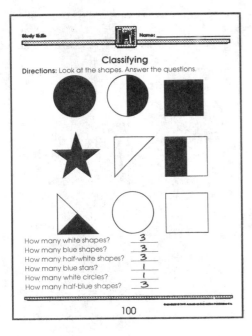

How many white shapes? **3**
How many blue shapes? **3**
How many half-white shapes? **3**
How many blue stars? **1**
How many white circles? **1**
How many half-blue shapes? **3**

100

Story Order

Directions: The pictures tell a story, but they are in the wrong order. Write a number under each box to show the order they belong in.

1   3   2

3   1   2

101

Tigers

Directions: Read about tigers. Then answer the questions.

Tigers sleep during the day. They hunt at night. Tigers eat meat. They hunt deer. They like to eat wild pigs. If they cannot find meat, tigers will eat fish.

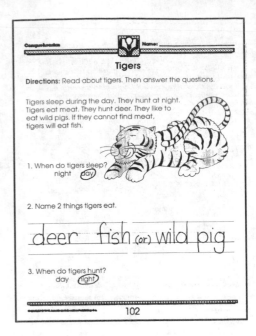

1. When do tigers sleep?
   night (day)

2. Name 2 things tigers eat.

   deer fish (or) wild pig

3. When do tigers hunt?
   day (night)

102

Shapes: Rectangle

A rectangle is a figure with four corners and four sides. Sides opposite each other are the same length. This is a rectangle ☐ .

Directions: Find the rectangles and put a circle around them.

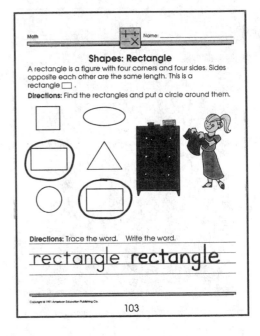

Directions: Trace the word.   Write the word.

rectangle rectangle

103

Beginning and Ending Sounds Discrimination

Directions: Say the name of each picture. Draw a triangle around the letter that makes the beginning sound. Draw a square around the letter that makes the ending sound. Color the pictures.

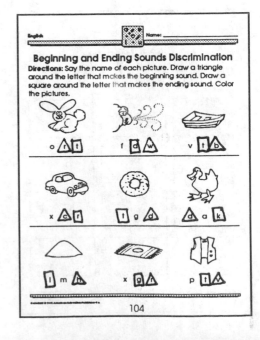

o △r▢ t   f □c △v   v △t □b

x △c r   □g g △d   △d a k

□l m △t   x □g □t   p □t △t

104

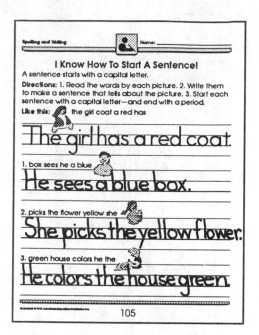

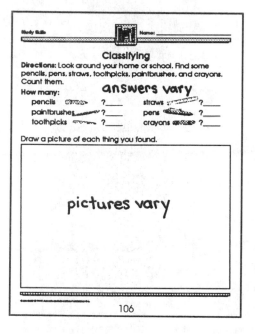

Citizenship

The Declaration of
Independence

Refer to page **525**
for Answer Key

Citizenship

The Declaration of
Independence Activity

Refer to page **525**
for Answer Key

Environmental Science

Keep Our Land Clean

Refer to page **539**
for Answer Key

Environmental Science

Keep Our Land Clean
Activity

Refer to page **539**
for Answer Key

Story Order

Directions: 1) Look at the picture story. 2) Read the sentences. 3) Write 1, 2, 3 or 4 by each sentence to show the order of the story.

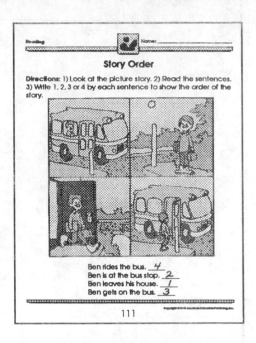

Ben rides the bus. _4_
Ben is at the bus stop. _2_
Ben leaves his house. _1_
Ben gets on the bus. _3_

111

Beginning and Ending Sounds Discrimination

Directions: Look at the example. Say the beginning and ending sounds for the word **pipe**. Write the letter that makes the beginning and ending sound for each picture.

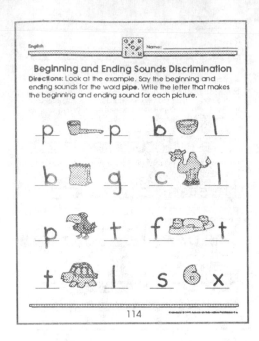

114

Tiger Puzzle

Directions: Re-read the story about tigers on page 14. Then fill in the puzzle with the right answers about tigers.

Across
3. The food tigers like best.
4. Tigers like to eat this meat: wild ___.

Down
1. Tigers do this during the day.
2. When tigers cannot get meat, they eat this.

112

I Can Play A Word Game!

Directions: Finish the name of each color. Some words go down and some go across. Can you spell them by yourself?

115

Shapes: Oval And Diamond

An oval is an egg-shaped figure. A diamond is a figure with four sides of the same length. Its corners form points at the top, sides, and bottom. This is an oval ⬭. This is a diamond ◇.

Directions: Color the ovals red. Color the diamonds blue.

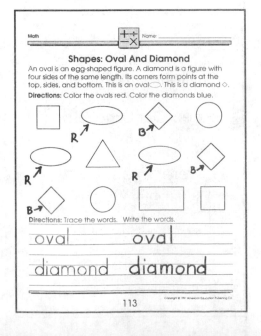

Directions: Trace the words. Write the words.

oval   oval

diamond   diamond

113

Classifying

Directions: Look at the shapes with Mary. Then answer the questions.

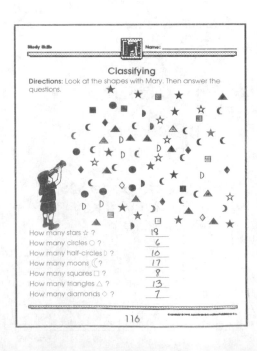

How many stars ☆ ?   18
How many circles ○ ?   6
How many half-circles ◗ ?   10
How many moons ☽ ?   17
How many squares □ ?   8
How many triangles △ ?   13
How many diamonds ◇ ?   7

116

466

Skills Review: Sequencing, Classifying

Directions: 1) Write numbers by the sentences to show the order they belong in. 2) Write each word from the word box in its correct place.

Kim picks out food. __2__

Kim pays the man. __3__

Kim goes to the store. __1__

apple	ice cream	cookie	banana	orange	cake

Fruits	Sweets
apple	ice cream
banana	cookie
orange	cake

117

Cookies

Directions: Read about cookies. Then answer the questions.

Cookies are made with many things. All cookies are made with flour. Some cookies have nuts in them. Some cookies do not. Some cookies have chips. Some cookies do not. Cookbooks give directions on how to make cookies. First turn on the oven. Then get all the things out that go in the cookies. Mix them together. Cut out or roll out the cookies. Bake the cookies. Now eat them!

1. Tell 1 way all cookies are the same.

made with flour

2. Name 2 different things in cookies.

chips   nuts

3. Where do you find directions for making cookies?

cookbooks

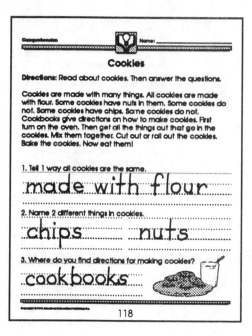

118

Review

Directions: Color the shapes in the picture as shown.

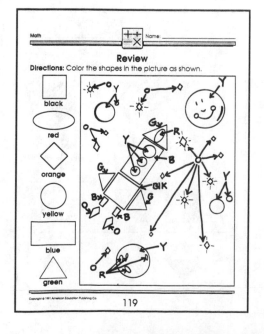

black

red

orange

yellow

blue

green

119

Review

Directions: Say the name of each object which has a consonant near it. Color the object orange if it begins with the sound of the letter. Color the object purple if it ends with the sound of the letter.

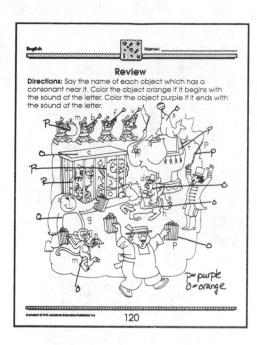

P=purple
O=orange

120

Review

Directions: 1. Write three sentences that tell about this picture. Use a color word in each one. Can you write the names of the colors and the pets by yourself now? 2. Remember to begin each sentence with a capital letter and end with a period.

Here are some more words you could use: walks, sees, runs, flies, grows, eats, looks, jumps, sits.

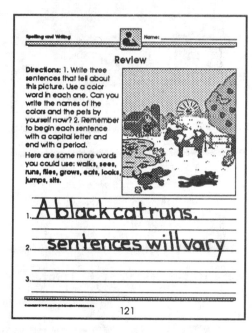

1. A black cat runs.

2. sentences will vary

3. _____

121

Review

Directions: Color the stars ☆ blue.

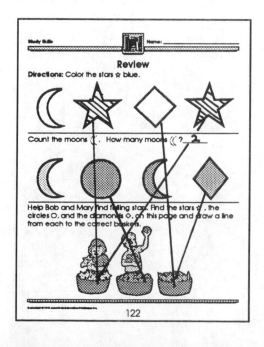

Count the moons ☾. How many moons ☾? __2__

Help Bob and Mary find falling stars. Find the stars ☆, the circles ○, and the diamonds ◇, on this page and draw a line from each to the correct baskets.

122

467

Rhyming Trains: Words with a

Directions: Each train has a group of pictures. Write the word that names the pictures. Read your rhyming words.

The short a sounds like the a in cat.

pan   can   fan   man

rat   cat   bat   hat

The long a sounds like the a in lake.

skate   gate   plate

rake   cake   snake

123

Short Vowel Sounds

The short vowel sounds used in this book are found in the following words: ant, egg, igloo, on, up.

Directions: Say the name of each picture. The short vowel sound may be in the front of the word or in the middle of the word. Color the pictures in each row that have the correct short vowel sound.

a

e

i

o

u

126

Find The Fruit

Directions: Fruit tastes good. It is sweet! Look at the pictures. Find the fruit. Then copy the name of each fruit in the blanks below.

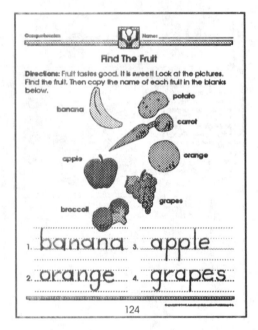

banana   potato
    carrot
apple   orange
broccoli   grapes

1. banana   3. apple

2. orange   4. grapes

124

I Can Write The Names Of Food!

Directions: 1. Follow the lines to write the names of food.
2. Write the names by yourself. 3. Color the pictures. 4. Read the words to someone.

Like this:

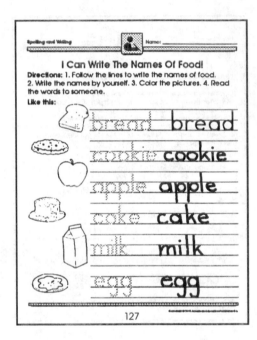

bread   bread
cookie   cookie
apple   apple
cake   cake
milk   milk
egg   egg

127

Addition 1, 2

Addition means "putting together" or adding two or more numbers to find the sum.

Directions: Count the cats and tell how many.

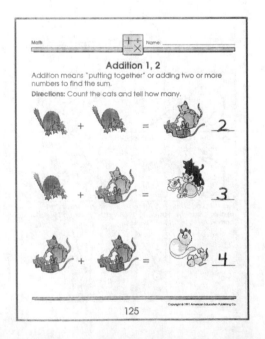

+   =   2

+   =   3

+   =   4

125

Duplicating

Directions: Look at the colored shape. Color the one beside it the same. Then draw the shape.

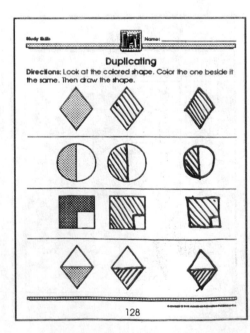

128

468

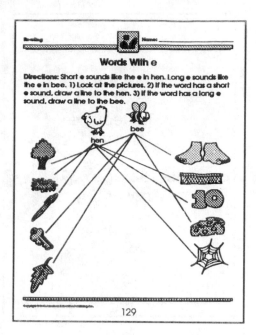

Words With e

Directions: Short e sounds like the e in hen. Long e sounds like the e in bee. 1) Look at the pictures. 2) If the word has a short e sound, draw a line to the hen. 3) If the word has a long e sound, draw a line to the bee.

hen   bee

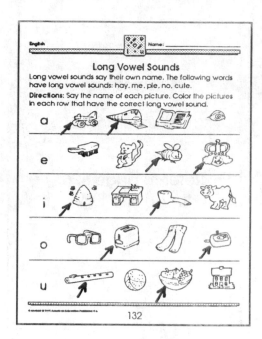

Long Vowel Sounds

Long vowel sounds say their own name. The following words have long vowel sounds: hay, me, pie, no, cute.

Directions: Say the name of each picture. Color the pictures in each row that have the correct long vowel sound.

a

e

i

o

u

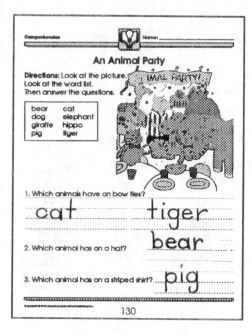

An Animal Party

Directions: Look at the picture. Look at the word list. Then answer the questions.

bear	cat
dog	elephant
giraffe	hippo
pig	tiger

1. Which animals have on bow ties?

cat   tiger

bear

2. Which animal has on a hat?

3. Which animal has on a striped shirt?   pig

I Know Which Ones Are Questions!

A question is a sentence that asks something.

Directions: 1. Write each sentence on the line. 2. Start all the sentences with capital letters. 3. Put a period at the end of the telling sentences. 4. Put a question mark at the end of the asking sentences.

Like this: do you like ice cream

Do you like ice cream?

1. milk comes from cows

Milk comes from cows.

2. is that cookie good

Is that cookie good?

3. did you eat your apple

Did you eat your apple?

Addition 3, 4, 5, 6

Directions: Practice writing the numbers and then add.

3 3
4 4
5 5
6 6

$$\begin{array}{r} 2 \\ +4 \\ \hline 6 \end{array} \qquad \begin{array}{r} 1 \\ +4 \\ \hline 5 \end{array}$$

$$\begin{array}{r} 3 \\ +2 \\ \hline 5 \end{array} \qquad \begin{array}{r} 1 \\ +2 \\ \hline 3 \end{array}$$

Duplicating

Directions: Color your circle O to look the same.

Color your square □ to look the same.

Trace the triangle △. Color it to look the same.

Trace the star ☆. Color it to look the same.

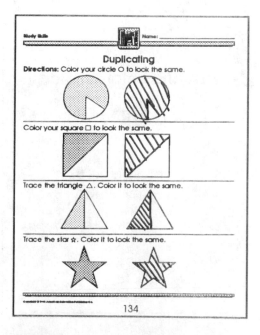

Citizenship

The White House

Refer to page **526**
for Answer Key

Citizenship

The White House
Activity

Refer to page **526**
for Answer Key

Environmental Science

Start To Recycle

Refer to page **539**
for Answer Key

Environmental Science

Start To Recycle
Activity

Refer to page **539**
for Answer Key

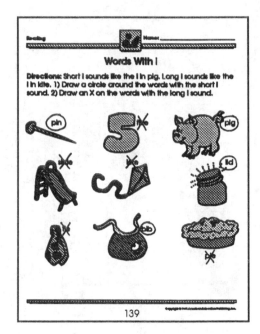

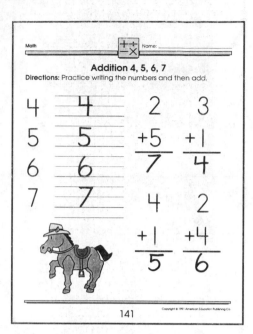

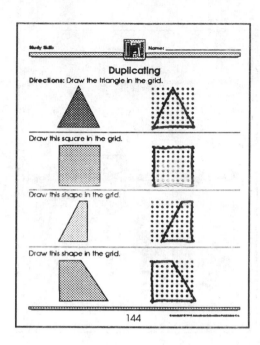

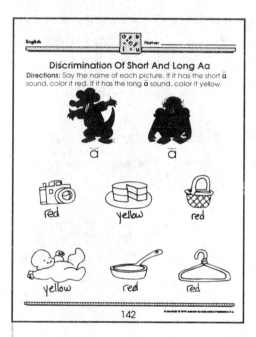

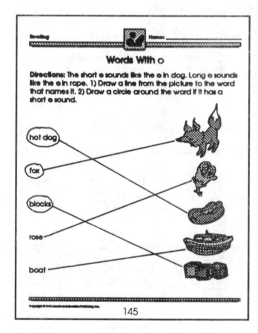

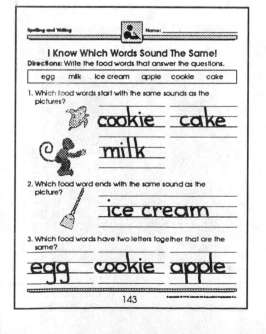

471

Addition 6, 7, 8
Directions: Practice writing the numbers and then add.

6 __6__
7 __7__
8 __8__

$$3 \atop {+4} \over 7$$ $$5 \atop {+1} \over 6$$

$$2 \atop {+6} \over 8$$ $$4 \atop {+4} \over 8$$

147

Duplicating
Directions: Draw this shape in the grid.

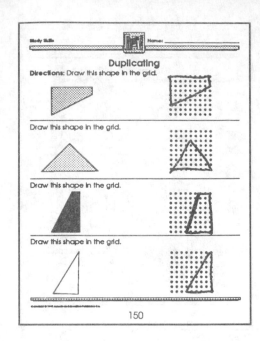

Draw this shape in the grid.

Draw this shape in the grid.

Draw this shape in the grid.

150

Discrimination Of Short And Long Ee
Directions: Say the name of each picture. Draw a circle around the pictures which have the short ĕ sound. Draw a triangle around the pictures which have the long ē sound.

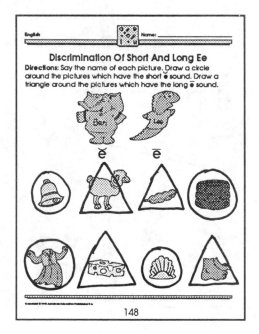

Ben   Lee

ĕ   ē

148

Words With u
Directions: The short u sounds like the u in bug. The long u sounds like the u in blue. 1) Draw a circle around the words with short u. 2) Draw an X on the words with long u.

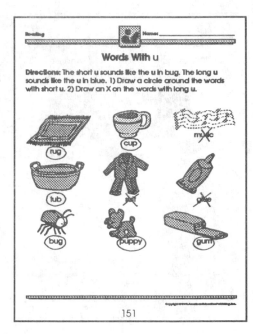

rug   cup   mule

tub   glue

bug   puppy   gum

151

I Can Ask Question!
Directions: Change each telling sentence into a question by moving the words around. Remember to put a question mark at the end of your question.

Like this: The girl is eating ice cream.

Is the girl eating ice cream?

1. The boy is giving a cookie.

Is the boy giving a cookie?

2. He is drinking milk.

Is he drinking milk?

3. She is making a cake.

Is she making a cake?

149

Put Teddy Bear to Bed
Directions: Re-read the story about the teddy bear. Look at the pictures. Number them in 1-2-3-4 order.

152

472

Addition 7, 8, 9

Directions: Practice writing the numbers and then add.

7   7   8   3

8   8   +1   +5

9   9   —   —
          9   8

            2   6

         +7   +1

         —   —
          9   7

153

Discrimination Of Short And Long Ii.

Directions: Say the name of each picture. Color it yellow if it has the short **i** sound. Color it red if it has the long **ī** sound.

RED   YELLOW   YELLOW   YELLOW

YELLOW   RED   RED   RED

154

I Know The Answers!

Directions: Use the food words to answer each question. The first letter is done for you. Can you write the other letters by yourself?

1. Which one can you drink?   milk

2. Which one do you have to keep very cold?   ice cream

3. Which one grows on trees?   apple

4. Which one do you put birthday candles on?   cake

5. Which one do people sometimes eat in the mornings?   egg

6. Which one do you like best?   ans. vary

155

Duplicating

Directions: Go outside. Look at your house. Now draw a picture of the shapes that make up your house. Name the shapes you see.

pictures vary

156

Short Vowel Sounds

Directions: In each box are three pictures. The words that name the pictures have missing letters. Write a, e, i, o, or u to finish the words.

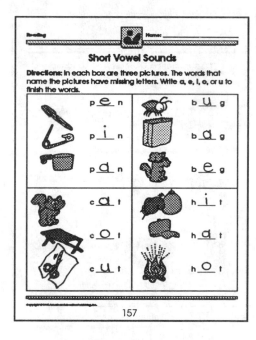

p_e_n   b_u_g

p_i_n   b_a_g

p_a_n   b_e_g

c_a_t   h_i_t

c_o_t   h_a_t

c_u_t   h_o_t

157

How We Eat

Directions: Read about meals. Look at the word list. Then answer the questions.

Big kids eat with spoons and forks. They use a knife to cut their food. They use a spoon to eat soup and ice cream. They use a fork to eat peas and corn. They say "Thank you. It was good!" when they are done.

| fork | ice cream | knife | soup |

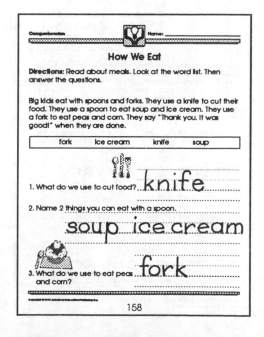

1. What do we use to cut food?   knife

2. Name 2 things you can eat with a spoon.

soup   ice cream

3. What do we use to eat peas and corn?   fork

158

473

Subtraction

Subtraction means "taking away" or subtracting one number from another.

Directions: Practice writing the numbers and then subtract.

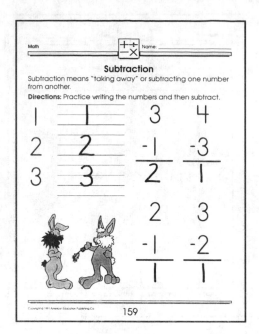

159

Finding Patterns

Directions: Find the hidden shape. Then color it.

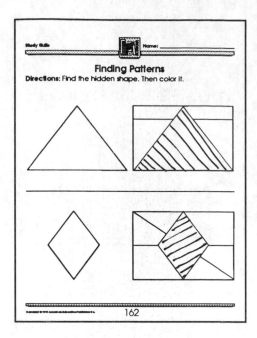

162

Discrimination Of Short And Long Oo

Directions: Say the name of each picture. If the picture has a long **o** sound, write a green **L** in the space. If the picture has a short **o** sound, write a red **S** in the space.

160

Citizenship

Christopher Columbus

Refer to page **527**
for Answer Key

163

I Can Write My Own Sentences!

Directions: 1. For each sentence, write a word in the first space to tell who is doing something. Here are some words you could use: boy, girl, mother, father, baby. 2. Write one of the food words in the second space. 3. Draw a picture to show what is happening in your sentence.

Like this:

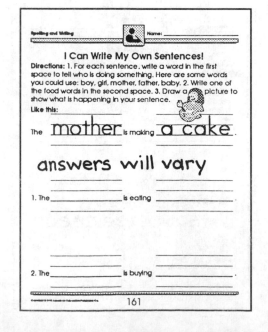

The _mother_ is making _a cake_

answers will vary

1. The _____ is eating _____.

2. The _____ is buying _____.

161

Citizenship

Christopher Columbus Activity

Refer to page **527**
for Answer Key

164

Environmental Science

Summary

Refer to page **540**
for Answer Key

165

Environmental Science
Review

Refer to page **540**
for Answer Key

166

Long Vowel Sounds

Directions: Write a, e, i, o, or u in each blank to finish the word. Draw a line from the word to its picture.

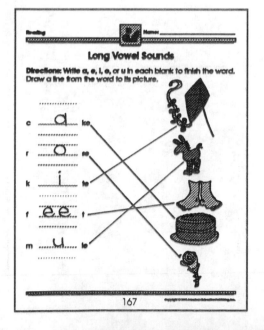

c _a_ te
r _o_ se
k _i_ te
f _ee_ t
m _u_ le

167

Things That Belong

Directions: Look at the pictures in each row across. Circle the ones in each row that belong. Write the names of the pictures that do not belong.

Row 1 — knife, key, fork, spoon
Row 2 — orange, apple, sucker, banana
Row 3 — beach ball, soccer ball, baseball, apple

These do not belong:

Row 1	Row 2	Row 3
key	sucker	apple

168

Subtraction 3, 4, 5, 6
Directions: Practice writing the numbers and then subtract.

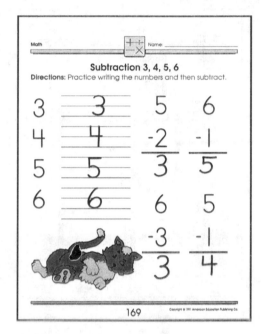

3 3
4 4
5 5
6 6

$$5 - 2 = 3$$
$$6 - 1 = 5$$
$$6 - 3 = 3$$
$$5 - 1 = 4$$

169

Discrimination Of Short And Long Uu
Directions: Say the name of the picture. If it has the long u sound, write a u in the unicorn column. If it has a short u sound, write a u in the umbrella column.

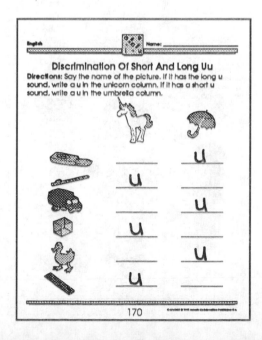

170

475

I Can Finish A Story!

Directions: Write the words in the story. Then read your story to someone.

Kim got up in the morning.

"Do you want an __egg__ 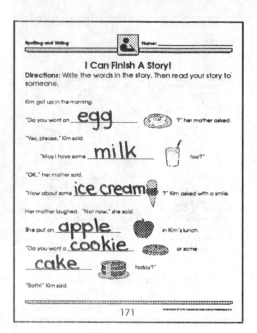 ?" her mother asked.

"Yes, please," Kim said.

"May I have some __milk__ too?"

"OK," her mother said.

"How about some __ice cream__ ?" Kim asked with a smile.

Her mother laughed. "Not now," she said.

She put an __apple__ in Kim's lunch.

"Do you want a __cookie__ or some

__cake__ today?"

"Both!" Kim said.

171

Finding Patterns

Directions: Find the hidden letter in each box. Trace it with a crayon.

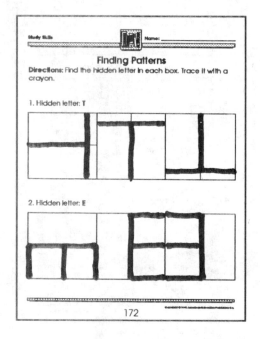

1. Hidden letter: T

2. Hidden letter: E

172

Skills Review: Vowel Sounds

Directions: Draw a circle around the word if it has a long vowel sound. Remember: a long vowel says its name.

feet · snake · cup

hose · tie · hat

dog · rake · bug

bone · bib · net

173

Skiing Is Fun

Directions: Read about how to ski. Answer the questions. Then put the skiing pictures in 1-2-3-4 order.

Skiing Is Fun
You need to dress warmly to ski. Two skis will fit on your boots. You wear the skis to a chair. The chair is called a ski lift. It takes you up in the air to a hill. When you get off, ski down the hill. Be careful! Sometimes you will fall.

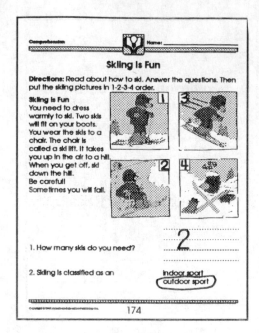

1. How many skis do you need? __2__

2. Skiing is classified as an — indoor sport / (outdoor sport)

174

Review

Directions: Trace the numbers. Work the problems.

1 2 3 4 5 6 7 8 9 10

9	6	3	2
−3	+2	+4	−1
6	8	7	1
5	9	7	8
+4	−5	+2	−6
9	4	9	2
4	6	9	1
−2	+3	−7	+7
2	9	2	8

175

Short And Long Vowel Sounds

Directions: Say the name of the picture. Write the correct vowel on each line to finish the word. Color the short vowel pictures yellow. Circle the long vowel pictures.

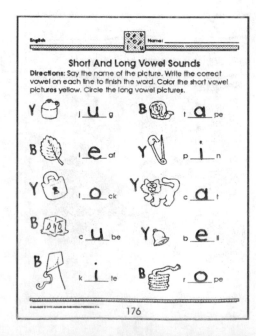

Y j__u__g   B t__a__pe

B l__e__af   Y p__i__n

Y l__o__ck   Y c__a__t

B c__u__be   Y b__e__ll

B k__i__te   B r__o__pe

176

476

Review

Directions: Write two telling sentences and one question about this picture. Be sure to use the food words you know — and the color and pet words.

Here are some more words you could use: boy, girl, water, table, candles, finds, birthday, out, eats, jumps, helps, sees, looks, stops, falls.

Two telling sentences:

1. The bird eats the apple.

2. answers vary

One question:
_____
_____
_____

Review

Directions: Color your shape to look the same.

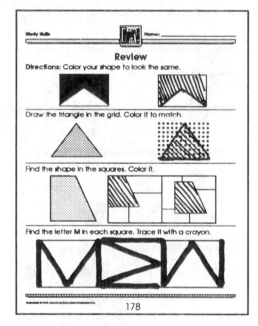

Draw the triangle in the grid. Color it to match.

Find the shape in the squares. Color it.

Find the letter M in each square. Trace it with a crayon.

Consonant Blends: bl, cl, fl, gl, pl, sl

Directions: The name of each picture begins with a blend. Draw a circle around the beginning blend for each picture.

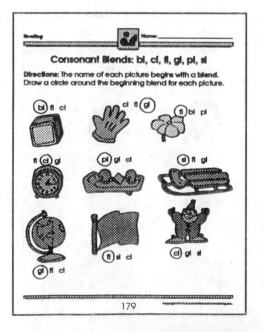

Clowns

Directions: Color the clowns. Then answer the questions. Use your crayons this way: 1 = red, 2 = blue, 3 = orange, 4 = pink.

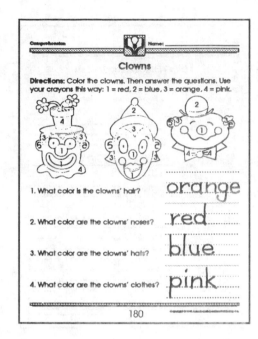

1. What color is the clowns' hair?   orange

2. What color are the clowns' noses?   red

3. What color are the clowns' hats?   blue

4. What color are the clowns' clothes?   pink

Zero

Directions: Write the number.

Example:

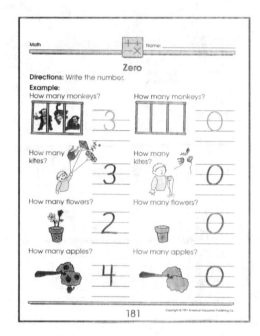

How many monkeys?   3   How many monkeys?   0

How many kites?   3   How many kites?   0

How many flowers?   2   How many flowers?   0

How many apples?   4   How many apples?   0

ABC Order

Use the first letter of each word to put the words in alphabetical order.

Directions: Draw a circle around the first letter of each word. Then, put the words in ABC order.

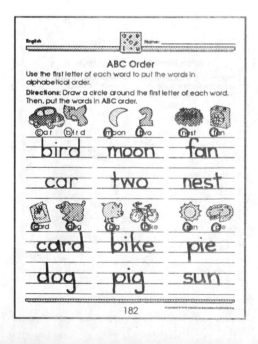

| car | moon | nest |
| bird | two | fan |

bird   moon   fan

car   two   nest

card   bike   pie

dog   pig   sun

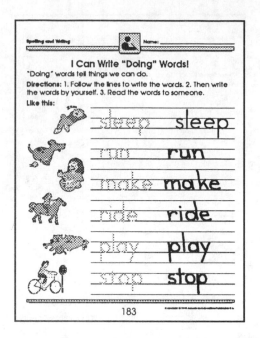

I Can Write "Doing" Words!

"Doing" words tell things we can do.

Directions: 1. Follow the lines to write the words. 2. Then write the words by yourself. 3. Read the words to someone.

Like this:

sleep — sleep

run — run

make — make

ride — ride

play — play

stop — stop

183

Simon Says

Directions: Read about how to play Simon Says. Then answer the questions.

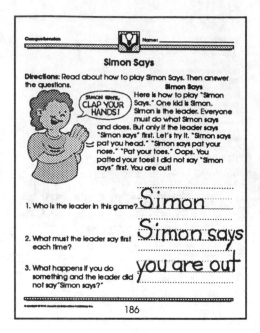

Simon Says

Here is how to play "Simon Says." One kid is Simon. Simon is the leader. Everyone must do what Simon says and does. But only if the leader says "Simon says" first. Let's try it. "Simon says pat you head." "Simon says pat your nose." "Pat your toes." Oops. You patted your toes! I did not say "Simon says" first. You are out!

1. Who is the leader in this game? **Simon**

2. What must the leader say first each time? **Simon says**

3. What happens if you do something and the leader did not say "Simon says?" **you are out**

186

Finding Patterns

Directions: Draw a line from the shape on the left to the box of shapes on the right that has the same pattern.

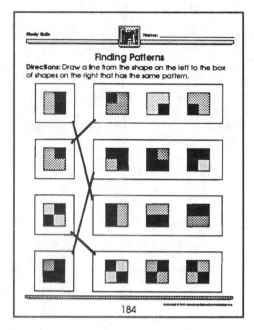

184

Zero

Directions: Write the number that tells how many.

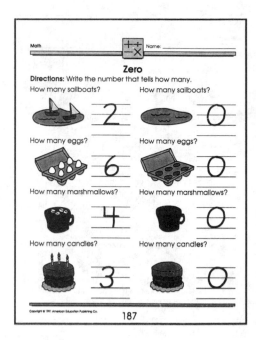

How many sailboats? **2**   How many sailboats? **0**

How many eggs? **6**   How many eggs? **0**

How many marshmallows? **4**   How many marshmallows? **0**

How many candles? **3**   How many candles? **0**

187

Consonant Blends: br, cr, dr, fr, pr, tr

Directions: The beginning blend for each word is missing. Using the list, fill in the correct blend to finish the word. Draw a line from the word to its picture.

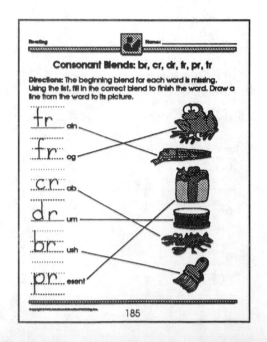

tr___ain

fr___og

cr___ab

dr___um

br___ush

pr___esent

185

ABC Order

Directions: Circle the first letter of each animal's name. Write a 1, 2, 3, 4, 5, or 6 on the line next to the animals' names to put the words in **ABC** order.

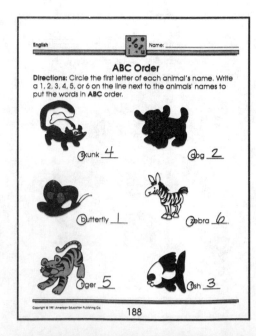

Skunk **4**   dog **2**

butterfly **1**   zebra **6**

tiger **5**   fish **3**

188

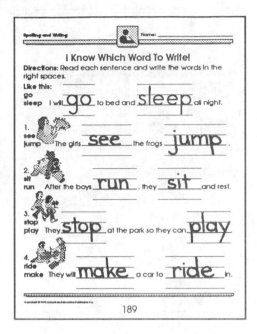

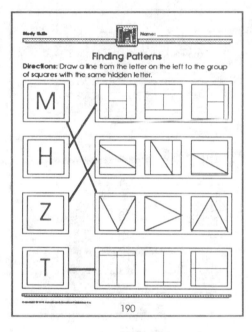

190

Citizenship

The Statue of Liberty
Activity

Refer to page **528**
for Answer Key

192

Citizenship

The Statue of Liberty

Refer to page **528**
for Answer Key

191

Environmental Science

Energy To Heat Our Homes

Refer to page **540**
for Answer Key

193

Environmental Science

Energy To Heat Our Homes
Activity

Refer to page **540**
for Answer Key

194

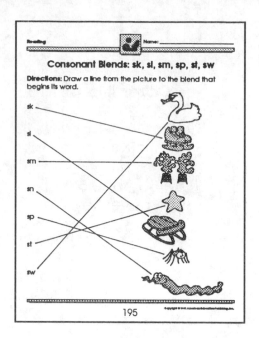

Consonant Blends: sk, sl, sm, sp, st, sw

Directions: Draw a line from the picture to the blend that begins its word.

sk
sl
sm
sn
sp
st
sw

195

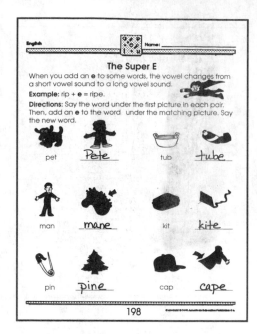

The Super E

When you add an **e** to some words, the vowel changes from a short vowel sound to a long vowel sound.

Example: rip + **e** = ripe.

Directions: Say the word under the first picture in each pair. Then, add an **e** to the word under the matching picture. Say the new word.

pet   Pete   tub   tube

man   mane   kit   kite

pin   pine   cap   cape

198

Look At Simon

Directions: Look at both pictures. Find 4 things in picture #2 that are not in picture #1. Look at the word list to see how to spell the word. Write your answers in the numbered spaces.

hat	head	socks	bare	feet
feather	watch	untied shoes	tied shoes	

1. watch
2. socks
3. feather
4. untied shoes

196

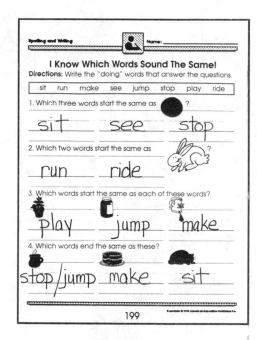

I Know Which Words Sound The Same!

Directions: Write the "doing" words that answer the questions.

sit	run	make	see	jump	stop	play	ride

1. Which three words start the same as ?

sit   see   stop

2. Which two words start the same as ?

run   ride

3. Which words start the same as each of these words?

play   jump   make

4. Which words end the same as these?

stop/jump   make   sit

199

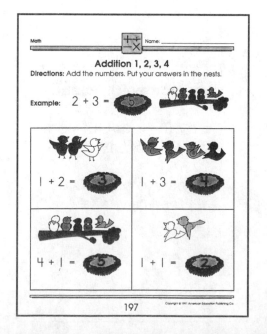

Addition 1, 2, 3, 4

Directions: Add the numbers. Put your answers in the nests.

Example: 2 + 3 = 5

1 + 2 = 3

1 + 3 = 4

4 + 1 = 5

1 + 1 = 2

197

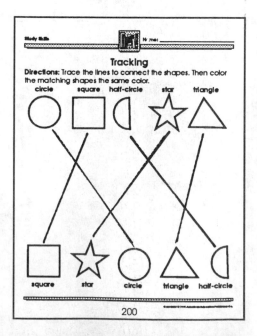

Tracking

Directions: Trace the lines to connect the shapes. Then color the matching shapes the same color.

circle   square   half-circle   star   triangle

square   star   circle   triangle   half-circle

200

Consonant Digraphs: ch, sh, th, wh

Directions: Look at the first picture in each row. Circle the pictures in the row that start with the same sound.

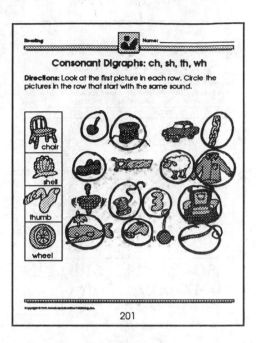

Do You Like Crayons?

Directions: Read about crayons. Then answer the questions.

Some crayons come in bright colors. Some crayons come in light colors. There are many colors of crayons. All crayons have wax in them. Wax makes the crayon stick together.

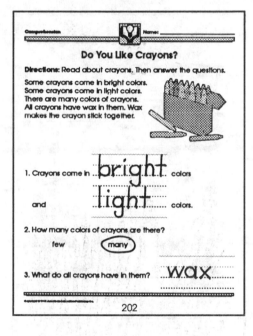

1. Crayons come in bright colors

and light colors.

2. How many colors of crayons are there?

few (many)

3. What do all crayons have in them? wax

201 / 202

Compound Words

Compound words are two words that are put together to make one word.

Directions: Look at the pictures and read the two words that are next to each other. Now, put the words together to make a new word. Write the new word.

Example:

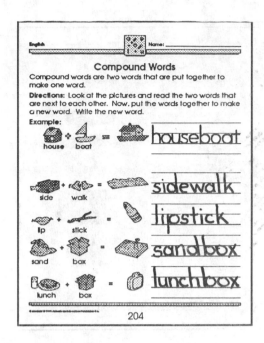

house + boat = houseboat

side walk = sidewalk

lip stick = lipstick

sand box = sandbox

lunch box = lunchbox

204

I Can Show Two Of Something!

To show two or more of something, most of the time we add "s" to the end of the word.

Like this: one cat   two cats

Directions: For each sentence, add "s" to show two or more. Then write in the "doing" word that finishes the sentence.

| sit | jump | stop | ride |

Like this:

The frog s sleep in the sun.

1. The boy s sit on the fence.

2. The car s stop at the sign.

3. The girl s jump in the water.

4. The dog s ride in the wagon.

205

Addition 6, 7, 8, 9, 10

Directions: Add the numbers. Put your answers in the doghouses.

Example: 4 + 2 = 6

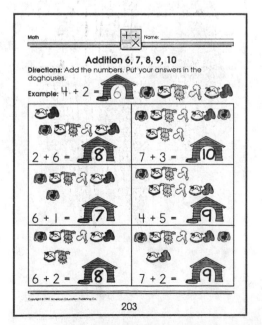

2 + 6 = 8   7 + 3 = 10

6 + 1 = 7   4 + 5 = 9

6 + 2 = 8   7 + 2 = 9

203

Tracking

Directions: Connect the letter on the left with the same letter on the right. Use a different color crayon for each line.

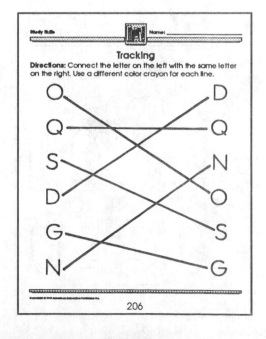

O   D
Q   Q
S   N
D   O
G   S
N   G

206

481

Consonant Blends: ft, lt

Directions: Write lt or ft to complete the words.

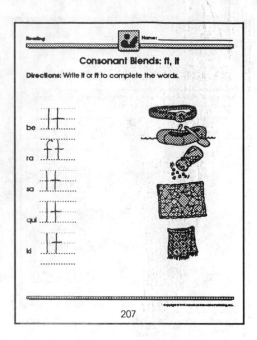

be **lt**

ra **ft**

sa **lt**

qui **lt**

ki **lt**

207

Synonyms

Synonyms are words that mean the same thing. Start and begin are synonyms.

Directions: Find the two words that describe each picture. Write the words in the boxes below the picture.

small funny large sad silly little big unhappy

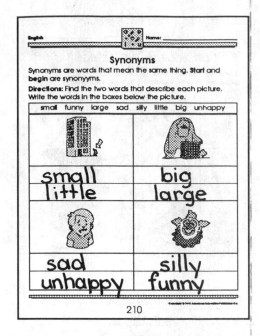

small little | big large

sad unhappy | silly funny

210

Can You Find Me?

Directions: To find the hidden picture, color only the shapes with a number inside. Do not color the shapes with a letter inside.

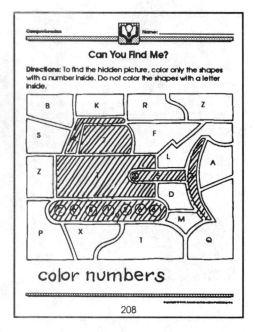

color numbers

208

I Know Which Spelling Is Right!

Directions: Circle the word that is spelled right. Then write the word the right way.

Like this:

seep
(sleep)
slep — sleep

paly
pay
(play) — play

seee
cee
(see) — see

rum
(run)
runn — run

(jump)
jumb
junp — jump

mack
maek
(make) — make

211

Subtraction 1, 2, 3, 4, 5

Directions: Count the fruit in each bowl. Write your answers on the blanks. Circle the problem that matches your answer.

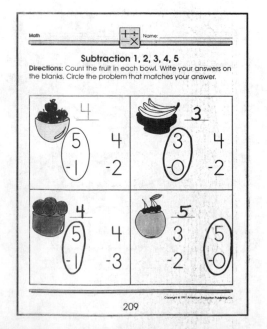

209

Tracking

Directions: Draw a straight line from A to B. Use a different color crayon for each line.

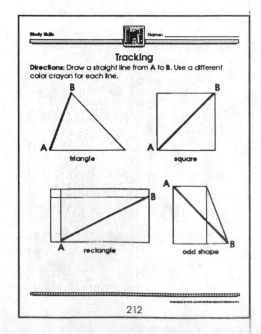

triangle

square

rectangle

odd shape

212

482

Consonant Blends: lf, lk, sk, sp, st

Directions: Draw a line from the picture to the blend that ends its word.

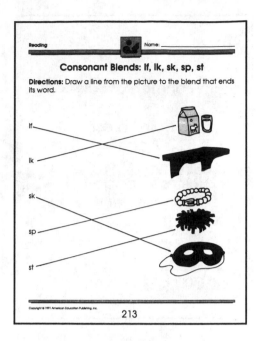

lf

lk

sk

sp

st

213

Antonyms

Antonyms are words that are opposites. Hot and cold are antonyms.

Directions: Draw a line between the words that are opposites. Can you think of other words that are opposites?

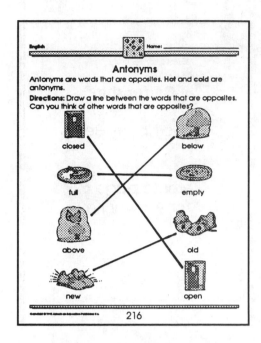

closed

below

full

empty

above

old

new

open

216

Rhyme Time

Directions: Read about words that rhyme. Then answer the questions.

Words that rhyme have the same end sounds. "Wing" and "sing" rhyme. "Boy" and "toy" rhyme. "Rhyme" and "time" rhyme. Can you think of other words that rhyme?

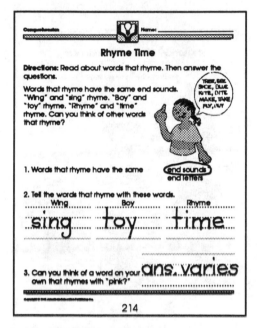

1. Words that rhyme have the same _end sounds_ (end letters)

2. Tell the words that rhyme with these words.

Wing   Boy   Rhyme

sing   toy   time

3. Can you think of a word on your own that rhymes with "pink?" _ans. varies_

214

I Can Ask Questions!

Directions: Write a question about each picture. Start with "can." Add a "doing" word. Remember that a question starts with a capital letter and ends with a question mark.
Like this:

I with you can

Can I sit with you?

cookies she can

Can she make cookies?

with you can I

Can I play with you?

I can in the box

Can I see in the box?

217

Subtraction 6, 7, 8, 9, 10

Directions: Count the flowers. Write your answers on the blanks. Circle the problems with the same answer.

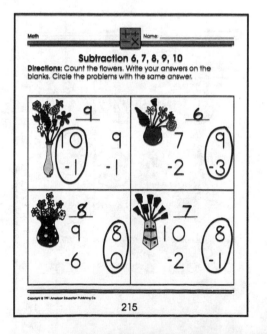

$$\begin{array}{r} 9 \\ -1 \end{array} \quad \begin{array}{r} 9 \\ -1 \end{array}$$

$$\begin{array}{r} 6 \\ 9 \\ -2 \end{array} \quad \begin{array}{r} 9 \\ -3 \end{array}$$

$$\begin{array}{r} 8 \\ 9 \\ -6 \end{array} \quad \begin{array}{r} 8 \\ -0 \end{array}$$

$$\begin{array}{r} 7 \\ 10 \\ -2 \end{array} \quad \begin{array}{r} 8 \\ -1 \end{array}$$

215

Tracking

Directions: Trace 3 paths from A to B.

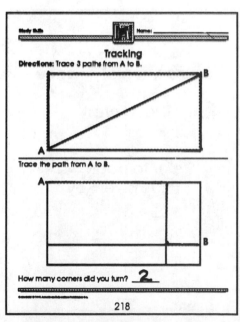

Trace the path from A to B.

How many corners did you turn? **2**

218

Citizenship

The Liberty Bell

Refer to page **529**
for Answer Key

219

Citizenship

The Liberty Bell
Activity

Refer to page **529**
for Answer Key

220

Environmental Science

Rain Forest

Refer to page **541**
for Answer Key

221

Environmental Science

Rain Forest
Activity

Refer to page **541**
for Answer Key

222

Consonant Blends: mp, nd, nk, ng

Directions: In every box is a word ending and a list of letters.
Add each of the letters to the word ending to make rhyming
words.

223

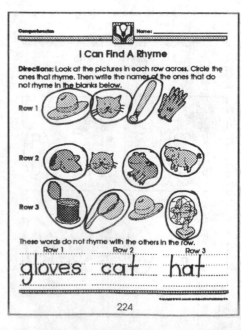

I Can Find A Rhyme

Directions: Look at the pictures in each row across. Circle the
ones that rhyme. Then write the names of the ones that do
not rhyme in the blanks below.

Row 1

Row 2

Row 3

These words do not rhyme with the others in the row.

Row 1	Row 2	Row 3
gloves	cat	hat

224

Addition And Subtraction

Directions: Work the problems. Remember, addition means "putting together" or adding two or more numbers to find the sum. Subtraction means "taking away" or subtracting one number from another.

$1 + 3 =$ **4** $4 - 3 =$ **1** $4 + 5 =$ **9**

$6 + 1 =$ **7** $7 - 2 =$ **5** $8 - 4 =$ **4**

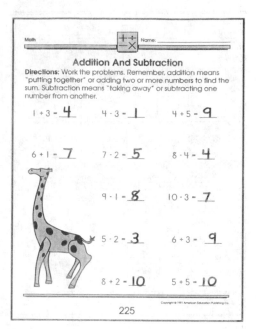

$9 - 1 =$ **8** $10 - 3 =$ **7**

$5 - 2 =$ **3** $6 + 3 =$ **9**

$8 + 2 =$ **10** $5 + 5 =$ **10**

225

Tracking

Directions: Help Megan find Randy. How many paths can she follow to reach him? **4**

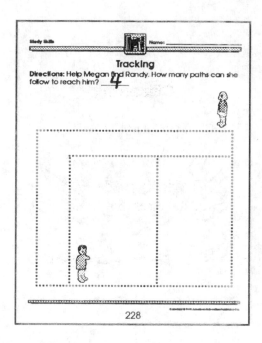

228

Homonyms

Homonyms are words that sound the same but are spelled differently and mean something different. **Blew** and **blue** are homonyms.

Directions: Look at the word pairs. Choose the word that describes the picture. Write the word on the line next to the picture.

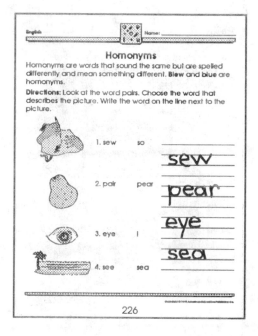

1. sew   so   **sew**

2. pair   pear   **pear**

3. eye   I   **eye**

4. see   sea   **sea**

226

Skills Review: Consonant Reviews

Directions: Finish each sentence with a word from the word box.

| sting | shelf | drank | plant | stamp |

1. Tom **drank** his milk.

2. A bee can **sting** you.

3. I put a **stamp** on my letter.

4. The **plant** is green.

5. The book is on the **shelf**

229

I Can Finish A Story!

Directions: Write in the "doing" words to finish the story. The first letter of each "doing" word is done for you.

One day Mom said I could **ride** the school bus home with Pat.   We watched Pat's **play** with a ●.   Then Pat told me, "My mother said she would **make** some I will get us some."

Pat went inside to get the .   Just then I saw a **run** into the yard.   Oh, no!   He might chase Pat's .   I have to **stop** him!

Pat came back with the .   The began to **jump** on Pat and lick Pat's face.   Then he ran off with the .

227

Moving Along

Directions: Read about words that tell about how you move. Circle the right answer on 1. Then answer the other questions.

You can move in many ways. There are many words that tell how. You can run. When you run, one foot hits the ground at a time. You can jump. When you jump, you land on two feet. You can hop. To hop, first stand on one leg. Then jump up and down.

1. Running and jumping are different because

A) One foot hits the ground at a time when you run. Two feet hit the ground at a time when you jump.

OR

B) Two feet at a time hit the ground when you run. One foot hits the ground at a time when you jump.

2. Fill in the missing directions on how to hop.

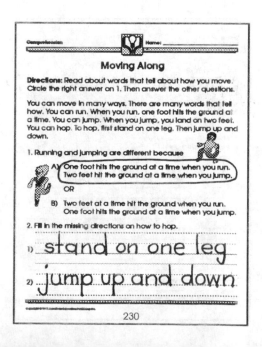

1) **stand on one leg**

2) **jump up and down**

230

485

Review

Directions: Work the problems. Color the picture.

$5 - 4 = 1$

$9 + 1 = 10$

231

Review

Directions: Circle the boxes that have P in them.

Color the triangles.

Trace all the paths from **A** to **B** with different colors.

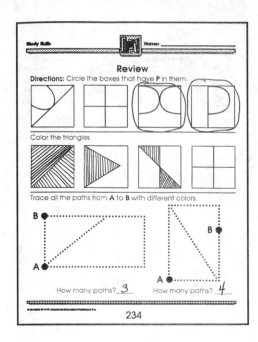

How many paths? 3   How many paths? 4

234

Review

Directions: Read the sentences below. Fill in the blanks with the correct word. Then circle the first letter of each word and write them in ABC order on the lines below.

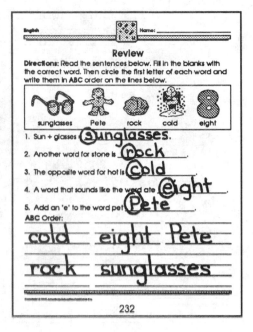

sunglasses   Pete   rock   cold   eight

1. Sun + glasses = sunglasses.
2. Another word for stone is rock.
3. The opposite word for hot is cold.
4. A word that sounds like the word ate is eight.
5. Add an 'e' to the word pet Pete.

ABC Order:

cold   eight   Pete

rock   sunglasses

232

Picture Clues

Directions: 1) Look at the big picture. 2) Now read the sentences. 3) Draw a line from each little picture to the word that tells about it.

I see the   tree

I see the   boy

I see the   swing

I see the   dog

I see the   sun

235

Review

Directions: 1. Write three telling sentences and one question about this picture. Put a "doing" word in each sentence. 2. Read your sentences to someone.

Here are some more words you could use: boys, girls, mothers, fathers, people, they, sand, bikes, tree.

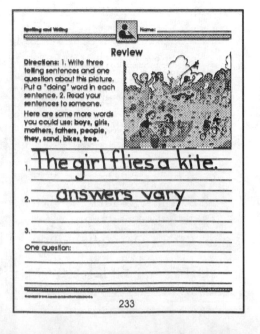

1. The girl flies a kite.

2. answers vary

3.

One question:

233

These Don't Belong

Directions: Look at the pictures in each row across. Circle the ones that go together. Then write the names of the ones that do not belong in the blanks below.

Row 1   cookies   cake   beans   ice cream

Row 2   apple   banana   orange   cookies

Row 3   kite   dice   checkers   chess

Row 1   Row 2   Row 3

beans   cookies   kite

236

486

Place Value: Tens And Ones

The place value of a digit, or numeral, is shown by where it is in the number. For example, in the number **123**, **1** has the place value of **hundreds**, **2** is **tens**, and **3** is **ones**.

Directions: Count the groups of ten crayons and write the number by the word **tens**. Count the other crayons and write the number by the word **ones**.

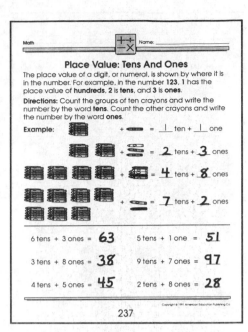

Example:

+ = _1_ ten + _1_ one

+ = **2** tens + **3** ones

+ = **4** tens + **8** ones

+ = **7** tens + **2** ones

6 tens + 3 ones = **63**	5 tens + 1 one = **51**
3 tens + 8 ones = **38**	9 tens + 7 ones = **97**
4 tens + 5 ones = **45**	2 tens + 8 ones = **28**

237

Finding Similarities

Directions: Circle the picture in each row that is most like the first picture.

Example:

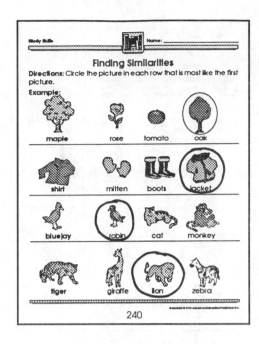

maple   rose   tomato   (oak)

shirt   mitten   boots   (jacket)

bluejay   (robin)   cat   monkey

tiger   giraffe   (lion)   zebra

240

Nouns Are Naming Words

Nouns tell the name of a person, place, or thing.

Directions: Look at each picture. Color it red if it names a person. Color it blue if it names a place. Color it green if it names a thing.

238

Vocabulary Building with Visual Clues

Directions: Draw a line from the sentence to its picture.

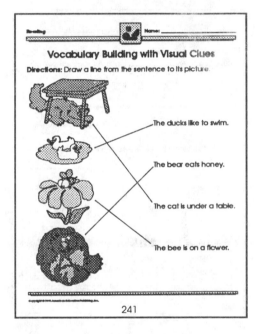

The ducks like to swim.

The bear eats honey.

The cat is under a table.

The bee is on a flower.

241

I Can Write "Weather" Words!

Directions: 1. Follow the lines to write the words. 2. Write the words by yourself. 3. Color the pictures. 4. Read the words to someone.

Like this:

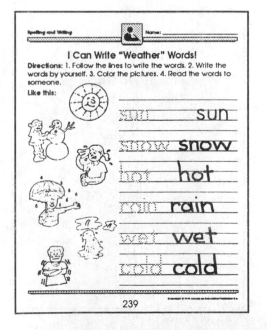

sun

snow

hot

rain

wet

cold

239

Babies

Directions: Read about babies. Then answer the questions.

Babies are small. Some babies cry a lot. They cry when they are wet. They cry when they are hungry. They smile when they are dry. They smile when they are fed.

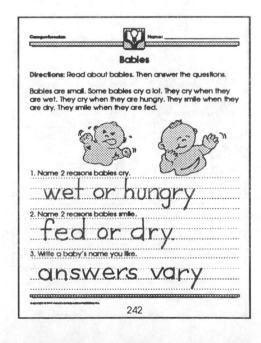

1. Name 2 reasons babies cry.

wet or hungry

2. Name 2 reasons babies smile.

fed or dry

3. Write a baby's name you like.

answers vary

242

Place Value: Tens And Ones
Directions: Write the answers in the correct spaces.

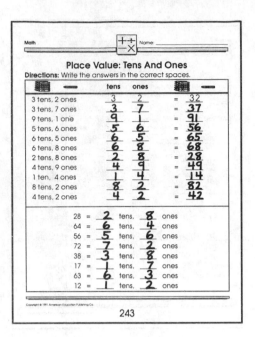

	tens	ones		
3 tens, 2 ones	3	2	=	32
3 tens, 7 ones	3	7	=	37
9 tens, 1 one	9	1	=	91
5 tens, 6 ones	5	6	=	56
6 tens, 5 ones	6	5	=	65
6 tens, 8 ones	6	8	=	68
2 tens, 8 ones	2	8	=	28
4 tens, 9 ones	4	9	=	49
1 ten, 4 ones	1	4	=	14
8 tens, 2 ones	8	2	=	82
4 tens, 2 ones	4	2	=	42

28 = **2** tens, **8** ones
64 = **6** tens, **4** ones
56 = **5** tens, **6** ones
72 = **7** tens, **2** ones
38 = **3** tens, **8** ones
17 = **1** tens, **7** ones
63 = **6** tens, **3** ones
12 = **1** tens, **2** ones

243

Finding Similarities
Directions: Circle the picture in each row that is most like the first picture.
Example:

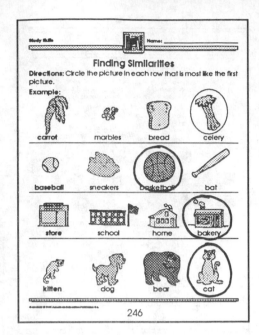

carrot   marbles   bread   celery

baseball   sneakers   basketball   bat

store   school   home   bakery

kitten   dog   bear   cat

246

Nouns Are Naming Words
Directions: Write these naming words in the correct box.

store	zoo	child	baby	teacher	table
cat	park	gym	woman	sock	horse

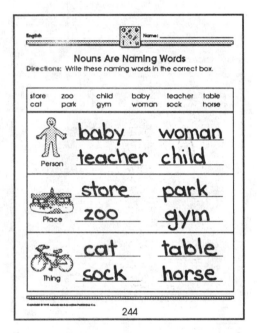

Person: baby   woman   teacher   child

Place: store   park   zoo   gym

Thing: cat   table   sock   horse

244

Citizenship

The Bald Eagle

Refer to page **530** for Answer Key

247

I Can Finish Sentences!
Directions: 1. Write in the right words to finish these sentences. Use each word only one time. 2. Put a period at the end of the telling sentences. 3. Put a question mark at the end of the asking sentences.
Like this:
Do flowers grow in the **sun** ?

rain	water	wet	hot

1. The sun makes me **hot** .

2. When it rains, the grass gets **wet** .

3. Do you think it will **rain** on our picnic ?

4. Should you drink the **water** from the rain ?

245

Citizenship

The Bald Eagle
Activity

Refer to page **530** for Answer Key

248

Environmental Science

Refuges

Refer to page **541**
for Answer Key

249

Saving Our Planet

Refuges
Activity

Refer to page **541**
for Answer Key

250

More Than One

Directions: An s at the end of a word often means there is more than one.1) Look at each picture. 2) Draw a circle around the right word. 3) Write the word on the line.

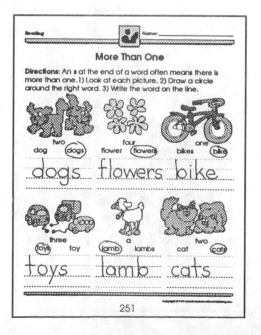

dog (dogs)   four flower (flowers)   bikes (bike)

dogs   flowers   bike

three (toys) toy   a (lamb) lambs   cat two (cats)

toys   lamb   cats

251

489

All About Ann And Ben

Directions: Read the story. Look at the pictures of Ben and Ann. Then use the word list to spell the answers to the questions.

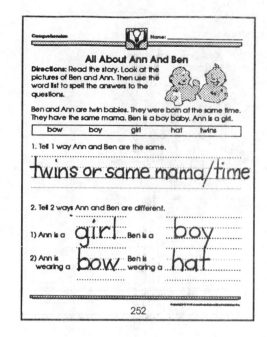

Ben and Ann are twin babies. They were born at the same time. They have the same mama. Ben is a boy baby. Ann is a girl.

bow	boy	girl	hat	twins

1. Tell 1 way Ann and Ben are the same.

twins or same mama/time

2. Tell 2 ways Ann and Ben are different.

1) Ann is a girl   Ben is a boy

2) Ann is wearing a bow   Ben is wearing a hat

252

Ordinal Numbers

Ordinal numbers are used to indicate order in a series, such as **first**, **second**, or **third**.

Directions: Draw a line to the picture that corresponds to the ordinal number in the left column.

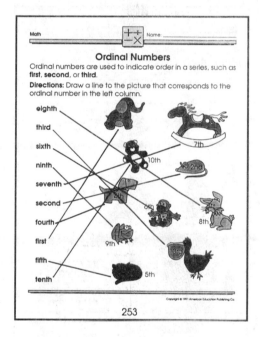

eighth
third
sixth
ninth
seventh
second
fourth
first
fifth
tenth

253

More Than One

Some nouns name more than one person, place or thing.

Directions: Add an "s" to make the words tell about the picture.

frog **s**   pan **s**

boy **s**   egg **s**

horn **s**   girl **s**

254

I Know Which Letters Are The Same!

Directions: 1. Read the letter that starts each row. 2. Find the two pictures in each row that start with that letter. 3. Write the letter under those pictures.

Like this:

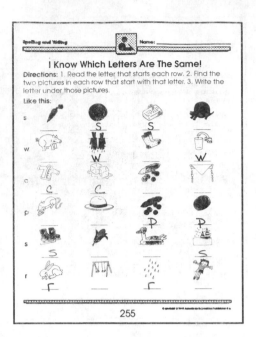

255

Hats

Directions: Read about hats. Then answer the questions.

There are many kinds of hats. Some hats have brims. Some hats have feathers. Some knit hats pull down over your ears. Some straw hats set on top of your head. Do you like hats?

1. Name 4 kinds of hats.

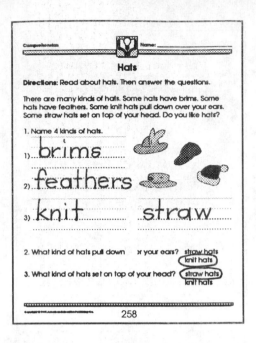

1) brims

2) feathers

3) knit   straw

2. What kind of hats pull down over your ears? straw hats / **knit hats**

3. What kind of hats set on top of your head? **straw hats** / knit hats

258

Finding Similarities

Directions: Randy and Megan are looking for sea shells. They only want the shells that look similar to this. Color the shells that Randy and Megan take home.

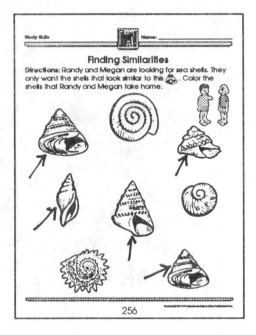

256

Counting By Tens

Directions: Count in order by tens to draw the path the boy takes to the store.

Copyright © 1991 American Education Publishing Co.

259

Going For A Ride

Directions: 1) Read the sentence. 2) Draw a circle around the word that tells about the picture. 3) Write the word.

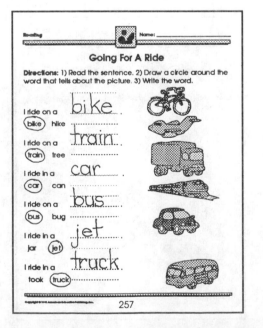

I ride on a (bike) hike — bike

I ride on a (train) tree — train

I ride in a (car) can — car

I ride on a (bus) bug — bus

I ride in a jar (jet) — jet

I ride in a took (truck) — truck

257

More Than One

Directions: Read the nouns under the pictures. Then, write the noun under One or More Than One.

One

barn

wagon

horse

More Than One

cows

ducks

pigs

260

I Know Where The Sentences Stop!

Directions: 1. Read the two sentences on each line. 2. Draw a line between them. 3. Write them again. 4. Remember to begin each sentence with a capital letter. Put a period or a question mark at the end of each one.

Like this: will it rain / the sky is very dark

Will it rain? The sky is dark.

1. she jumped in the water she got wet

She jumped in the water. She got wet.

2. do you like my snowman does he need a hat

Do you like my snowman? Does he need a hat?

261

I Like Hats

Directions: Look at the pictures. Then number them in 1-2-3-4 order.

264

Finding Similarities

Directions: Circle the word in each row that is most like the first word in the row.

Example:

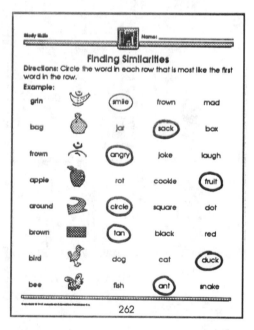

grin	(smile)	frown	mad
bag	jar	(sack)	box
frown	(angry)	joke	laugh
apple	rot	cookie	(fruit)
around	(circle)	square	dot
brown	(tan)	black	red
bird	dog	cat	(duck)
bee	fish	(ant)	snake

262

Counting By Fives

Directions: Count by fives to draw the path to the playground.

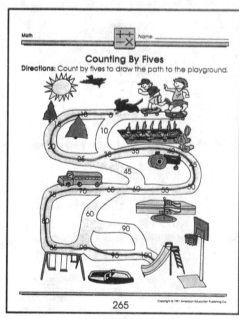

265

Sentences With Not

Directions: 1) Say the word. 2) Write the word. 3) Read the sentences. 4) Look at the picture. 5) Draw a circle around the sentence that tells about the picture.

not   not not

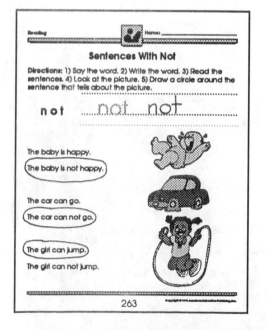

The baby is happy.
(The baby is not happy.)

The car can go.
(The car can not go.)

(The girl can jump.)
The girl can not jump.

263

Verbs Are Action Words

Verbs are words that tell what a person or a thing can do.

Example: The girl pats the dog.
The word "pat" is the verb. It shows action.

Directions: Draw a line between the verbs and the pictures that show the action.

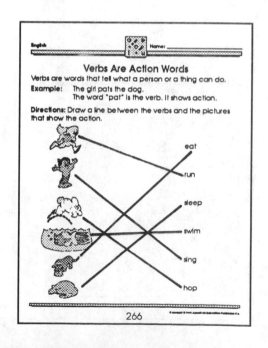

eat
run
sleep
swim
sing
hop

266

I Know How The Letters Go!

Directions: Put the letters in the right order.
Like this:

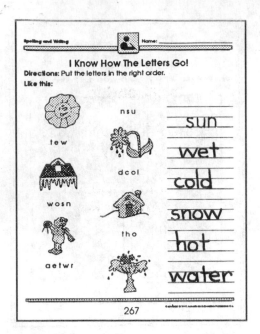

nsu

tew

dcol

wosn

tho

aetwr

sun
wet
cold
snow
hot
water

Name The Cats

Directions: Look at the pictures of the cats. Read about the cats. Then write the correct name beside each cat.

Fluffy, Blackie and Tiger are playing. Tom is sleeping. Blackie has spots. Tiger has stripes.

Tiger   Fluffy

Blackie   Tom

Finding Opposites

Directions: Find and circle the picture in each row that is the opposite of the first picture.

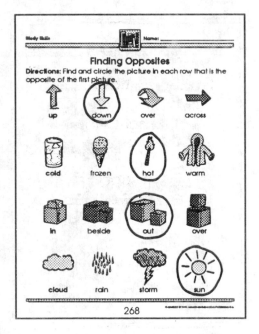

up   down   over   across

cold   frozen   hot   warm

in   beside   out   over

cloud   rain   storm   sun

Fractions

Directions: Color half of each object.
Example:

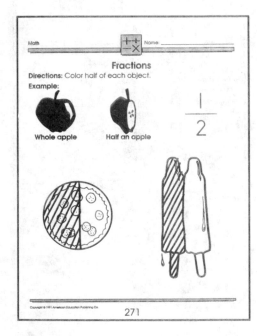

Whole apple   Half an apple

$\frac{1}{2}$

My House

Directions: 1) Read the word. 2) Write the word. 3) Write the word to finish the sentences. 4) Draw a picture of your house.

house   house house

Here is my house .   I like my house .

PICTURE VARIES

Verbs Are Action Words.

Directions:
Look at the pictures.
Read the words.
Write an action word in each sentence below.

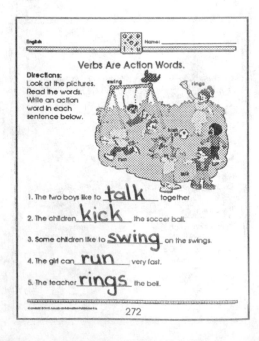

swing   rings

1. The two boys like to **talk** together

2. The children **kick** the soccer ball.

3. Some children like to **swing** on the swings.

4. The girl can **run** very fast.

5. The teacher **rings** the bell.

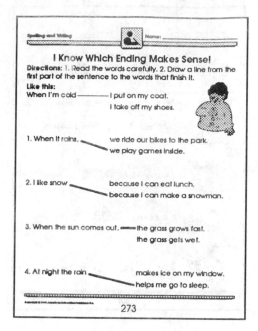

I Know Which Ending Makes Sense!
Directions: 1. Read the words carefully. 2. Draw a line from the first part of the sentence to the words that finish it.
Like this:
When I'm cold ——— I put on my coat.
I take off my shoes.

1. When it rains, — we ride our bikes to the park.
we play games inside.

2. I like snow — because I can eat lunch.
because I can make a snowman.

3. When the sun comes out, — the grass grows fast.
the grass gets wet.

4. At night the rain — makes ice on my window.
helps me go to sleep.

273

Finding Opposites
Directions: Color the things that are the opposite of "up" in this picture.

274

Citizenship

The Fourth of July

Refer to page **531**
for Answer Key

275

Citizenship

The Fourth of July
Activity

Refer to page **531**
for Answer Key

276

Environmental Science

Conservation

Refer to page **542**
for Answer Key

277

Environmental Science

Conservation
Activity

Refer to page **542**
for Answer Key

278

You And Me

Directions: 1) Read the word. 2) Write the word. 3) Draw a circle around the right word to finish each sentence. 4) Write the word on the lines.

you and me   you and me
you and me

I will play with _you_ .   (you)   me

You can go with _me_ .   you   (me)

Can you run with _me_ ?   you   (me)

279

Is And Are Are Special Words

Use "is" when talking about one person or one thing. Use "are" when talking about more than one person or thing.

Example: The dog is barking.
The dogs are barking.

Directions: Write "is" or "are" in the sentences below.

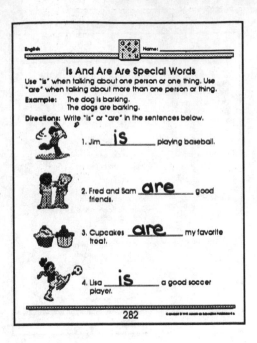

1. Jim _is_ playing baseball.

2. Fred and Sam _are_ good friends.

3. Cupcakes _are_ my favorite treat.

4. Lisa _is_ a good soccer player.

282

See The Cats!

Directions: Look at the pictures of Tom, Fluffy, Tiger and Blackie. In picture 2, one thing about each cat is different. Look at the word list. Then write your answers.

ball	bow	brush	collar

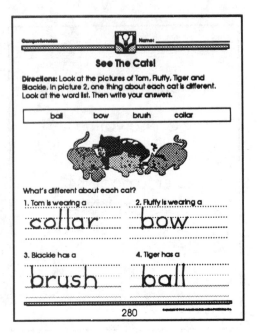

What's different about each cat?

1. Tom is wearing a
collar

2. Fluffy is wearing a
bow

3. Blackie has a
brush

4. Tiger has a
ball

280

I Can Finish A Story!

Directions: Write the missing words in the story. The first letter of each word is there. Can you write the other letters by yourself?

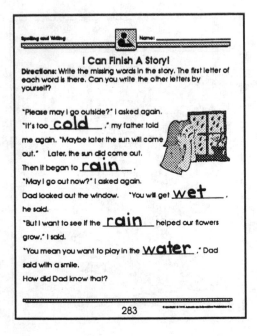

"Please may I go outside?" I asked again.

"It's too _cold_ ," my father told me again. "Maybe later the sun will come out." Later, the sun did come out. Then it began to _rain_ .

"May I go out now?" I asked again.

Dad looked out the window.   "You will get _wet_ , he said.

"But I want to see if the _rain_ helped our flowers grow," I said.

"You mean you want to play in the _water_ ," Dad said with a smile.

How did Dad know that?

283

Fractions: Thirds And Fourths

A fraction is a number that names part of a whole, such as 1/2 or 3/4.

Directions: Each object has 3 equal parts. Color one section.

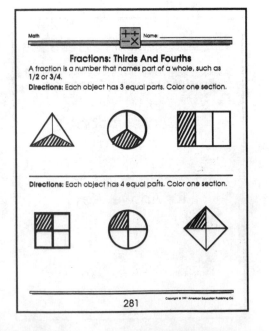

Directions: Each object has 4 equal parts. Color one section.

281

Finding Opposites

Directions: Draw a line between the words that are opposite.

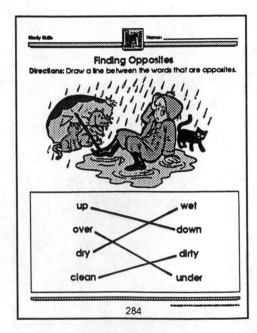

up — wet
over — down
dry — dirty
clean — under

284

494

Skills Review: Vocabulary

Directions: Write the word from the word box that finishes the sentences.

house	me	you	not	ride

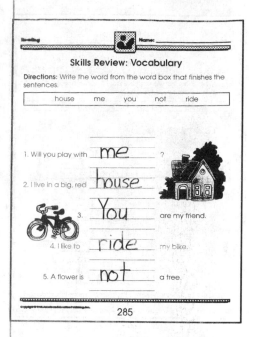

1. Will you play with **me** ?

2. I live in a big, red **house**

3. **You** are my friend.

4. I like to **ride** my bike.

5. A flower is **not** a tree.

285

Clothes For Winter And Summer

Directions: Read the story. Look at the pictures. Then answer the questions.

Some clothes are for winter. Some clothes are for summer. Winter clothes keep us warm. Summer clothes keep us cool. In summer, I first put on shorts. Then a shirt. Then sandals. These clothes keep me cool!

1. Tell the order of clothes I put on in summer.

1) **shorts** 2) **shirt** 3) **sandals**

2. List the winter clothes pictured.

coat **hat** **scarf**

3. How are summer and winter clothes different?
Summer clothes keep us **cool** Winter clothes keep us **warm**

286

Review

Directions: Write the missing numbers by counting by tens and fives.

10 , 20 , **30** **40** **50** **60** , 70 , **80** , **90** , 100

5 , **10** , 15 , **20** **25** , 30 , **35** **40** **45** , **50**

Directions: Color the object with thirds red. Color the object with halfs blue. Color the object with fourths green.

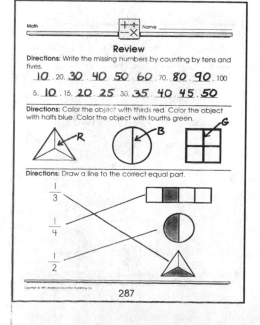

Directions: Draw a line to the correct equal part.

$\frac{1}{3}$

$\frac{1}{4}$

$\frac{1}{2}$

287

Nouns And Verbs

Directions: Read the sentences below. Draw a red circle around the nouns. Draw a blue line under the verbs.

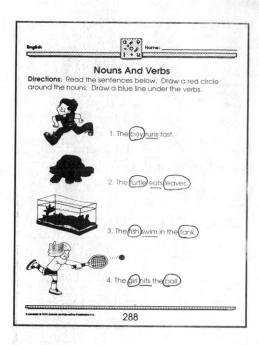

1. The boy runs fast.

2. The turtle eats leaves.

3. The fish swim in the tank.

4. The girl hits the ball.

288

Review

Directions: Write a telling sentence about each of these pictures. Then write an asking sentence about one of the pictures. Use the weather words and the other words you know how to write.

Here are some more words you could use: people, coats, hats, bikes, puddles.

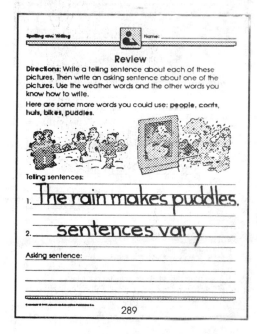

Telling sentences:

1. **The rain makes puddles.**

2. **sentences vary**

Asking sentence: _____

289

Review

Directions: Color the picture in the row that is similar to the first picture.

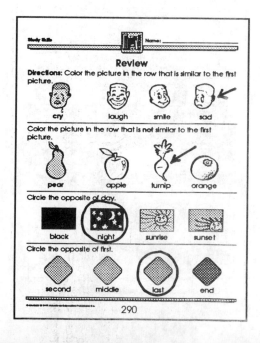

cry   laugh   smile   sad

Color the picture in the row that is not similar to the first picture.

pear   apple   turnip   orange

Circle the opposite of day.

black   night   sunrise   sunset

Circle the opposite of first.

second   middle   last   end

290

495

Compound Words

Directions: Draw lines to make compound words. Write the six new words on the lines.

Example: song + bird = songbird.

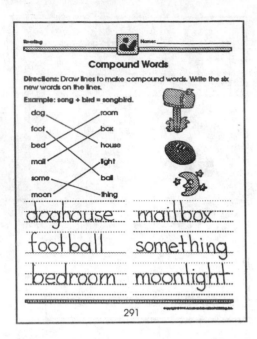

dog   room
foot   box
bed   house
mail   light
some   ball
moon   thing

doghouse   mailbox
football   something
bedroom   moonlight

291

Words That Describe

Describing words tell us more about a person, place, or thing.

Directions: Read the words in the box. Choose a word that describes the picture. Write it next to the picture.

happy	round	sick	cold	long

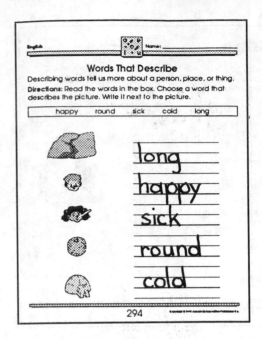

long
happy
sick
round
cold

294

The Zoo And The Farm

Directions: Read the story about the zoo and the farm. Then fill in the the puzzle with the right answers about the animals.

The zoo is for wild animals. Tigers live at the zoo. Snakes live at the zoo. The farm is for tame animals. Ducks and donkeys live on farms.

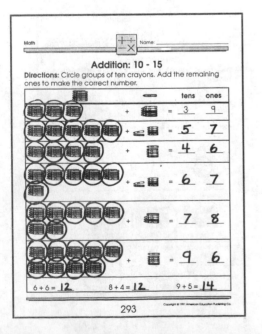

(crossword)
3. t i g e r s (down)
4. d u c k s (down)
1. d o n k e y s (across)
2. s n a k e s (across)

Across
1. These animals say "hee-haw." They live on the farm.
2. These animals are long and thin. They live in the zoo.

Down
3. These animals have stripes. They live in the zoo.
4. These animals say "quack." They live on the farm.

292

I Can Write "Opposite" Words!

Some words are opposites. "Big" and "little" are opposites. Today you will write more opposite words.

Directions: Follow the lines to write the words. Then write the words by yourself.

Like this: _____

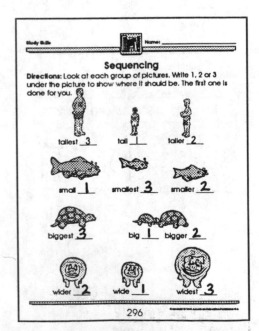

new   new
old   old
big   big
little   little
lost   lost
found   found

295

Addition: 10 - 15

Directions: Circle groups of ten crayons. Add the remaining ones to make the correct number.

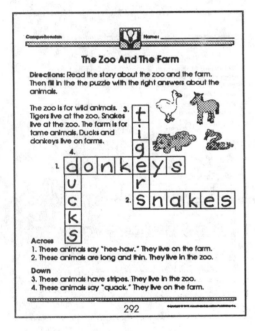

	tens	ones
+ =	3	9
+ =	5	7
+ =	4	6
+ =	6	7
+ =	7	8
+ =	9	6

6 + 6 = 12   8 + 4 = 12   9 + 5 = 14

293

Sequencing

Directions: Look at each group of pictures. Write 1, 2 or 3 under the picture to show where it should be. The first one is done for you.

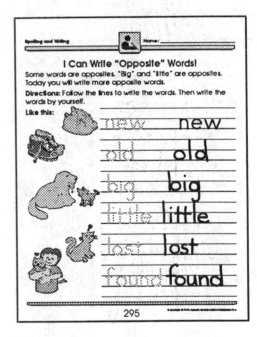

tallest 3   tall 1   taller 2

small 1   smallest 3   smaller 2

biggest 3   big 1   bigger 2

wider 2   wide 1   widest 3

296

Compound Words

Directions: Draw a circle around the compound word to finish each sentence. Write the words on the lines.

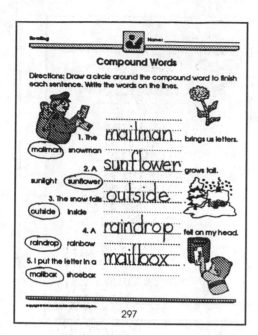

1. The (mailman) snowman _mailman_ brings us letters.

2. A sunlight (sunflower) _sunflower_ grows tall.

3. The snow falls (outside) inside _outside_

4. A (raindrop) rainbow _raindrop_ fell on my head.

5. I put the letter in a (mailbox) shoebox _mailbox_

297

Words That Describe

Directions: Read the words in the box. Choose the word that describes the picture. Write it on the line below.

wet	round	funny	soft	sad	tall

soft   _tall_

funny   _sad_

round   _wet_

300

Week Days

Directions: Read about the days of the week. Then answer the questions.

Do you know the names of the 7 days of the week? Here they are: Monday, Tuesday, Wednesday, Thursday, Friday, Saturday, Sunday. Each name has a meaning. Thursday is "Thor's day." Long ago, some people thought a man named Thor was in charge of wars.

1. What day is "Thor's day?"

Thursday

2. What was Thor in charge of?

war

3. How many days are in each week?

_7_

298

I Can Write About A Picture!

Directions: 1. Read the sentence about the first picture.
2. Write another sentence about the picture beside it. Use the "opposite" words. 3. Start your sentences with a capital and end with a period.

Like this: This apple is little.

This apple is big

dark	old	first	new	light	last

1. This coat is light green.

This bird is dark green.

2. This woman is first in line.

This woman is last in line

3. This is Mike's old friend.

This is Mike's new friend.

301

Subtraction: 10 - 15

Directions: Count the crayons in each group. Put an **X** through the number of crayons being subtracted. How many are left?

		− 5	=	10
		− 4	=	7
		− 7	=	6
		− 6	=	8
		− 5	=	7
		− 8	=	6

13 - 8 = _5_   11 - 5 = _6_   12 - 9 = _3_

14 - 7 = _7_   10 - 7 = _3_   13 - 3 = _10_

15 - 9 = _6_   11 - 8 = _3_   12 - 10 = _2_

299

Sequencing

Directions: Look at the pictures in each row. Put a number next to the word to show whether it comes 1, 2 or 3 in the row.

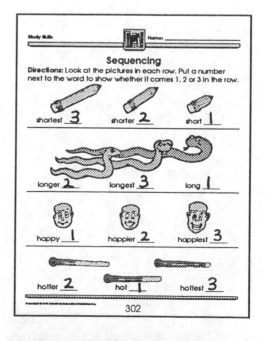

shortest _3_   shorter _2_   short _1_

longer _2_   longest _3_   long _1_

happy _1_   happier _2_   happiest _3_

hotter _2_   hot _1_   hottest _3_

302

497

Citizenship

The Bill of Rights

Refer to page **532**
for Answer Key

303

Citizenship

The Bill of Rights
Activity

Refer to page **532**
for Answer Key

304

Environmental Science

Summary

Refer to page **542**
for Answer Key

305

Environmental Science

Review

Refer to page **542**
for Answer Key

306

307

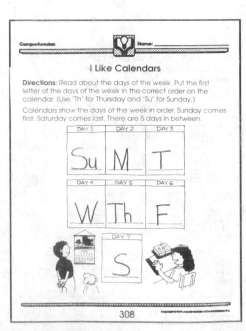

308

Addition And Subtraction

...member, addition means "putting together" or adding two or more numbers to find the sum. Subtraction means "taking away" or subtracting one number from another.

Directions: Work the problems. From your answers, use the code to color the quilt.

Color:
6 = blue
7 = yellow
8 = green
9 = red
10 = orange

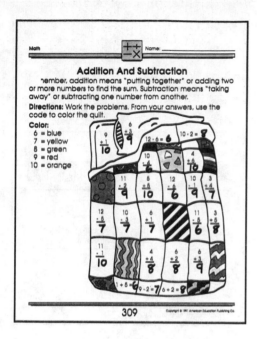

309

Copyright © 1991 American Education Publishing Co.

Sequencing

Directions: These children are waiting to see a movie. Look at the group and follow the instructions.

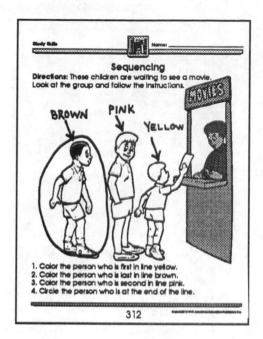

1. Color the person who is first in line yellow.
2. Color the person who is last in line brown.
3. Color the person who is second in line pink.
4. Circle the person who is at the end of the line.

312

Words That Describe

Directions: Circle the describing word in each sentence. Draw a line from the word to the picture.

1. The hungry dog is eating.
2. The tiny bird is flying.
3. Horses have long legs.
4. She is a fast runner.
5. The little boy was lost.

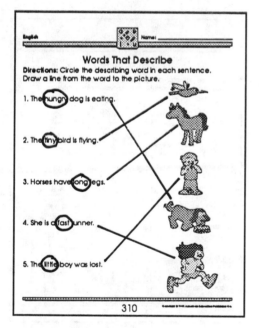

310

How Do I Play?

Directions: 1) Read the word. 2) Write the word. 3) Write the word to finish the sentences. 4) Draw a picture of how you play.

play   play play

I can   play

I like to   play

How do I   play ?

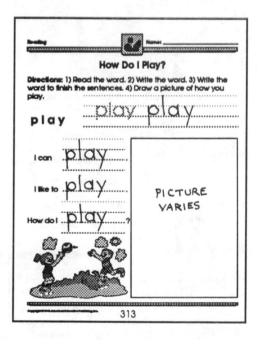

PICTURE VARIES

313

I Know Which Words Sound The Same!

Directions: Write the "opposite" words that answer the questions.

dark	found	old	light	new	first	lost	last

1. Which three words start the same as ⧉ ?

light   lost   last

2. Which two words start the same as 🐟 ?

found   first

3. Which words start the same as each of these words?

dark   new   🐩   9

4. Which two words end the same as 🐕 ?

found   old

311

See The Boats

Directions: Read about boats. Then answer the questions.

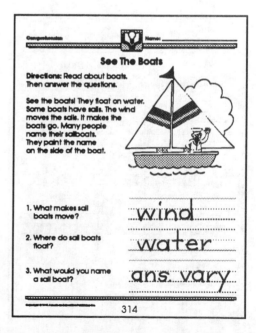

See the boats! They float on water. Some boats have sails. The wind moves the sails. It makes the boats go. Many people name their sailboats. They paint the name on the side of the boat.

1. What makes sail boats move?

wind

2. Where do sail boats float?

water

3. What would you name a sail boat?

ans. vary

314

Time: Hour

The short hand of the clock tells the hour. The long hand tells how many minutes after the hour. When the minute hand is on the 12, it is the beginning of the hour.

Directions: Look at each clock. Write the time.

Example:

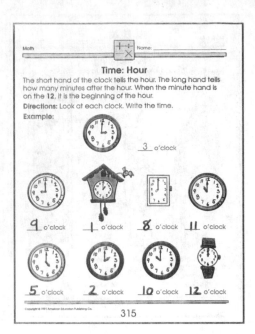

_3_ o'clock

_9_ o'clock   _1_ o'clock   _8_ o'clock   _11_ o'clock

_5_ o'clock   _2_ o'clock   _10_ o'clock   _12_ o'clock

315

Names Of People

The names of people begin with a capital letter.

Directions: Choose a name from the box to go with each child. Write the name on the line. Start each name with a capital letter.

Sam	Fred
Jack	Lisa
Ann	Jenny

ANSWERS VARY

1. Sam   4. Lisa

2. Ann   5. Fred

3. Jack   6. Jenny

316

I Can Tell What Happens Next!

Directions: Read the sentence under the first picture. Then look at the next picture. Write a sentence that tells about it.

Like this: The little dog eats.

The dog grows big.

| found | new | first | lost | old | last |

1. His book is lost.

His book is found.

2. She feeds her dog first.

She feeds her fish last.

3. I like my old shirt.

I like my new shirt.

317

Sequencing

Directions: Look at each group of shapes. Figure out the order. Fill in the missing shape. Color it.

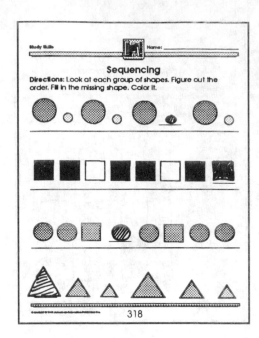

318

Over or Under?

Directions: 1) Read the words. 2) Write the words. 3) Draw a circle around the correct word to finish each sentence. 4) Write it on the line.

over   over over

under   under under

The kite is over (under)   **under** the tree.

The kite is (over) under   **over** the tree.

319

Boats That Are The Same

Directions: Look carefully at the picture. Find the boats that are the same. Color them all the same. Only 1 boat is different. Color it a different color.

320

Time: Hour, Half-Hour

The short hand of the clock tells the hour. The long hand tells how many minutes after the hour. When the minute hand is on the **6**, it is on the half-hour. A half-hour is thirty minutes. It is written **:30**, such as **5:30**.

Directions: Look at each clock. Write the time.

Example:

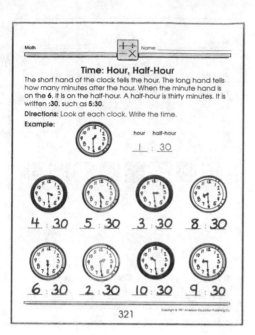

hour   half-hour
1 : 30

4 : 30   5 : 30   3 : 30   8 : 30

6 : 30   2 : 30   10 : 30   9 : 30

321

Sequencing

Directions: Draw red flowers in holes 1 and 2. Draw yellow flowers in holes 3 and 4. Draw blue flowers in holes 5 and 6.

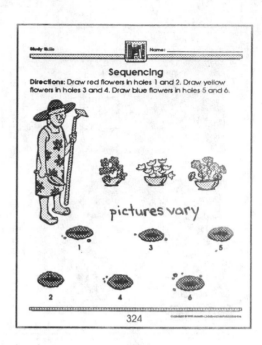

pictures vary

1   3   5

2   4   6

324

Name That Cat

The name of a pet begins with a capital letter.

Directions: Read the names in the box. Choose one name for each cat. Write the name in the space under the cat.

| Fritz | Fuzzy | Boots | King | Queenie | Lola |

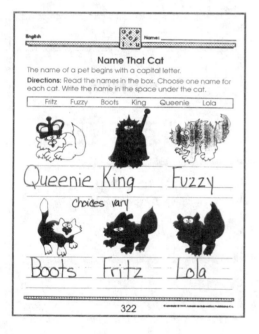

Queenie   King   Fuzzy

choices vary

Boots   Fritz   Lola

322

Day Or Night?

Directions: 1) Read the words. 2) Write the words. 3) Look at each picture. 4) Write day or night on the lines to show if they happen at day or night.

day   day   day

night   night   night

night   day

night   day

325

I Can Find The Spelling Mistakes!

Directions: Circle any words that are not spelled right. Then write the word correctly.

| dark | found | old | first | lost |

Like this:

The house is (litle.)   little

1. Are those your (older) shoes?   old

2. I (fond) your book.   found

3. He is (frist) in line.   first

4. She (loss) her lunch.   lost

5. I am afraid of the (drak.)   dark

323

Let's Go On A Trip!

Directions: Read about going on trips. Then answer the questions.

Pack your bag. Shall we go by car, plane or train? Shall we go to the sea? When we get there, let's go on a sail boat!

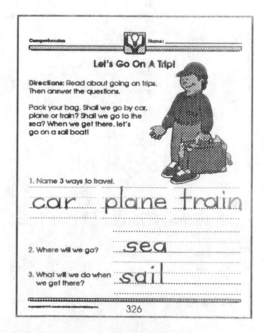

1. Name 3 ways to travel.

car   plane   train

2. Where will we go?   sea

3. What will we do when we get there?   sail

326

501

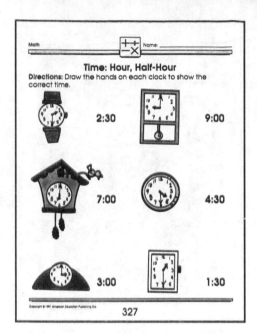

Time: Hour, Half-Hour
Directions: Draw the hands on each clock to show the correct time.

2:30

9:00

7:00

4:30

3:00

1:30

327

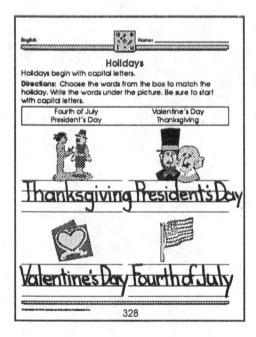

Holidays
Holidays begin with capital letters.

Directions: Choose the words from the box to match the holiday. Write the words under the picture. Be sure to start with capital letters.

Fourth of July President's Day	Valentine's Day Thanksgiving

Thanksgiving

President's Day

Valentine's Day

Fourth of July

328

I Can Write The Answer!
Directions: Look at each picture. Write the answer to the question.

Like this: Is the cookie big?

No, the cookie is little.

1. Has the boy found his boat?

No, the boat is lost.

2. Is she eating her apple last?

No, she is eating her apple first.

3. Is the book light brown? dark blue

No, the book is dark blue.

329

Sequencing
Directions: Put the following groups in ABC order. Then number them in 1, 2, 3 order.

Example:

cold	warm	hot
1	3	2

small	big	cute
3	1	2

baby	mother	family
1	3	2

doll	truck	ball
2	3	1

man	boy	grandma
3	1	2

330

Citizenship

Mary McLeod Bethune

Refer to page **533** for Answer Key

331

Citizenship

Mary McLeod Bethune Activity

Refer to page **533** for Answer Key

332

Environmental Science

Using Paper at School

Refer to page **543**
for Answer Key

333

Environmental Science

Using Paper at School
Activity

Refer to page **543**
for Answer Key

334

Bo Bo The Clown

Directions: 1) Read the story. 2) Write a word from the story to finish the following sentences. 3) Draw a circle around Yes or No.

Bo Bo is a clown. He works at the circus. Bo Bo plays with a seal.

Bo Bo is a clown. Bo Bo plays with a seal

Does Bo Bo work at the zoo?   Yes   No

335

Let's Go To The Beach!

Directions: Look at the picture. Use your crayon to draw the way to the beach. On the way, you will stop for (1) food and (2) gas. Then you will (3) cross a bridge. Finally, you will be at the sea (4)! Write the correct number 1, 2, 3 or 4 in the box before each of your stops.

336

Math   Name:

Money: Penny And Nickel

A penny is worth one cent. It is written 1¢ or $.01. A nickel is worth five cents. It is written 5¢ or $.05.

Directions: Count the money and write the answers.

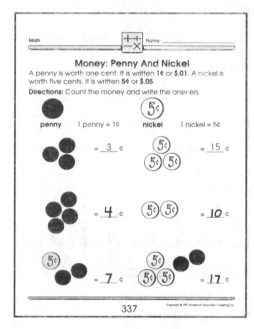

337

English   Name:

Days of the Week

The days of the week begin with capital letters.

Directions: Write the days of the week in the spaces below. Put them in order. Be sure to start with capital letters.

Tuesday	Sunday
Saturday	Monday
Monday	Tuesday
Friday	Wednesday
Thursday	Thursday
Sunday	Friday
Wednesday	Saturday

338

I Know Which Word To Write!

Directions: Write the opposite words that finish these sentences. Can you spell them all by yourself?

Like this:

The rain made my $\underline{little}$ flower grow $\underline{big}$.

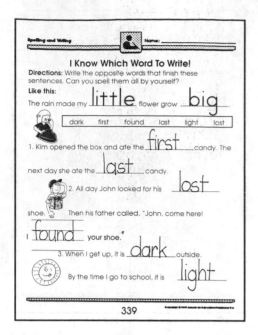

| dark | first | found | last | light | lost |

1. Kim opened the box and ate the $\underline{first}$ candy. The

next day she ate the $\underline{last}$ candy.

2. All day John looked for his $\underline{lost}$

shoe. Then his father called, "John, come here!

I $\underline{found}$ your shoe."

3. When I get up, it is $\underline{dark}$ outside.

By the time I go to school, it is $\underline{light}$.

339

Sequencing

Directions: Follow the instructions under each glass. Use crayons to draw your favorite drink in the ones that are full and half-full.

full   half-full   empty

empty   half-full   full

340

Skills Review: Vocabulary

Directions: 1) Look at each picture. 2) Draw a circle around the correct word to finish the sentence. 3) Write it on the line.

1. Mike can make a $\underline{snowman}$
(snowman) snowball

2. Beth can $\underline{work}$ outside.
play (work)

3. The cat is $\underline{under}$ the chair.
over (under)

4. I sleep in the $\underline{night}$.
day (night)

341

Coins

Directions: Read about coins. Look at the pictures of coins. Then answer the questions.

You can use all coins to buy things. Some coins are worth more than others. Do you know the names of coins? A penny is worth 1 cent. A nickel is worth 5 cents. A dime is worth 10 cents.

1. What can you use all coins to do?

$\underline{to\ buy\ things}$

2. How are coins different?

$\underline{some\ are\ worth\ more}$

3. Number the coins in order, from the coin that is worth the least to the coin that is worth the most. Under each picture, write how many pennies each coin is worth.

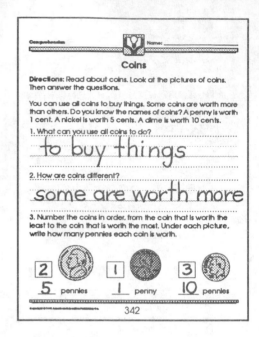

[2] $\underline{5}$ pennies   [1] $\underline{1}$ penny   [3] $\underline{10}$ pennies

342

Review

Directions: What time is it?

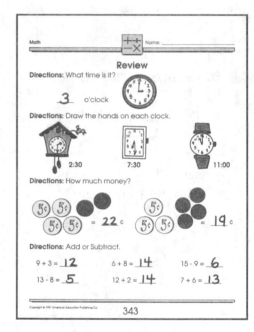

$\underline{3}$ o'clock

Directions: Draw the hands on each clock.

2:30   7:30   11:00

Directions: How much money?

= $\underline{22}$ ¢   = $\underline{19}$ ¢

Directions: Add or Subtract.

$9 + 3 = \underline{12}$ $6 + 8 = \underline{14}$ $15 - 9 = \underline{6}$

$13 - 8 = \underline{5}$ $12 + 2 = \underline{14}$ $7 + 6 = \underline{13}$

343

Review

Directions: Circle the letters that should be capital letters. Underline the describing words.

1. (J)an has <u>red</u> flowers for (m)other's (d)ay.

2. We eat a <u>hot</u> lunch on (m)onday.

3. (J)im and (F)red are <u>fast</u> runners.

4. (S)pot is a <u>small</u> dog.

5. We go to the <u>big</u> store on (f)riday.

344

504

Review

Directions: 1. Look at all three pictures in each row. 2. Write one sentence about the last picture in each row. 3. Start each sentence with a capital letter and end with a period.

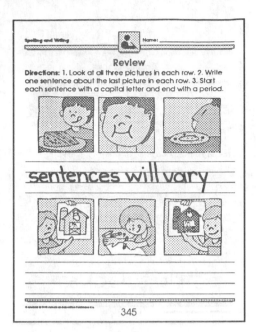

sentences will vary

345

Things To Drink

Directions: Look at the pictures. Find the pictures of things you can drink. Write the names of those things in the blanks.

milk   ice
juice
soup
pop   ice cream bar

milk   juice   pop

348

Review

Directions: Put the boys in 1, 2, 3 order from shortest to tallest.

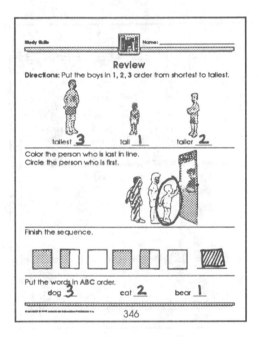

tallest **3**   tall **1**   taller **2**

Color the person who is last in line.
Circle the person who is first.

Finish the sequence.

Put the words in ABC order.
dog **3**   cat **2**   bear **1**

346

Picture Problems: Addition 0 - 9

Directions: Work the number problem under each picture.

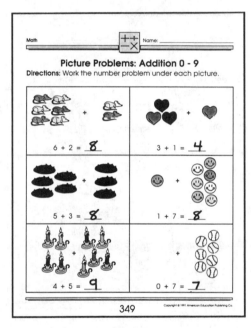

$6 + 2 = 8$ $3 + 1 = 4$

$5 + 3 = 8$ $1 + 7 = 8$

$4 + 5 = 9$ $0 + 7 = 7$

---
349   Copyright © 1991 American Education Publishing Co.

Find The Synonyms

Directions: 1) Look at the underlined word in each sentence. 2) Draw a circle around the word that means the same thing. 3) Write the new words.

1. The _little_ dog ran.   tall   funny   (small)
2. The _happy_ girl smiled.   (glad)   sad   good
3. The bird is in the _big_ tree.   green   pretty   (tall)
4. He was _nice_ to me.   (kind)   mad   bad
5. The baby is _tired_.   (sleepy)   sad   little

small   tall   sleepy
glad   kind

347

Telling Sentences

Sentences can tell us something. Telling sentences begin with a capital letter. They end with a period.

Directions: Read the sentences. Draw a yellow circle around the capital letter at the beginning of the sentence. Draw a purple circle around the period at the end of the sentence.

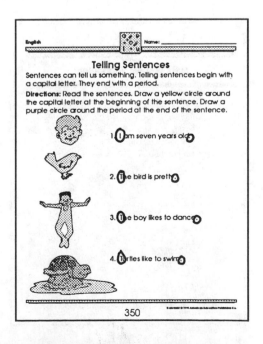

1. I am seven years old.
2. The bird is pretty.
3. The boy likes to dance.
4. Turtles like to swim.

350

I Can Write More "Doing" Words!

Directions: 1. Follow the lines to write the words. 2. Write the words by yourself. 3. Read the words to someone.

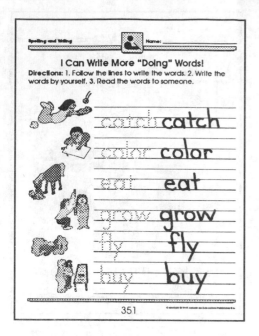

catch

color

eat

grow

fly

buy

351

Ticking Clocks

Directions: Read about clocks. Then answer the questions.

Many clocks make 2 sounds. The sounds are tick tock. Big clocks often make loud tick tocks. Little clocks often make small tick tocks. Sometimes people put little clocks in the box with a new puppy. The puppy likes the sound. The tick tock makes the puppy feel safe.

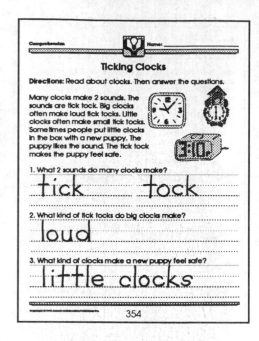

1. What 2 sounds do many clocks make?

tick   tock

2. What kind of tick tocks do big clocks make?

loud

3. What kind of clocks make a new puppy feel safe?

little clocks

354

Classifying

Directions: Color the clothes Scott should wear outside to build a snowman.

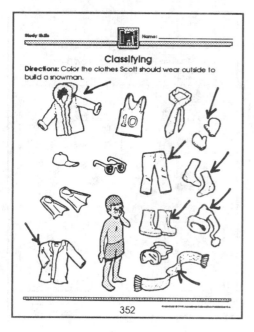

352

Picture Problems: Addition 0 - 9

Directions: Work the number problem under each picture.

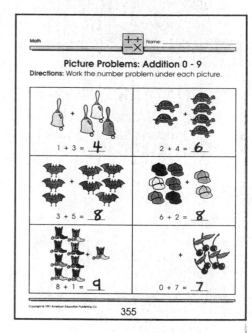

1 + 3 = 4
2 + 4 = 6
3 + 5 = 8
6 + 2 = 8
8 + 1 = 9
0 + 7 = 7

355

Getting The Main Idea

Directions: 1) Look at each picture. 2) Read the sentences. 3) Draw a circle around Yes or No.

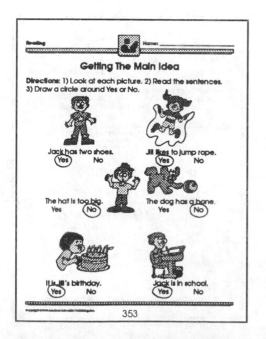

Jack has two shoes.
(Yes)   No

Jill likes to jump rope.
(Yes)   No

The hat is too big.
Yes   (No)

The dog has a bone.
Yes   (No)

It is Jill's birthday.
(Yes)   No

Jack is in school.
(Yes)   No

353

Telling Sentences

Directions: Read the sentences. Write the sentences on the lines below. Begin each sentence with a capital letter. End each sentence with a period.

1. most children like pets
2. some children like dogs
3. some children like cats
4. some children like snakes
5. some children like all animals

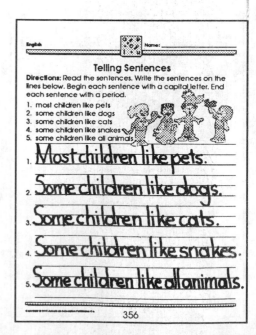

1. Most children like pets.

2. Some children like dogs.

3. Some children like cats.

4. Some children like snakes.

5. Some children like all animals.

356

506

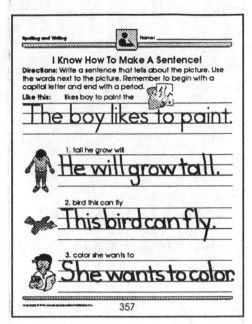

I Know How To Make A Sentence!

Directions: Write a sentence that tells about the picture. Use the words next to the picture. Remember to begin with a capital letter and end with a period.

Like this: likes boy to paint the

The boy likes to paint.

1. tall he grow will

He will grow tall.

2. bird this can fly

This bird can fly.

3. color she wants to

She wants to color.

357

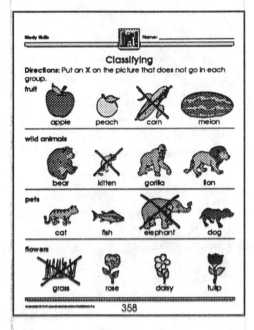

Classifying

Directions: Put an X on the picture that does not go in each group.

fruit: apple, peach, corn, melon

wild animals: bear, kitten, gorilla, lion

pets: cat, fish, elephant, dog

flowers: grass, rose, daisy, tulip

358

Citizenship

Pioneer Children

Refer to page **534**
for Answer Key

359

Citizenship

Pioneer Children
Activity

Refer to page **534**
for Answer Key

360

Environmental Science

Conserve Heat Energy

Refer to page **543**
for Answer Key

361

Environmental Science

Conserve Heat Energy
Activity

Refer to page **543**
for Answer Key

362

Matching Pictures And Sentences

Directions: Draw a line from the picture to the sentence that tells about it.

Kelly has flowers in her basket.

A red apple is on the green tree.

Four ducks swim in the lake.

The toy train goes fast!

The brown bear is eating honey.

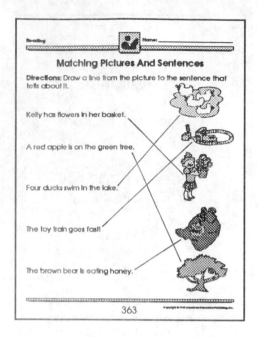

363

Telling Sentences

Directions: Read the sentences. Write the sentences below. Start each sentence with a capital letter and end with a period.
1. I like to go to the store with Mom
2. we go on Friday
3. I get to push the cart
4. I get to buy the cookies
5. I like to help Mom

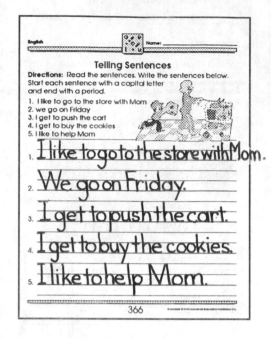

1. I like to go to the store with Mom.

2. We go on Friday.

3. I get to push the cart.

4. I get to buy the cookies.

5. I like to help Mom.

366

Help The Puppy Feel Safe

Directions: Re-read the story about clocks. Look at the pictures. Then number them in 1-2-3-4 order.

364

I Know Which Words Sound The Same!

Directions: Write the words that answer the questions.

| catch | fly | eat | grow | buy | color |

1. Which words start the same as 🎂 ?

catch   color

2. Which word starts the same as each of these pictures?

buy   fly   grow

3. Which words rhyme with 🐶 ?

fly   buy

4. Which "doing" word rhymes with these?

eat   grow

367

Picture Problems: Subtraction

Directions: Work the number problem under each picture.

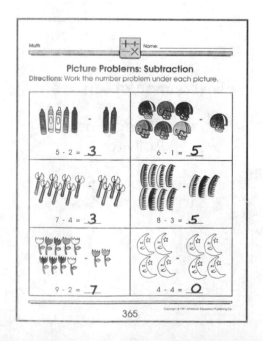

5 - 2 = **3**   6 - 1 = **5**

7 - 4 = **3**   8 - 3 = **5**

9 - 2 = **7**   4 - 4 = **0**

365

Classifying

Directions: Help Ben clean up the park. Circle the litter. Underline the coins. Put a box around the balls.

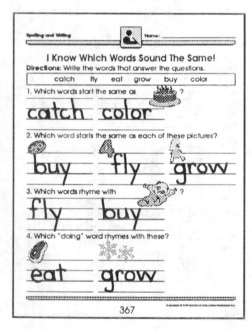

368

What Do You See?

Directions: 1) Look at the picture. 2) Read the sentences.
3) Draw a circle around Yes or No.

1. The clown has five balloons.   (Yes)   No
2. The girl has a hat on.   (Yes)   No
3. There are three children.   Yes   (No)
4. Two children are sad.   Yes   (No)
5. The clown has no shoes.   Yes   (No)
6. The clown has a big nose.   (Yes)   No
7. One child is waving.   (Yes)   No

369

Asking Sentences

Asking sentences ask a question. An asking sentence begins with a capital letter. It ends with a question mark.

Directions: Draw a green line under the sentences that ask a question.

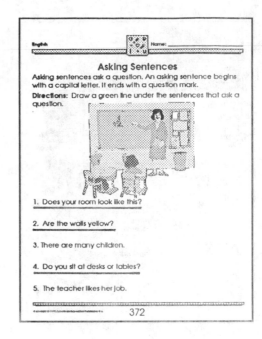

1. Does your room look like this?

2. Are the walls yellow?

3. There are many children.

4. Do you sit at desks or tables?

5. The teacher likes her job.

372

I Like Soup

Directions: Read about soup. Then answer the questions.

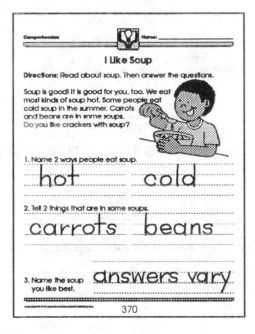

Soup is good! It is good for you, too. We eat most kinds of soup hot. Some people eat cold soup in the summer. Carrots and beans are in some soups. Do you like crackers with soup?

1. Name 2 ways people eat soup.

hot   cold

2. Tell 2 things that are in some soups.

carrots   beans

3. Name the soup you like best.

answers vary

370

I Can Write My Own Sentences!

Directions: You will write five sentences with the "doing" words. Read your sentences to someone.
Words to start your sentences: I, we, they, boys, girls, people, birds, dogs, airplanes, flowers, apples, cats.
Words to end your sentences: balls, frogs, ice cream, cookies, pictures, bigger, in my house, in the sky, in a tree, in the rain, in a bed, at school, at home.

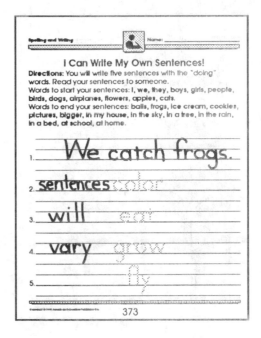

1. We catch frogs.

2. sentences color

3. will eat

4. vary grow

5. fly

373

Picture Problems: Subtraction

Directions: Work the number problem under each picture.

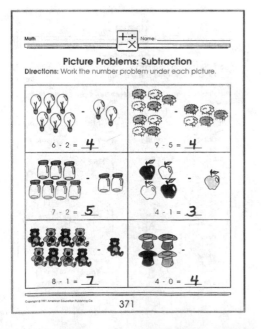

6 - 2 = **4**   9 - 5 = **4**

7 - 2 = **5**   4 - 1 = **3**

8 - 1 = **7**   4 - 0 = **4**

371

Classifying

Directions: Write each word in the correct row at the bottom of the page.

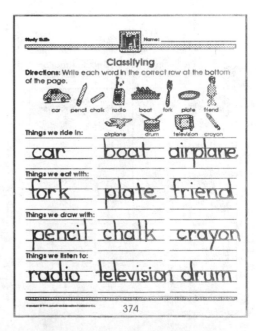

car   pencil   chalk   radio   boat   fork   plate   friend

airplane   drum   television   crayon

Things we ride in:

car   boat   airplane

Things we eat with:

fork   plate   friend

Things we draw with:

pencil   chalk   crayon

Things we listen to:

radio   television   drum

374

Page 375 — What Am I?

What Am I?

Directions: 1) Read the word. 2) Write the word. 3) Read each riddle. 4) Draw a line to the picture it tells about.

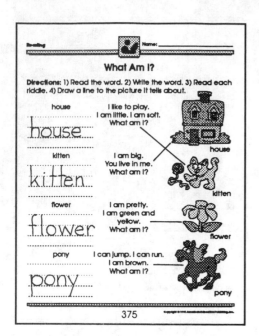

house
house

kitten
kitten

flower
flower

pony
pony

I like to play.
I am little. I am soft.
What am I?

I am big.
You live in me.
What am I?

I am pretty.
I am green and yellow.
What am I?

I can jump. I can run.
I am brown.
What am I?

house
kitten
flower
pony

375

Page 378 — Asking Sentences

Asking Sentences

Directions: Draw a blue line under the sentences that ask a question.

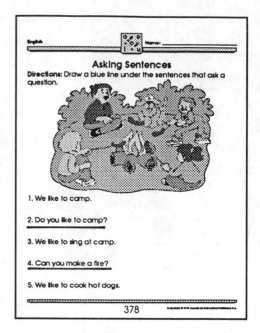

1. We like to camp.

2. Do you like to camp?

3. We like to sing at camp.

4. Can you make a fire?

5. We like to cook hot dogs.

378

Page 376 — Eating Soup

Eating Soup

Directions: 1) Look at both pictures. 2) Find 4 things in picture #1 that are not in picture #2. 3) Say your answers aloud. 5) Draw a circle around them.

#1   #2

376

Page 379 — I Know Which Letters Are Missing!

I Know Which Letters Are Missing!

Directions: Write in the missing letters. Can you spell the words by yourself now?

Like this:

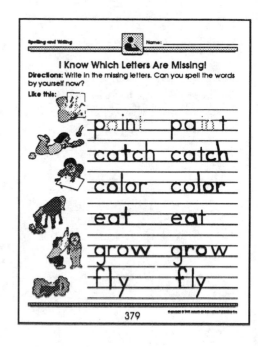

paint   paint
catch   catch
color   color
eat   eat
grow   grow
fly   fly

379

Page 377 — Picture Problems: Addition And Subtraction

Picture Problems: Addition And Subtraction

Directions: Work the number problem under each picture.

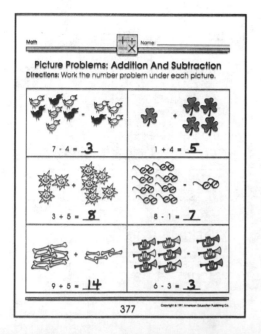

7 - 4 = **3**   1 + 4 = **5**

3 + 5 = **8**   8 - 1 = **7**

9 + 5 = **14**   6 - 3 = **3**

377

510

Page 380 — Classifying

Classifying

There are four food groups: meat, fruit and vegetables, breads, and dairy (milk and cheese).

Directions: Color the meats brown. Color the fruits and vegetables green. Color the breads tan. Color the dairy items yellow.

hotdog B   bread T   apple G   cheese Y

rolls T   celery G   orange G   hamburger B

steak B   pear G   milk Y   butter Y

ice cream Y chicken B potato G   muffin T

380

Animal Riddles

Directions: 1) Read the word. 2) Write the word. 3) Draw a line from the sentences to the animal they tell about.

long _long_ _long_

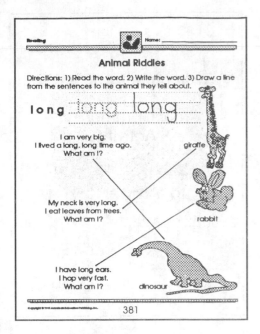

I am very big.
I lived a long, long time ago.
What am I? — giraffe

My neck is very long.
I eat leaves from trees.
What am I? — rabbit

I have long ears.
I hop very fast.
What am I? — dinosaur

381

Asking Sentences

Directions: Write the first word of each asking sentence. Be sure to start each question with a capital letter. End each question with a question mark.

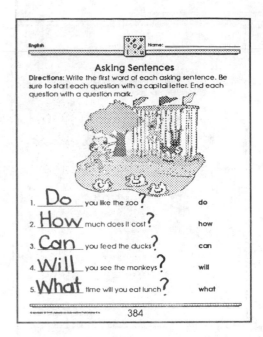

1. **Do** you like the zoo **?**   do
2. **How** much does it cost **?**   how
3. **Can** you feed the ducks **?**   can
4. **Will** you see the monkeys **?**   will
5. **What** time will you eat lunch **?**   what

384

Put The 3 Bears To Bed

Directions: Read about the 3 bears. Then match the bears with their beds. Put # 1 beside Papa Bear's bed. Put # 2 beside Mama Bear's bed. Put # 3 beside Baby Bear's Bed.

Do you know the story of the 3 bears? Papa Bear was the biggest bear. He had the biggest bed. Mama Bear was a middle-size bear. She had the middle-size bed.
Baby Bear was the little bear. He had the baby bed.

382

I Can Make Two Sentences Into One!

Directions: Make two sentences into one.
Like this: The ball is red. The ball is blue.

The ball is red and blue.

1. I eat apples. I eat cookies.

I eat apples and cookies.

2. We buy milk. We buy eggs.

We buy milk and eggs.

3. I color a horse. I color a cow.

I color a horse and a cow.

4. Flowers grow. Trees grow.

Flowers and trees grow.

385

Picture Problems: Addition and Subtraction

Directions: Work the number problem under each picture. Write + or - to show if you should add or subtract.

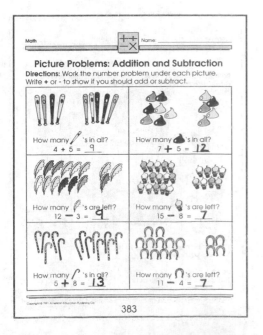

How many ✎ 's in all?
4 + 5 = **9**

How many 🍫's in all?
7 **+** 5 = **12**

How many 🖋 's are left?
12 − 3 = **9**

How many 🍦's are left?
15 − 8 = **7**

How many 🦯 's in all?
5 **+** 8 = **13**

How many ∩ 's are left?
11 − 4 = **7**

383

Classifying

Directions: Draw food you like to eat. Draw one meat, one fruit or vegetable, one bread and something with milk in it. Then answer the questions.

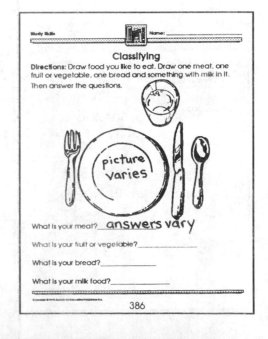

picture varies

What is your meat? **answers vary**

What is your fruit or vegetable? _____

What is your bread? _____

What is your milk food? _____

386

Citizenship

Samantha Smith

Refer to page **535**
for Answer Key

387

Citizenship

Samantha Smith
Activity

Refer to page **535**
for Answer Key

388

Environmental Science

Your Community

Refer to page **544**
for Answer Key

389

Environmental Science

Your Community
Activity

Refer to page **544**
for Answer Key

390

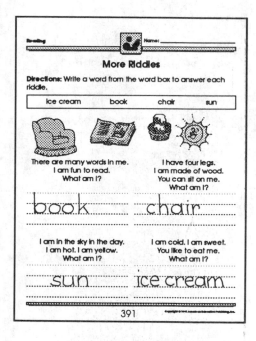

Reading   Name: _____

More Riddles

Directions: Write a word from the word box to answer each riddle.

| ice cream | book | chair | sun |

There are many words in me.
I am fun to read.
What am I?

b o o k

I have four legs.
I am made of wood.
You can sit on me.
What am I?

c h a i r

I am in the sky in the day.
I am hot. I am yellow.
What am I?

s u n

I am cold. I am sweet.
You like to eat me.
What am I?

i c e c r e a m

391

Comprehension   Name: _____

3 Bears Puzzle

Directions: Re-read the story of the 3 bears. Then fill in the puzzle with the right answers about the bears.

Across
1. Papa Bear was the _____ bear.
3. All the bears slept in _____.

Down
1. This bear was the little bear.
2. Mama Bear was middle - _____.

392

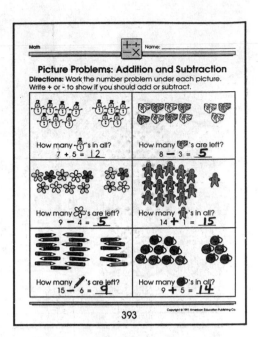

Picture Problems: Addition and Subtraction

Directions: Work the number problem under each picture. Write + or − to show if you should add or subtract.

How many ☃'s in all?
7 + 5 = 12

How many 🦇's are left?
8 − 3 = 5

How many ✿'s are left?
9 − 4 = 5

How many 🧍's in all?
14 + 1 = 15

How many ✏'s are left?
15 − 6 = 9

How many 🍪's in all?
9 + 5 = 14

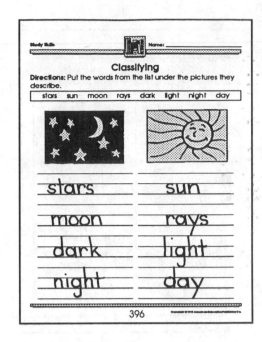

Classifying

Directions: Put the words from the list under the pictures they describe.

stars	sun	moon	rays	dark	light	night	day

stars   sun

moon   rays

dark   light

night   day

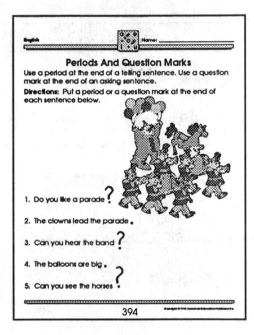

Periods And Question Marks

Use a period at the end of a telling sentence. Use a question mark at the end of an asking sentence.

Directions: Put a period or a question mark at the end of each sentence below.

1. Do you like a parade ?
2. The clowns lead the parade .
3. Can you hear the band ?
4. The balloons are big .
5. Can you see the horses ?

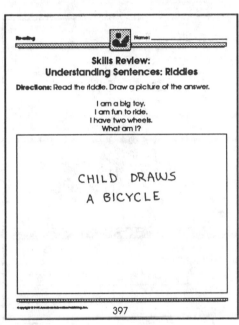

Skills Review:
Understanding Sentences: Riddles

Directions: Read the riddle. Draw a picture of the answer.

I am a big toy.
I am fun to ride.
I have two wheels.
What am I?

CHILD DRAWS
A BICYCLE

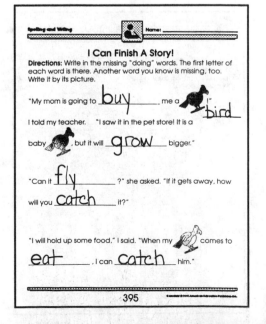

I Can Finish A Story!

Directions: Write in the missing "doing" words. The first letter of each word is there. Another word you know is missing, too. Write it by its picture.

"My mom is going to **buy** me a **bird**!"

I told my teacher. "I saw it in the pet store! It is a baby **bird**, but it will **grow** bigger."

"Can it **fly** ?" she asked. "If it gets away, how will you **catch** it?"

"I will hold up some food," I said. "When my **bird** comes to **eat**, I can **catch** him."

No-Cook Candy

Directions: Read how to make no-cook candy. Then answer the questions.

Some candy needs to be cooked on a stove. But you do not need to cook this candy. It is a good candy for kids to make. You will need a large bowl to mix the things in. You will need 5 things to make this candy.

No-Cook Candy
1/2 cup peanut butter
4 cups powdered sugar
1 cup cocoa
pinch of salt
4 tablespoons milk
A pinch of salt is just a tiny bit!
Mix everything in the bowl. Roll it into small balls.

1. What is # 3 on the list of cooking? **1 cup cocoa**

2. What is different about no-cook candy? **not cooked on a stove**

3. First mix everything in a bowl. Then **roll it into small balls**

393

396

394

397

395

513

398

Review

Directions: Work the number problem under each picture. Write + or - to show if you should add or subtract.

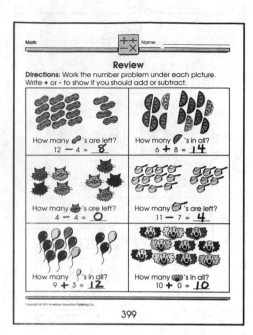

How many 🥜's are left?
12 − 4 = **8**

How many 🍊's in all?
6 **+** 8 = **14**

How many 🐱's are left?
4 − 4 = **0**

How many 🍃's are left?
11 − 7 = **4**

How many 🎈's in all?
9 **+** 3 = **12**

How many 🐑's in all?
10 **+** 0 = **10**

399

Review

Directions: Look at the picture. In the space below, write one telling sentence about the picture. Then, write one asking sentence about the picture.

A telling sentence.

answers vary

An asking sentence.

400

Review

Directions: Use the words you know to write sentences that tell about these pictures. Write a question about the last picture.

Here are some more words you could use in your sentences: **boys, girls, he, she, they.**

Like this:

Rain makes flowers grow

sentences will vary

Write a question about this picture:

401

Review

Directions: Color the item that does not belong in the group.

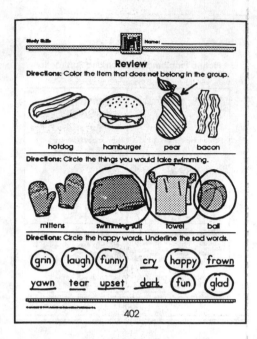

hotdog   hamburger   pear   bacon

Directions: Circle the things you would take swimming.

mittens   swimming suit   towel   ball

Directions: Circle the happy words. Underline the sad words.

grin   laugh   funny   cry   happy   frown

yawn   tear   upset   dark   fun   glad

402

A Poem

Directions: Read the poem. Write the correct words in the blanks.

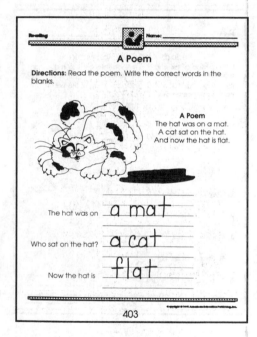

A Poem
The hat was on a mat.
A cat sat on the hat.
And now the hat is flat.

The hat was on   **a mat**

Who sat on the hat?   **a cat**

Now the hat is   **flat**

403

See The Barnyards

Directions: Look at the 2 pictures of the barnyard. Find 5 things that are different in the 2 pictures. Color only the things that are different.

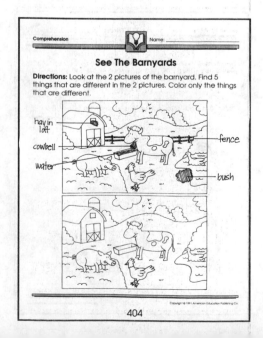

hay in loft
cowbell
water
fence
bush

404

514

Money: Penny, Nickel, Dime

A penny is worth one cent. It is written 1¢ or $.01. A nickel is worth five cents. It is written 5¢ or $.05. A dime is worth ten cents. It is written 10¢ or $.10.

Directions: Add the coins pictured and write the total amounts in the blanks.

Example:

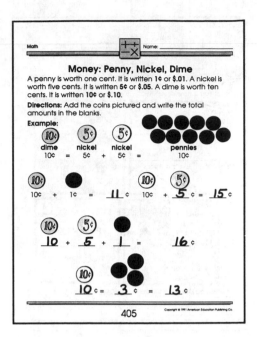

10¢ dime   5¢ nickel   5¢ nickel   pennies

10¢ = 5¢ = 5¢ =

10¢ + 1¢ = __11__ ¢   10¢ + __5__¢ = __15__ ¢

__10__ + __5__ + __1__ = __16__ ¢

__10__¢ = __3__ ¢ = __13__ ¢

405

Predicting Outcome

Directions: Finish the story by drawing a picture in the last box.

Dan likes to paint.   He likes to help his dad.

1   2   3   4

picture varies

He is tired when he's finished.

408

Word Order

Word order is the logical order of words in a sentence.

Directions: Put the words in each sentence in order. Write the sentence on the lines.

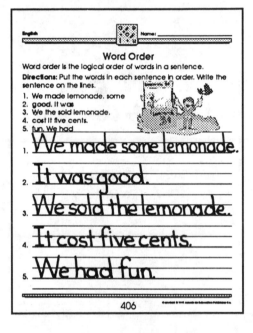

1. We made lemonade. some
2. good. It was
3. We the sold lemonade.
4. cost It five cents.
5. fun. We had

1. We made some lemonade.

2. It was good.

3. We sold the lemonade.

4. It cost five cents.

5. We had fun.

406

Draw A Picture

Directions: Read the sentences. Draw the picture the sentences tell about.

A boy and a girl play ball.   The ball is red.
The girl has a hat on.   There is a big, green tree.
See the yellow sun!   The dog can run.

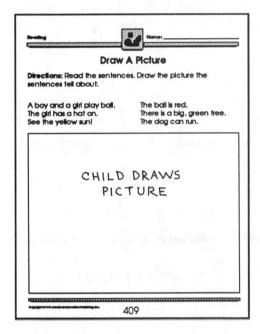

CHILD DRAWS PICTURE

409

I Can Write "People" Words!

Directions: 1. Follow the lines to write the words. 2. Then write the words again by yourself. 3. Read the words to someone.

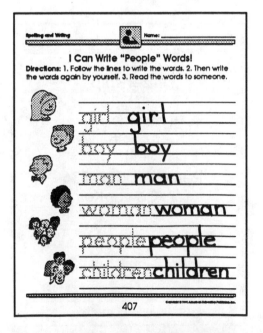

girl
boy
man
woman
people
children

407

Hey Diddle Diddle

Directions: Read "Hey Diddle Diddle." Then answer the questions.

Hey diddle diddle
The cat and the fiddle
The cow jumped over the moon.
The little dog laughed
To see such sport
And the dish ran away with the spoon!

1. Who jumped over the moon?
cow

2. Who laughed?
dog

3. Who ran away?
dish   and   spoon

410

515

Time: Hour, Half-Hour
Directions: Tell what time it is on the clocks.

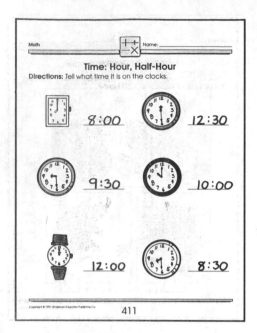

8:00

12:30

9:30

10:00

12:00

8:30

411

Predicting Outcome
Directions: Read the story. Fill in the first and last box. How do you think the story will end?

Susan is new at school.

Hello, I'm Amy.

1

picture varies

2

3

4

picture varies

Do you like to jump rope?

414

Word Order
Directions: Look at the picture. Put the words in the correct order. Write the sentences on the lines below.

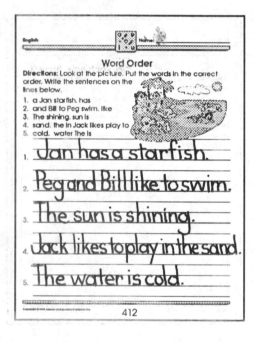

1. a Jan starfish. has
2. and Bill to Peg swim. like
3. The shining. sun is
4. sand. the in Jack likes play to
5. cold. water The is

1. Jan has a starfish.

2. Peg and Bill like to swim.

3. The sun is shining.

4. Jack likes to play in the sand.

5. The water is cold.

412

Citizenship

Labor Day

Refer to page **536** for Answer Key

415

I Can Finish Sentences!
Directions: Find the sentence that goes with each picture. Then write in the word that finishes the sentence.

| people | man | girl | children | boy | woman |

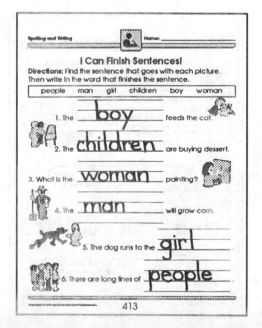

1. The **boy** feeds the cat.

2. The **children** are buying dessert.

3. What is the **woman** painting?

4. The **man** will grow corn.

5. The dog runs to the **girl**.

6. There are long lines of **people**.

413

Citizenship

Labor Day Activity

Refer to page **536** for Answer Key

416

Name:

Fill In The Blanks

Directions: Look at the picture. Write the words from the word box to finish the sentences.

frog	log	bird	fish	ducks

The turtle is on a _log_

The _frog_ can jump.

The boy wants a _fish_

A _bird_ is in the tree.

I see three _ducks_

419

Name:

Hey Diddle Diddle, Again!

Directions: Re-read the story of "Hey Diddle Diddle." Then put the pictures of the story in 1-2-3-4 order.

420

Name:

Shapes: Square, Circle, Rectangle, Triangle
Directions: Use the code to color the shapes.

Squares - Orange
Circles - Red
Rectangles - Blue
Triangles - Green

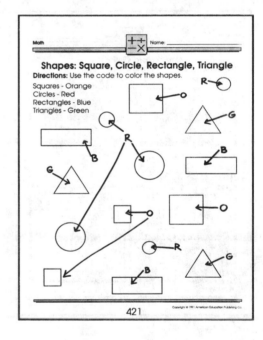

421

Name:

Word Order Can Change Meaning
If you change the order of the words in a sentence, you can change the meaning of the sentence.

Directions: Read the sentences. Draw a purple circle around the sentence that describes the picture.
Example:

The fox jumped over the dogs.
The dogs jumped over the fox.

1. The cat watched the bird.
The bird watched the cat.

2. The girl looked at the boy.
The boy looked at the girl.

3. The turtle ran past the rabbit.
The rabbit ran past the turtle.

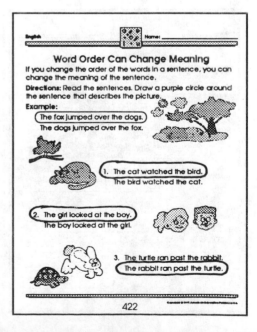

422

Name: _____

I Can Play A Word Game!

Directions: Find each of the "people" words. Put circles around them, like the circle around "baby."

people	boy	woman	girl	children	man

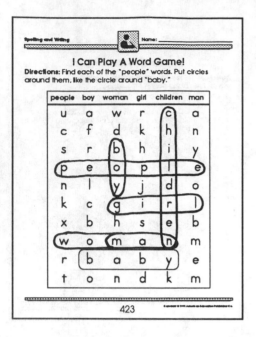

```
u  a  w  r  c  a
c  f  d  k  h  n
s  r  b  h  i  y
p  e  o  p  l  e
l  y  j  i  d  o
k  g  i  r  l
x  b  h  s  e  b
w  o  m  a  n  m
r  b  a  b  y  e
t  o  n  d  k  m
```

423

Name: _____

Predicting Outcome

Directions: Read the story. Fill in the last box.

That's my ball!   I got it first.

| 1 | 2 |
| 3 | 4 picture varies |

It's mine!

424

Name: _____

A Short Story

Directions: Read the story. Write the word from the story that completes each sentence.

Ben and Sue have a bug.
It is red with black spots.
They call it Spot.
Spot likes to eat green
leaves and grass.
The children keep him in a box.

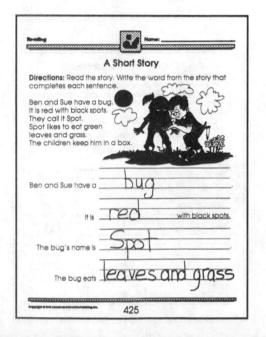

Ben and Sue have a **bug**

It is **red** with black spots.

The bug's name is **Spot**

The bug eats **leaves and grass**

425

Name: _____

Bluebird

Directions: Read about the bluebird. Look at the word list. Choose the words that tell what blue things the bluebird sees.

Bluebird, bluebird
Up in the tree
How many blue things
Do you see?

book	flowers
girl	grass
hat	sky
shoes	tree

Here are the blue things
the bluebird sees:

1. **flowers**
2. **sky**   3. **hat**
4. **book**   5. **shoes**

426

Name: _____

Place Value: Tens, Ones And One Hundred

The place value of each digit, or numeral, is shown by where it is in the number. For example, in the number **123**, **1** has the place value of **hundreds**, **2** is **tens**, and **3** is **ones**.

Directions: Count the groups of crayons and add.

Example:

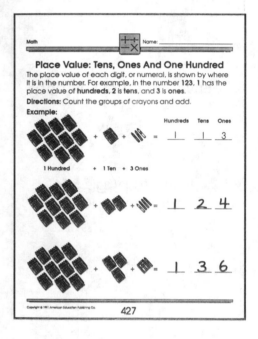

		Hundreds	Tens	Ones
	=	1	1	3

1 Hundred   + 1 Ten   + 3 Ones

| = | 1 | 2 | 4 |

| = | 1 | 3 | 6 |

427

Name: _____

I Can Write Sentences

A story has more than one sentence.

Directions: Use the words from the pictures to write a story.

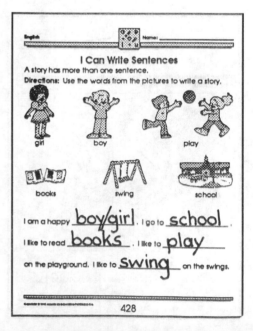

girl   boy   play

books   swing   school

I am a happy **boy/girl**. I go to **school**.

I like to read **books**. I like to **play**

on the playground. I like to **swing** on the swings.

428

518

I Know Other Words For People!

Sometimes we use other words to mean people: For boy or man, we can use "he." For girl or woman, we can use "she." For two or more people, we can use "they."

Directions: Write "he," "she," or "they" in these sentences.

Like this:

The boy likes cookies. **He** likes cookies.

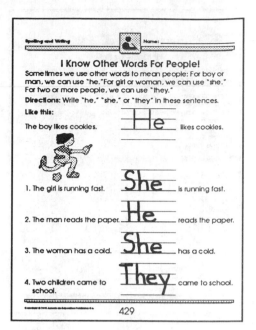

1. The girl is running fast. **She** is running fast.

2. The man reads the paper. **He** reads the paper.

3. The woman has a cold. **She** has a cold.

4. Two children came to school. **They** came to school.

429

Making Inferences

Dave likes baseball. He likes to win. He hits the ball hard. Dave's team does not win.

Directions: Circle the right answers.

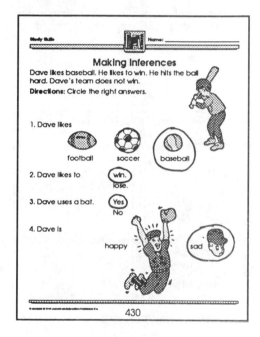

1. Dave likes

football   soccer   (baseball)

2. Dave likes to   (win.)   lose.

3. Dave uses a bat.   (Yes)   No

4. Dave is   happy   (sad)

430

A Rainy Day Story

Directions: Read the story. Write the words from the story in the blanks to finish the sentences.

Jane and Bill like to play in the rain. They take off their shoes and socks. They splash in the puddles. It feels cold! It is fun to splash!

Jane and Bill like to **play in the rain**

They take off their **shoes and socks**

They splash in **puddles**

Do you like to splash in puddles?   **ANSWER VARIES**   Yes   No

431

Inside And Outside

Directions: 1) Read about inside animals and outside animals. 2) Look at the pictures. 3) Circle the animals that can live inside. 4) Write the names of the ones that belong outside.

Some animals belong inside. Some animals belong outside. Wild animals belong outside. Large animals belong outside. Small, tame animals can live inside.

Animals that belong outside:

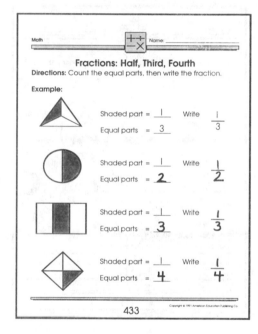

1. **tiger**
2. **bird**
3. **horse**
4. **cow**

432

Fractions: Half, Third, Fourth

Directions: Count the equal parts, then write the fraction.

Example:

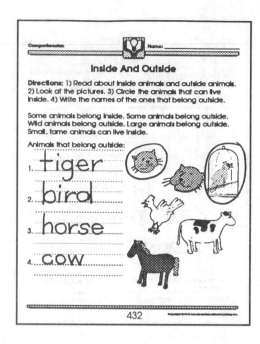

Shaded part = **1**   Write $\frac{1}{3}$
Equal parts = **3**

Shaded part = **1**   Write $\frac{1}{2}$
Equal parts = **2**

Shaded part = **1**   Write $\frac{1}{3}$
Equal parts = **3**

Shaded part = **1**   Write $\frac{1}{4}$
Equal parts = **4**

433

I Can Write Sentences

Directions: Draw a picture of yourself in the box marked Me. Then write three sentences about yourself on the lines.

Me

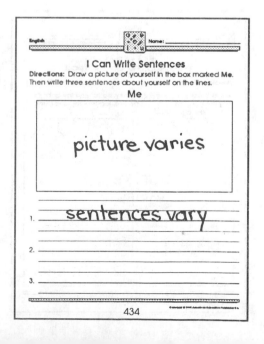

picture varies

1. sentences vary

2. _____

3. _____

434

I Can Spell By Myself!

Directions: 1. Write a "people" word in each sentence to tell who is doing something. The first letter is there. Can you spell the rest of the word by yourself? 2. Then, on your own paper, draw a picture to show what is happening.

1. The **boy** was last in line at the toy store.

2. The **children** took a walk in the woods.

3. The **girl** had to help her father.

4. The **woman** had a surprise for the children.

5. Some **people** like to eat outside.

6. Something came out of the box when the **man** opened it.

435

All Kinds Of Balls

Directions: Read about the ways we can play with balls. Then answer the questions.

Some balls are soft. A beach ball is soft. Some balls are hard. We play baseball with a hard ball. Basketballs bounce. Can you throw a basketball through a hoop? First bounce it 3 times. Then hold the basketball high. Now, throw it toward the hoop. Did you make a basket?

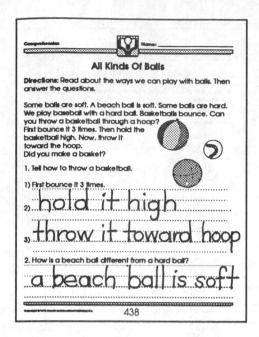

1. Tell how to throw a basketball.

1) First bounce it 3 times.

2) **hold it high**

3) **throw it toward hoop**

2. How is a beach ball different from a hard ball?

a beach ball is soft

438

Making Inferences

Lynn looks at the stars. She sings a song about them. She makes a wish on them. The stars are there. The stars help Lynn sleep.

Directions: Answer the questions about Lynn.

1. Lynn likes the:

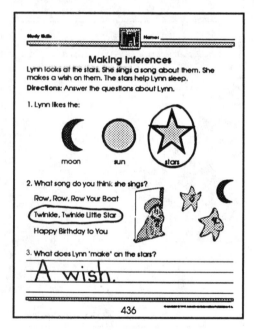

moon   sun   stars

2. What song do you think she sings?

Row, Row, Row Your Boat

(Twinkle, Twinkle Little Star)

Happy Birthday to You

3. What does Lynn 'make' on the stars?

A wish.

436

Review

Directions: Follow the instructions.
1. How much money?

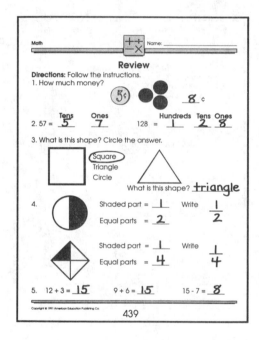

8 ¢

2. 57 = Tens **5** Ones **7**   128 = Hundreds **1** Tens **2** Ones **8**

3. What is this shape? Circle the answer.

(Square)
Triangle
Circle

What is this shape? **triangle**

4. Shaded part = **1**   Equal parts = **2**   Write **1/2**

Shaded part = **1**   Equal parts = **4**   Write **1/4**

5. 12 + 3 = **15**   9 + 6 = **15**   15 - 7 = **8**

439

Skills Review:
Understanding What Is Read

Directions: Read the story. Draw a picture about the story.

Dee and Duke are at the zoo. They like to feed the animals. They like the giraffe. The giraffe eats leaves. Dee and Duke give leaves to the giraffe.

PICTURE
VARIES

437

Review

Directions: Put the words in the right order to make a sentence. The sentences will tell a story.

1. a gerbil. has Ann
2. is The Mike. named gerbil
3. likes eat. Mike to
4. play. to Mike likes
5. happy a is gerbil. Mike

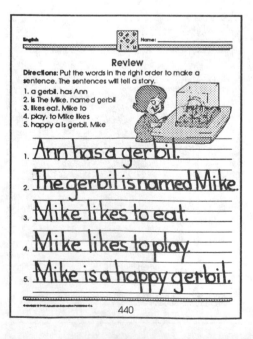

1. **Ann has a gerbil.**

2. **The gerbil is named Mike.**

3. **Mike likes to eat.**

4. **Mike likes to play.**

5. **Mike is a happy gerbil.**

440

520

Look What I Can Write!

Here are all the words you know now - **Pets:** dog, fish, cat, bird. **Colors:** blue, yellow, red, green, black, brown. **Food:** cake, apple, milk, egg, ice cream, cookie. **"Doing" Words:** ride, sit, stop, color, make, eat, run, grow, play, fly, see, catch, jump, buy. **Weather:** rain, snow, cold, hot, wet, water. **Opposites:** new, old, first, last, found, light, dark. **People:** girl, boy, man, woman, people, children.

Directions: 1. Write three telling sentences below. Use three or more of these words in each one. Remember to start with a capital letter and end with a period. 2. Write one question. Remember to end with a question mark. 3. Read your sentences to someone.

1. My black cat likes milk.

2. sentences will vary

3. _____

A question:
_____
_____
_____
_____

441

Review

Directions: Read each story. Follow the instructions.

Complete this story.
1. Ed's dog runs away.
2. Ed chases it.
3. The dog runs into a store.

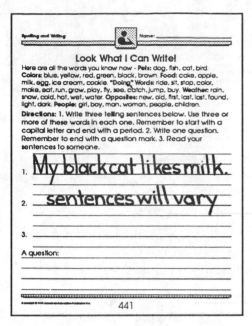

4. answer
   varies

Liz plays games with her little sister. Sometimes she hides from her. Her sister calls her name over and over. Liz does not answer. Liz thinks it is funny.

1. Is Liz being nice or mean to her sister?   mean
2. Do you think her sister likes Liz to hide?   Yes   (No)
3. What would you do if you were Liz's sister?

answer varies

442

TEACHING SUGGESTIONS

Citizens Now

Purposes:
To recognize that children are citizens
To identify the United States on a map

Materials:
classroom map, crayons, paste, large sheet(s) of paper

Prework:
Locate the United States on the Classroom map. Then read page 23 together. Point out that most people become citizens of the United States just by being born in this country. If the situation warrants, you may want to discuss circumstances in which children may not be United States citizens.

Instructions:
On chart paper draw a large outline shape of the United States. Make a collage of the children's faces on the map outline and title it **Citizens Now**. Then make a comparison/contrast chart on the board. Invite children to tell how United States citizens are the same and how they are different. Lead children to conclude that although American citizens are all different, they all live and work together in the same country. You may wish to organize the collage to allow space for the Art and Family Extension activities.

Extensions:

- Reading: Place *People* by Peter Spier on the reading table. Challenge partners to talk about how the people in the book are alike and how they are different. When children are finished sharing the book, ask them what makes the United States different from other countries.

- Writing: Ask children to finish this sentence: I am proud to be a United States citizen because_____ . Compile the sentences on a Proud Citizens chart.

- Art: Encourage children to work cooperatively to cut out pictures of all kinds of people from old magazines. Make a new collage or add the pictures to the **Citizens Now** collage.

- Family: Invite children to bring in photographs of their families or family members. Add the photos to the classroom **Citizens Now** collage.

AMERICA 2000 Lesson 2

Purpose: To recognize that reading is important

Materials: crayons, familiar books

Prework: Read and discuss page 51 together. Be aware of children's backgrounds when presenting the idea that not all adults can read. Ask children to predict what they can do now as citizens to make AMERICA 2000 work.

Instructions: Display several familiar books. Discuss the titles and cover designs. Then read the directions on page 52. Be sure children understand that they will be drawing a cover for a book that a first grader would like to read. Ask children to cut out the book jackets. Then invite them to draw pictures of their older selves reading to first graders. Place the book jackets and the drawings on a bulletin board titled "Make AMERICA 2000 Come True."

Extensions:
- Reading: Read and discuss *My Mom Can't Read* by Muriel Stanek. In this book, first grader Tina discovers that her mother can't read and asks her teacher for help, so that she and her mother can learn to read together.

- Writing: Describe a problem a person who could not read might have.

- Math: Help children to calculate their ages in the year 2000.

- Family: Invite children to ask family members about their favorite books when they were in first grade. Compile a list and compare it with the books children enjoy today. Ask children to infer why some stories never grow old.

TEACHING SUGGESTIONS

The United States Flag Lesson 3

Purposes:
To recognize that the United States flag is a symbol of our country and its people
To recall places where the flag is displayed
To recognize that Sally Ride studied hard to become the first American woman astronaut

Materials:
United States flag, a piece of cloth approximately the same size as the flag, crayons

Prework:
Display the United States flag. Then show children a piece of cloth approximately the same size as the flag. Invite children to feel both the flag and the cloth. Then ask them to tell how the flag and the cloth are alike and how they are different. Lead them to conclude that the United States flag is more than just a piece of cloth because it stands for our country and its people.

Instructions:
After children have colored and cut out the flag patch on page 80, pin the patches to their left shoulder sleeves. Invite children to tell people who ask about the patch what the flag stands for.

Extensions:
- Reading: Read and discuss *Sally Ride, Astronaut: An American First* by June Behrens. Emphasize the importance of education in Sally's life by focusing on pages 12–17.

- Speaking: Remind children that the United States flag always flies over American schools. Invite small groups to discuss ways working hard in school can help them to be good **Citizens** . Instruct each group to appoint a spokesperson to share the group's responses with the class.

- Math: Invite children to work with a partner to count the stars and stripes on the United States flag.

- Family: Encourage children to ask family members to think of as many nicknames as they can for the United States flag (Old Glory, The Red, White, and Blue, The Stars and Stripes). Ask them to share their families' responses with the class.

The Declaration of Independence

Purposes: To recognize that Thomas Jefferson wrote the Declaration of Independence
To realize that the Declaration of Independence says that people have the right to be free

Materials: United States map

Prework: Point out the colonies on a United States map. Explain that this was the size of the country when the people in America decided they no longer wanted to follow England's rules. Point out that American leaders wanted a paper to be written that told why the people wanted to be free. Invite children to read page 107 to find out who wrote this important paper.

Instructions: Invite children to work with a partner to complete page 108. Circulate and give spelling assistance when necessary. Allow time for pairs to read their documents to the class.

Extensions:
- Reading: Read and discuss *A Picture Book of Thomas Jefferson* by David Adler. Ask children how Thomas Jefferson might have felt after he finished writing the Declaration of Independence.

- Speaking: Invite children to pretend they are the American leaders who approved the Declaration of Independence. Challenge them to write some comments the men may have written on Jefferson's rough draft of the Declaration. Ask: Would they mark for capital letters and periods? What about spelling? Would they talk about Jefferson's ideas?

- Physical Education: After moving outdoors or to a large open area, encourage children to demonstrate motions that make them feel free (running, arms rotating, skipping, leaping).

- Family: Encourage children to discuss with their families other kinds of official papers or documents such as licenses and diplomas. Share responses with the class and list them on the board.

TEACHING SUGGESTIONS

The White House

Purpose: To recognize that the White House is where the President of the United States and his family live

Materials: map of the United States, crayons

Prework: Point out Washington D.C. on the map of the United States. Tell children that this is the city where a famous house called the White House is located. Ask children to read page 135 to find out who lives in the White House.

Instructions: Encourage children to tell about times when they have visited or seen pictures of the White House. Record their descriptions on a semantic map around the words *White House*. Talk about what the President and his family might do in their home. After children complete the living room designs, challenge groups to role play situations that might happen in the living room of the White House.

Extensions:
- Reading: Read *Arthur Meets the President* by Marc Brown. Encourage children to talk about how they would feel if they had to give a speech for the President of the United States.

- Writing: Challenge groups to use reference books and books from the library to find out interesting facts about the White House. Record the facts on a poster titled: The President's House.

- Art: Invite children to use common art material and empty boxes to design a house for the President and his family. Encourage them to name their houses.

- Family: Encourage children to discuss this question with their families: If the President of the United States and his family did not live in the White House, where else might they live? Ask them to share their responses.

Christopher Columbus

Purpose: To recognize that Columbus commanded three ships that reached a land unknown to Europeans

Materials: classroom map, a globe
For each child: a toothpick, a piece of flat, recycled plastic foam from the grocery store, scissors
For small groups: a shallow pan, water

Prework: Display pictures of Christopher Columbus. Tell children that Columbus made an ocean voyage in 1492 that opened up a whole new area of the world. Then use the classroom map to point out important places connected with Columbus's voyage: Europe, Spain, the Bahamas, North, South, and Central America.

Instructions: Use a globe to show why Columbus believed he could sail west from Spain to get to the East. Ask children to conclude why he did not reach India, as he had planned. Circulate and help children construct their boats. You may want groups of three to "sail" their boats in the same container of water. Encourage children to experiment with moving the sail to change the direction of the ship.

Extensions:
- Reading: Read and discuss *Christopher Columbus: A Great Explorer* by Carol Greene. Encourage partners to sit together and look at the famous artworks included in this book.

- Speaking: Explain that Columbus's crew members were afraid and wanted to return to Spain. Divide the class into Columbuses and sailors. Have the sailors make up excuses to turn around and go home. Allow the Columbuses to respond to the excuses, so the sailors will push on to try to complete the voyage successfully.

- Music: Play music with a nautical theme, such as "Sailing" by Christopher Cross or "Columbus Sailed with Three Ships" by Margaret Dugard. As in sports stadiums, invite children to do the "wave" as the music plays.

- Family: Invite children to take their sailing ships home. Encourage them to tell their families about Columbus's ships and his voyage across the ocean.

TEACHING SUGGESTIONS

The Statue of Liberty

Purpose: To recognize that the Statue of Liberty was a symbol of hope and freedom for immigrants

Prework: Draw attention to the illustration on page 191. Tell children they will be learning why the statue is important to American citizens.

Instructions: After children complete the conversation balloons, invite them to share them with the class. Compile the pages into a book titled: *We Want to be Citizens!*

Extensions:

- Reading: Encourage partners to read and discuss *The Long Way to a New Land* by Joan Sandin. After reading, ask partners to retell the story of the journey of the Swedish family to America during the famine of 1868.

- Writing: Ask children to pretend they are living in another country but would like to go to the United States to live. Encourage groups to make lists of questions they would like to know about the United States before leaving their own country. Invite children to share the questions and answer as many as possible.

- Language Arts: Challenge groups to role play this situation: A new student from another country has just come into the classroom. What will you do to make this new person feel welcome?

- Family: Encourage children to ask their family members what nationalities their ancestors were. When they share the responses with the class, tally the nationalities on the board. Challenge children to count the number of different countries that are represented.

The Liberty Bell

Purpose: To identify the Liberty Bell To recognize that the Liberty Bell is a symbol of our country

Materials: United States map, newspapers

Prework: Ask children to look at the picture of the Liberty Bell on page 219. Explain that like the United States flag, the Liberty Bell is a symbol of our country. Then locate Philadelphia, Pennsylvania, on a map of the United States. Tell children that this is the city where the Liberty Bell is displayed. Invite children who have visited Philadelphia to share their experiences.

Instructions: Display several simple newspaper headlines. Point out that the important words in the headlines begin with capital letters. Then have children brainstorm for possible headlines. Examples: Bell Rings for New Country, Bell Rings for Freedom. Write children's responses on the board. Use the headlines as a handwriting lesson by asking each child to carefully copy one onto page 220.

Extensions:
- Reading: For a glimpse of colonial life, read and discuss *Yankee Doodle* by Steven Kellogg. You may wish to use one of the detailed illustrations as a story starter.

- Speaking: Explain that in the 1700s ringing bells was a way people knew there was news. Point out that a town crier would often walk the streets ringing a bell and calling out the news. Invite children to take turns being the town crier by walking around the room, ringing a bell, and announcing school news.

- Art: Ask partners to make clay models of the Liberty Bell. Invite each pair to talk about what they have learned about the Liberty Bell as they work. Display the bells beneath a sign that says "Let Freedom Ring."

- Family: Challenge children to ask family members two questions about the Liberty Bell. Remind them that they should be able to answer the questions if the family member has difficulty.

TEACHING SUGGESTIONS

The Bald Eagle

Purpose: To recognize that the bald eagle is a symbol of our country

Materials: crayons, scissors, string, paper clips or clothespins

Prework: Ask children to look at the picture of the bald eagle on page 247. Ask them to discuss where they have seen pictures of the bald eagle (on a dollar, a quarter, mailboxes, clothing, sports equipment, courthouse, books, mail trucks). Then read and discuss page 247 before asking children to draw pictures.

Instructions: Read the directions on page 248 together. Invite children to fill in the blank with their favorite type of team. Assist them with spelling. When children are finished with the designs, ask them to cut out the T-shirts. Then, stretch a length of string across a corner of the room. Hang the T-shirts from the string with clothespins or paper clips.

Extensions:
- Reading: Read and discuss the poem "I Watched an Eagle Soar" from *Dancing Teepees* by Virginia Driving Hawk Sneve. You may wish to share other poems in this book which were passed down by word of mouth from various Native American tribes.

- Writing: Tell children that baby eagles are called eaglets. Explain that eaglets are hatched with their eyes open and are covered with a grayish-white fuzz. Point out that both parents guard the nest and bring food to the eaglets until they can fly well enough to take care of themselves. Then ask children to visualize an eagle's nest in the top of a tall tree. Tell them that two eaglets have just been born, and it is now lunch time for the babies. Invite children to draw a picture of the scene you described. After sharing their pictures, challenge children to write stories about the drawings. Display their work.

- Science: Challenge children to find out more interesting facts about our national bird by using reference books and library books, such as *Bald Eagles* by Emilie U. Lepthien. Compile the facts into a book titled: *Bald Facts.*

- Family: Ask family members to list as many places as they can where they have seen pictures of the bald eagle.

The Fourth of July

Purpose: To recognize that the Fourth of July is the birthday of the United States

Materials: crayons, United States flag

Prework: Discuss ways children celebrate their birthdays. Ask children to look at the picture on page 275 to find out how citizens celebrate America's birthday.

Instructions: When the mazes are complete, play patriotic music and invite children to take turns holding the United States flag in a parade around the room.

Extensions:
- Reading: Read the poem "The Fourth" by Shel Silverstein in *Where the Sidewalk Ends.* Challenge children to substitute other onomatopoeic words for the poet's.

- Listening: Play traditional patriotic songs, such as "America," "America the Beautiful," and the "Star-Spangled Banner" as well as more contemporary ones, such as "Proud to Be An American" and "Voices That Care." Encourage children to describe how the songs make them feel.

- Art: Ask: What words would you put on a birthday card for the United States? Challenge children to design birthday cards for our country that can be sent to family members on the next Fourth of July or other national holiday.

- Family: Encourage children to ask family members to name a person or group they think most Americans would enjoy listening to at a Fourth of July celebration. Share their responses with the class.

TEACHING SUGGESTIONS

The Bill of Rights

Purpose: To recognize that the Bill of Rights protects the rights of Americans

Prework: Say: You have the right to ask questions in school. Ask children to speculate about the meaning of the word *right* in your sentence. Then read and discuss page 303 together. Ask children to point out the ways the people in the picture are exercising the rights that are protected by the Bill of Rights.

Instructions: Have children write the name of their school on the line. Brainstorm for rights they have at school, such as the right to check out library books, the right to be treated equally, the right to use the playground at certain times. List the responses on the board, and invite children to copy two of them on page 304. Then ask them to name some rights they do not have (running in the halls, talking loudly in the library, shouting out in class, damaging school property).

Extensions:
- Reading: Read a version of the traditional fable, "The Boy Who Cried Wolf," such as *Anno's Aesop: A Book of Fables by Aesop and Mr. Fox.* Then discuss what might happen if citizens did not use their right to freedom of speech wisely.

- Listening: Invite an immigrant from another country to talk about differences between rights and freedoms in the United States and the country from which the person came. Allow time for questions.

- Art: Invite children to draw pictures of what might happen if citizens did not have each of the rights described on page 303 (worship house would be locked, only one newspaer would be at the newsstand, protesters would be arrested).

- Family: Ask children to discuss this statement with their families: You should have the right to do what you want as long as you don't hurt anyone. Invite them to share their discussions.

Mary McLeod Bethune

Lesson 12

Purpose: To recognize that Mary McLeod Bethune worked for equal rights

Prework: Direct children's attention to the drawing of Mary McLeod Bethune on page 331. Tell chidren that when Mary was growing up, black Americans did not always have the right to go to the same schools as white children. Explain that Mary worked very hard to change this because she believed everyone should be treated equally. Then ask children to read page 331 along with you to find out one way she helped. Discuss their responses.

Instructions: Challenge children to work in small groups to make up several verses of the song. Encourage groups to sing their verses to the class. Invite the class to join in repeated singings.

Extensions:
- Reading: Read and discuss *This is the Way We Go to School* by Edith Baer. Encourage children to repeat the rhyming couplets in unison as they look at the many different school scenes both in the United States and in other countries.

- Speaking: Tell children that in Mary McLeod Bethune's will, she left a message: She said that children must never stop wanting to build a better world. Ask small groups to discuss what she meant by this. Discuss their responses.

- Language Arts: Ask children to role play what would happen in Mary's classroom if a child who wasn't black came in and wanted to stay.

- Family: Invite children to ask family members if they recall a favorite teacher and why. Share their answers with the class. Point out that fairness and treating all students equally are usually qualities students remember and like in a teacher.

TEACHING SUGGESTIONS

Pioneer Children Lesson 13

Purpose: To recognize that children were participants in the settling of the United States

Materials: crayons

Prework: Encourage children to discuss the chores they do to help their families. Tell children they will be reading page 359 together to find out how pioneer children helped their families. Discuss the similarities and differences between family chores then and now.

Instructions: When children have finished their drawings, encourage them to pantomime the job they chose while others in the group try to guess what they are doing. Then display the drawings on a bulletin board titled: Children Helped to Settle Our Country

Extensions:
- Reading: Read and discuss *Aurora Means Dawn* by Scott Russell Sanders. Then as you reread the book, ask children to visualize what it would be like to be one of the Sheldon children, as they traveled from their home in Connecticut to an unsettled area of Ohio. Ask children to describe what it would be like to be the first family to start a new community.

- Speaking: Explain that often at night pioneers would sit around a huge campfire to tell and listen to stories. Point out that often the stories were scary ghost tales. Challenge small groups to tell round robin ghost stories around a "campfire." You may wish to darken the room first.

- Science: Invite partners to use reference books and library books to find out about one of the animals the pioneers may have encountered (buffaloes, prairie dogs, rattlesnakes, wolves, coyotes, jack rabbits). Encourage pairs to report their findings orally to the class.

- Family: Tell children that most pioneers didn't carry a United States flag with them. Explain that for Fourth of July celebrations, they had to make one out of materials they had in the wagon, such as a blue shirt, a red sock, or a white scarf. Challenge children to look through their homes to find things they would use to make a flag. Encourage them to share their findings with the class.

Samantha Smith

Lesson 14

Purposes: To recognize how important one person's efforts can be
To recognize that Samantha Smith made others think about working together for peace

Materials: world map, glass bottles

Prework: Tell children that you will be reading about a girl who traveled from her home in Maine all the way to the country that used to be called Soviet Union to make people think about peace. Point out Maine and the former Soviet Union on a world map.

Instructions: Read page 388 together. Then locate the Black Sea on the world map. Discuss what the campers may have expected to happen to their messages. After children share the messages they wrote on page 388, remove the pages and fold them into small squares. Put the squares in glass bottles. Invite children from other classes or parents at open house to pull a message from one of the bottles. Finally, discuss how this activity might have helped others to think of world peace.

Extensions:
- Reading: Encourage partners to read and discuss *Deborah Sampson Goes to War* by Bryna Stevens to find out about another young woman who cared about her country and got involved.

- Writing: Explain that when Samantha Smith wrote to the Soviet leader, she used a very simple address. Write the address on the board: Mr. Yuri Andropov/The Kremlin/Moscow, U.S.S.R. Challenge children to give the address that a child in the Soviet Union might use to mail a letter to our country's leader (President _____ /The White House/ Washington, D.C./U.S.A.).

- Language Arts: Present several simple Russian words to the class, and invite children to use them throughout the day. Examples: *da* = yes, *n'eyt* = no, *spa-SEE-ba* = thank you

- Family: Encourage children to ask their families how they would feel if a leader of a foreign country asked them to visit his or her country.

Labor Day

Purpose: To recognize that Labor Day is an American holiday that honors working people

Materials: crayons

Prework: Ask children to discuss the working people in their school. Tell children that there is a holiday that honors these school workers as well as all working people in the United States. Ask them to read page 415 to find out about this holiday.

Instructions: Read the directions on page 416. Be sure children understand that each drawing should have different types of workers. After the drawings are complete, encourage children to share them with the class. Point out that each of the jobs represented in the drawings could be held by either a male or female. Invite children to paste their drawings on empty boxes. Arrange the boxes in a community display.

Extensions:

- Reading: Encourage children to look at *All About Things People Do* by Melanie and Chris Rice. Ask children to make up riddles about some of the jobs included in the book. Compile the riddles into a book for the reading table.

- Speaking: Remind children that their work is school. Challenge groups to discuss what their jobs include.

- Art: Invite children to draw a pictures of themselves in the future doing the jobs they want to do when they grow up.

- Family: Invite family members to send to school with their child an object that relates to their job such as a hat or a tool. Challenge children to create a display of the workers' things.

TEACHING SUGGESTIONS

PURPOSE:
To understand the meaning of the term environment
To identify things that comprise the local environment

PREWORK:
Take a walk and ask children to point out everything around them. Lead them to discover that some of the things were made by people and others by nature. Ask them to tell if each of the things named is living or nonliving.

INSTRUCTIONS:
Read the directions on page 26 together. Then help children name each picture. After children complete the page independently, discuss the pictures they drew.

EXTENSIONS:
Challenge children to classify the items on the chart as Living and Nonliving, Made by People and Made by Nature.

Read and discuss *The Little House* by Virginia Lee Burton. (Houghton Mifflin, 1978). This 1943 Caldecott winner shows environmental changes that take place around a little house over a long period of time.

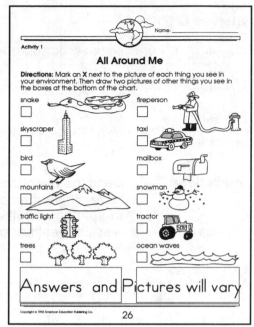

Activity 1

Name: _____

All Around Me

Directions: Mark an **X** next to the picture of each thing you see in your environment. Then draw two pictures of other things you see in the boxes at the bottom of the chart.

snake
fireperson
skyscraper
taxi
bird
mailbox
mountains
snowman
traffic light
tractor
trees
ocean waves

Answers and Pictures will vary

26

ANSWER KEY   Activity 1

TEACHING SUGGESTIONS

PURPOSE:
To recognize that all living things need clean water
To predict how polluted water can harm living things

MATERIALS:
cups, bean seeds, soil, detergent, cooking oil

PREWORK:
Ask children to name ways they use water in their homes. Discuss how they would feel if they couldn't use the water in their homes because it was dirty and unsafe.

INSTRUCTIONS:
Safety: While children are planting, observe them closely. Caution them to place the seeds only in the cups. Have them wipe up spilled water. Ask children to observe the plants daily and water them when necessary. After a period of growing time, have them return to the drawings on page 54. Discuss whether the predictions were correct.

EXTENSIONS:
Place a large processed feather in oil, and have children observe what happens. Encourage them to predict how oil spills hurt birds that live around water.

Invite children to use waterpaints to create pictures of water scenes showing clean water. Compile paintings in a book titled: "Save Our Water".

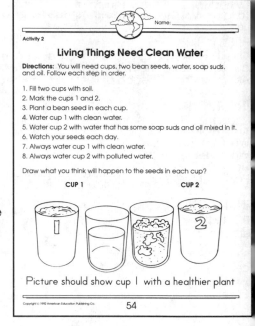

ANSWER KEY   Activity 2

PURPOSE:
To recognize that air pollution is harmful to living things
To identify ways people can help make air clean

MATERIALS:
petroleum jelly

PREWORK:
Spread a thin film of petroleum jelly on a piece of paper. Attach the paper to the outside window sill. After a few days, have children observe the paper. Encourage them to infer where the dirt came from.

INSTRUCTIONS:
Invite children to read the words in the bus. Do the first example together.

Lead children to conclude that one bus carrying 30 people gives off less pollution than 30 cars each carrying one person. You may want to mention car pooling as another way to stop air pollution.

EXTENSIONS:
Challenge children to use clay, blocks, paper and other readily available items to devise models of nonpolluting vehicles that people of the future may use. Display the inventions under the sign: "2092—No More Air Pollution!"

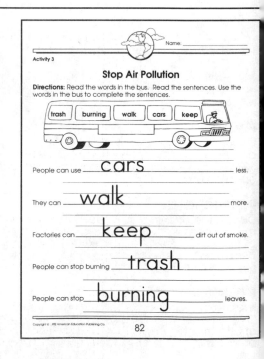

ANSWER KEY   Activity 3

PURPOSE:
To identify ways of keeping the school environment clean. To formulate questions

PREWORK:
Ask children to look around the room, and point out examples of pollution (trash). As each item is named, ask that child to place it in the trash can. Review sentence structure by helping children to write questions about the trash they found in the room.

EXAMPLES:
Who put the paper on the floor?
Where is the other half of the pencil?
How did the crayon break?
Point out beginning capital letters and question marks.

INSTRUCTIONS:
Alternatives to the activity on page 110.
Present children's questions to the custodian, and ask him or her to provide written answers.
Speak informally with the custodian, and record his or her answers to the children's questions.

EXTENSIONS:
Ask children to write thank you notes to the custodian. Invite them to include drawings of how they followed his or her suggestions for keeping the school clean.

Read and discuss *The Wump World* by Bill Peet. (Houghton Mifflin, 1970). Various forms of pollution are shown as the Pollutians take over the crystal clean world of the Wumps.

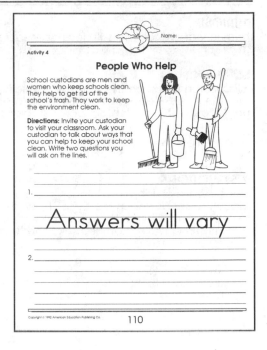

ANSWER KEY   Activity 4

PURPOSES:
To understand the meaning of the term recycle
To categorize items which can be recycled

MATERIALS:
newspapers, an empty glass bottle, a used metal can, address of the nearest recycling center

PREWORK:
Display a newspaper, an empty bottle and a used metal can. Help children determine what material each item is made of. Using "Paper", "Metal" and "Glass" as headings, challenge children to think of other items which would fit in each column.

INSTRUCTIONS:
Discuss the drawings and reasons for placing items in each category. Explain that in areas that do recycling, people have to use separate containers for glass, paper and metal. Have children copy the address of the nearest recycling center on the lines on page 138. Be sure they understand the location (next to the post office, in front of the grocery store, in the mall).

EXTENSIONS:
Use the drawings on page 138 as a model for a bulletin board titled; "Over and Over". Ask children to cut out their drawings or enlarge them on separate sheets of construction paper. Encourage them to bring in the items which they drew to be placed on a display table near the bulletin board.

Read and discuss "New Ways of Handling Garbage" pages 30-33 from the series A New True Book, *Soil Erosion and Pollution* by Darlene R. Stille (Childrens Press, 1990).

ANSWER KEY   Activity 5

TEACHING SUGGESTIONS

PURPOSE:
To review and evaluate skill development for lessons on air, water, land and the environment

PREWORK:
Ask children to turn to the glossary. Explain that a glossary is a list of hard words from the book. Read and discuss the glossary explanations for earth, environment, polluted, pollution, school custodians, and recycle.

INSTRUCTIONS:
Point out the front cover of the booklet on page 165. Ask each child to print his or her name on the line. Then read the sentences on pages 165 and 166 together. When children are finished drawing, help them order the pages. Staple the pages for each child.

EXTENSIONS:
Invite students to share their booklets with another class.

ANSWER KEY   Review #1

PURPOSE:
To evaluate information about solar homes

PREWORK:
Ask children to close their eyes and visualize sitting at the pool or beach on a hot summer day. Ask them to describe what the sun feels like.

INSTRUCTIONS:
For children having difficulty drawing a conclusion for question 2, ask:
What do the plates and sheets on the roofs of solar homes collect? (sunlight)
What kind of weather is best for collecting sunlight? (sunny)
Besides sunny days, what are some other kinds of days? (cloudy, rainy)
Do all places have a lot of sunny days? (no)

EXTENSIONS:
Invite children to design newspaper ads for solar homes. Attach their ads to the pages of a local newspaper and place the newspaper on the reading table.

Read and discuss the poem "sun" from *small poems* by Valerie Worth. (Farrar, Straus, Giroux, 1972). Challenge children to write small poems about the sun's heat. Display their poems in a place where the sun shines in the room.

Ask children to record the number of sunny days on a calendar. After a month, form discussion groups to determine whether solar homes would be practical for the month in which they recorded the weather.

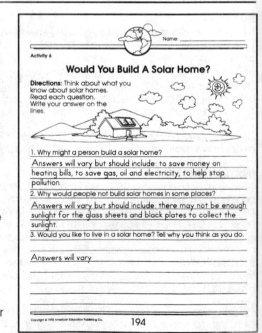

ANSWER KEY   Activity 6

PURPOSES:
To construct a simple if/then statement
To understand why rain forests should not be destroyed

MATERIALS:
crayons

PREWORK:
Ask children to describe what happens when they are sick. Record their responses in sentence form using the words if and then.

Examples:
If I am sick, then I will go to the doctor.
If I am sick, then I can't go to school.
Point out that the same event can have different outcomes.
Tell them it is important to think of all the different things that might happen.
Practice with other examples.

INSTRUCTIONS:
Ask children to recall what they read about the rain forest on page 221. Remind them that several different things might happen if the people chop down the trees. Ask them to choose just one thing to write on the line. Discuss the if/then statements and their drawings of what happened next.

EXTENSIONS:
Help children use research books to do oral reports on some of the strange plants and animals of a rain forest.

Read and discuss *The Great Kapok Tree* by Lynne Cherry (Harcourt, Brace, Jovanovich, 1990) In this beautifully illustrated book, animals who live in the branches of a Kapok tree in the Amazon rain forest beg a man with an ax not to destroy their home.

ANSWER KEY   Activity 7

PURPOSE:
To understand the purpose of wild animal refuges

PREWORK:
After reading page 249, draw children's attention to the illustrations. Explain that at one time only 21 whooping cranes were left in the world. Tell children that one way people have saved the whooping crane is by protecting them in refuges in Texas and Canada. Ask: What would a whooping crane need in its refuge? Point out that long ago thousands of elk died because people took over the places where they lived. Explain that refuges such as the National Elk Refuge in Wyoming have helped save the elk. Ask: What would a refuge for an elk be like?

INSTRUCTIONS:
Before reading page 250, ask children to think about books, movies and TV programs that showed the American bison, sometimes called the buffalo. Have them brainstorm for ideas about bison. Ask children to read page 250 to find out how the bison were saved. When the have completed the maze, invite them to

EXTENSIONS:
Invite children to devise mazes that help a lost elk or whooping crane find refuges. Compile their mazes in an Amazing Refuges book.

Read and discuss *Heron Street* by Ann Turner (Harper & Row, 1989). Invite children to repeat onomatopoeic words especially those of the animals as they are displaced from their marsh by the sea — "sqwonk-honk, chee-hiss, aroooo!".

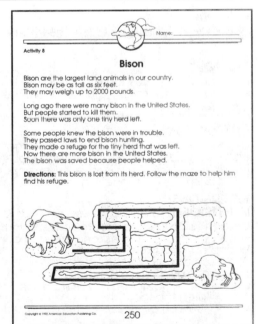

ANSWER KEY   Activity 8

TEACHING SUGGESTIONS

PURPOSE:
To communicate the goals of conservationists

PREWORK:
Before reading page 277, direct children's attention to the illustration of Theodore Roosevelt. Explain that Roosevelt was the President of the United States from 1901-1909. Ask them to name some of the jobs the President of the United States might do. List their responses. Then, ask children to read to find out how Theodore Roosevelt made taking care of the environment one of his main jobs.

INSTRUCTIONS:
After reading the directions together, organize the children in small groups to discuss what the President of the United States might say on TV. Circulate and give suggestions when needed. Then, ask children to write their ideas on the lines inside the TV screen. Accept invented spelling.

EXTENSIONS:
Help children use a large cardboard box to make a TV screen. Invite children to position themselves inside the screen to present the speeches they wrote on page 278.

Point out that Theodore Roosevelt's nickname was "Teddy." Tell children that when he was President a cartoon showed him holding a bear cub. Explain that soon afterwards toymakers began to make stuffed animals that are still called "Teddy bears." Display several teddy bears. Invite children to bring their favorite teddy bears to school. Allow them to keep their teddies near as they complete pages 305 and 306

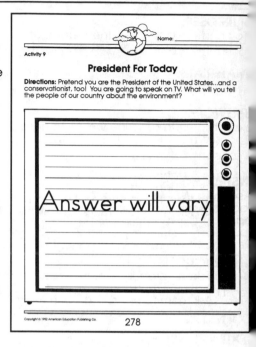

ANSWER KEY   Activity 9

PURPOSE:
To review and evaluate skill development for lessons on energy, plants, animals and conservation

PREWORK:
Invite children to use the tape recorder to record sentences about key terms: solar homes, rain forest, refuges, bison, Theodore Roosevelt, conservationist. Play the tape for the class.

INSTRUCTIONS:
Encourage children to work with a partner to complete page 305. Discuss each picture and allow time for children to tell shy the people or things hurt or helped the environment. Go over the first example on page 306 together. After children complete the page independently, discuss the answers.

EXTENSIONS:
Challenge children to create riddles about key words and concepts for the lessons on energy, plants, animals, and conservation.
Example: I am a kind of home.
    I use energy from the sun.
    What am I? (a solar home)
Compile their riddles on a worksheet and save it for a review later in the year.

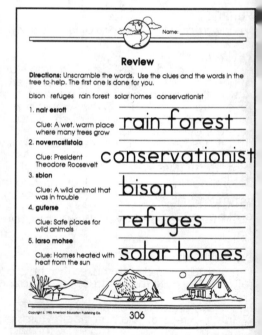

ANSWER KEY   Review #2

PURPOSES:
To identify ways paper is used at school
To recognize that using paper wisely helps the environment

MATERIALS:
Full trash can

PREWORK:
Empty the classroom trash can on newspapers. Carefully go through the contents for paper trash. Display the paper. Ask children to determine if each piece was used completely. Make a separate pile for sheets that were wasted.

INSTRUCTIONS:
Ask children to brainstorm for ways paper is used in the classroom and school (books, maps, notebooks, writing paper, name tags, bulletin boards, computer paper, napkins, paper towels, toilet paper, tissues, art work) Record the responses. Ask them to copy six of the words on the semantic map on page 333. Refer to the pile of wasted paper set aside in prework. Lead children to conclude that they could make the pile of paper smaller by using paper wisely. Read the story of "Perry Paper" on page 334 together. Point out the quotation marks and tell children that these special marks show the exact words someone said. Read and discuss children's predictions of what Perry said.

EXTENSIONS:
Challenge children to work in small groups to create a short play based on "Perry Paper." Ask them to prepare dialogue for Perry, Val and Luis. Simple props may be used. Invite groups to present the play to the class.

Review words that begin with the sound the letter p represents. Using the tongue twister on page 333 as a model, challenge children to orally devise other tongue twisters about paper.

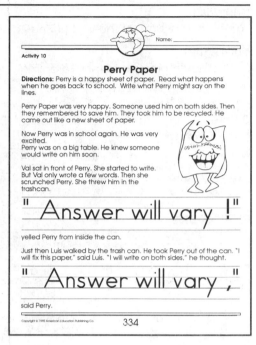

ANSWER KEY Activity 10

PURPOSE:
To identify ways of conserving heat at home

MATERIALS:
Furnace air filter

PREWORK:
Point out the room's thermostat. Explain that a thermostat controls the temperature in the room. Ask children to raise their hands if they think the room is comfortable. Help a volunteer read the temperature displayed on the thermostat. Write the temperature on the board. Display a clean furnace filter. Tell children that most furnaces use air filters. Explain that the filters are like screens that keep the dirt out of furnaces.

INSTRUCTIONS:
Read page 361 together. After each energy saving suggestion is read aloud, you may want to:
1. Explain that dirty filters make the furnace work harder to make heat so that means the furnace is using too much energy to heat the house. Tell them air filters should be changed several times a year.
2. Ask children what they like to wear around the house in the winter. Have them determine if the clothing keeps them warm enough without turning up the heat.
3. Point out that if everyone in America would turn the heat down to at least 68, thousands of barrels of oil would be saved each day.
4. Tell children that pulling down shades and closing curtains helps keep the heat inside the house at night.
Discuss the first example before children complete page 362 independently.

EXTENSIONS:
Invite children to use page 362 as a checklist. Ask them to take page 362 home and mark an z on the pictures of the things they see happening in their homes. have them report their findings. Discuss how the pictures in the CONSERVE column might be different in the summer.

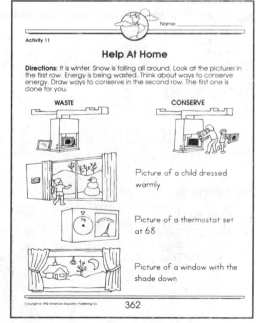

ANSWER KEY Activity 11

TEACHING SUGGESTIONS

PURPOSE:
To design a refuge for the wild animals and birds of the local community.

PREWORK:
Help children brainstorm for wild animals and birds of the community. Record the responses. Ask them to copy the names in the correct column on page 389.

INSTRUCTIONS:
Before reading the directions on page 390, explain that one of the jobs of community leaders is to protect wildlife. Then, discuss the homes and eating habits of the wild animals and birds listed on page 389. As an alternative, you may want each child to plan a refuge for just one of the birds or animals discussed. When they are finished, invite children to vote for the refuge name they like best. Then ask children to cut out their drawings. Display the drawings under a sign with the winning name.

EXTENSIONS:
Ask children to use small boxes, clay, paper and other common materials to create dioramas of the refuges they planned.

Display a large map of the local area. Point out the water and green areas. Help children draw conclusions as to where the best location for a refuge would be.

Invite a local conservationist or government environmental official to visit the class. Ask the person to speak about ways the community protects its wildlife.

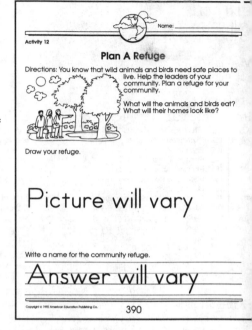

ANSWER KEY   Activity 12

PURPOSE:
To review and evaluate skill development

PREWORK:
Announce: "Only grown-ups can help to protect the environment."
Challenge children to explain why your statement is true or false.

INSTRUCTIONS:
Organize the class into two groups. Draw a large tic-tac-toe grid on the board, and have the two groups play the game with Xs and Os. Explain that the game on page 417 is played the same way. Tell them the only difference is that after a player marks an X or an O, they must say whether the picture is showing something that helps or hurts the environment.

When children finish page 418 compile the drawings in a book titled: Saving Our Planet: Part 2. Display it near the class room globe.

EXTENSIONS:
Challenge children to devise their own tic-tac-toe game like the one on page 417.

ANSWER KEY   Review #3